T0325829

Cyber–Physical System Solutions for Smart Cities

Vanamoorthy Muthumanikandan
Vellore Institute of Technology, Chennai, India

Anbalagan Bhuvaneswari
Vellore Institute of Technology, Chennai, India

Balamurugan Easwaran
University of Africa, Toru-Orua, Nigeria

T. Sudarson Rama Perumal
Rohini College of Engineering and Technology, India

A volume in the Advances in
Systems Analysis, Software
Engineering, and High Performance
Computing (ASASEHPC) Book Series

Published in the United States of America by
    IGI Global
    Engineering Science Reference (an imprint of IGI Global)
    701 E. Chocolate Avenue
    Hershey PA, USA 17033
    Tel: 717-533-8845
    Fax: 717-533-8661
    E-mail: cust@igi-global.com
    Web site: http://www.igi-global.com

Library of Congress Cataloging-in-Publication Data

Names: Muthumanikandan, Vanamoorthy, 1988- editor. | Bhuvaneswari,
    Anbalagan, 1989- editor. | Eswaran, Balamurugan, 1975- editor. |
    Perumal, T. Sudarson Rama, 1986- editor.
Title: Cyber-physical system solutions for smart cities / edited by
    Vanamoorthy Muthumanikandan, Anbalagan Bhuvaneswari, Balamurugan
    Eswaran, T Sudarson Rama Perumal.
Description: Hershey, PA : Engineering Science Reference, [2023] | Includes
    bibliographical references and index. | Summary: "Cyber-Physical System
    Solutions for Smart Cities considers the most recent developments in
    several crucial software services and cyber infrastructures that are
    important to smart cities. Covering key topics such as artificial
    intelligence, smart data, big data, and computer science, this premier
    reference source is ideal for industry professionals, government
    officials, policymakers, scholars, researchers, academicians,
    instructors, and students"-- Provided by publisher.
Identifiers: LCCN 2023004864 (print) | LCCN 2023004865 (ebook) | ISBN
    9781668477564 (h/c) | ISBN 9781668477571 (s/c) | ISBN 9781668477588
    (eISBN)
Subjects: LCSH: Smart cities. | Internet of things. | Cooperating objects
    (Computer systems) | Big data.
Classification: LCC TD159.4 .C88 2023 (print) | LCC TD159.4 (ebook) | DDC
    004.67/8--dc23/eng/20230215
LC record available at https://lccn.loc.gov/2023004864
LC ebook record available at https://lccn.loc.gov/2023004865

This book is published in the IGI Global book series Advances in Systems Analysis, Software Engineering, and High Performance Computing (ASASEHPC) (ISSN: 2327-3453; eISSN: 2327-3461)

British Cataloguing in Publication Data
A Cataloguing in Publication record for this book is available from the British Library.

All work contributed to this book is new, previously-unpublished material.
The views expressed in this book are those of the authors, but not necessarily of the publisher.

For electronic access to this publication, please contact: eresources@igi-global.com.

Advances in Systems Analysis, Software Engineering, and High Performance Computing (ASASEHPC) Book Series

ISSN:2327-3453
EISSN:2327-3461

Editor-in-Chief: Vijayan Sugumaran, Oakland University, USA

MISSION

The theory and practice of computing applications and distributed systems has emerged as one of the key areas of research driving innovations in business, engineering, and science. The fields of software engineering, systems analysis, and high performance computing offer a wide range of applications and solutions in solving computational problems for any modern organization.

The **Advances in Systems Analysis, Software Engineering, and High Performance Computing (ASASEHPC) Book Series** brings together research in the areas of distributed computing, systems and software engineering, high performance computing, and service science. This collection of publications is useful for academics, researchers, and practitioners seeking the latest practices and knowledge in this field.

COVERAGE

- Virtual Data Systems
- Computer System Analysis
- Computer Networking
- Network Management
- Performance Modelling
- Parallel Architectures
- Human-Computer Interaction
- Enterprise Information Systems
- Engineering Environments
- Storage Systems

IGI Global is currently accepting manuscripts for publication within this series. To submit a proposal for a volume in this series, please contact our Acquisition Editors at Acquisitions@igi-global.com or visit: http://www.igi-global.com/publish/.

Titles in this Series

For a list of additional titles in this series, please visit:
http://www.igi-global.com/book-series/advances-systems-analysis-software-engineering/73689

Perspectives and Considerations on the Evolution of Smart Systems
Maki K. Habib (American University in Cairo, Egypt)
Engineering Science Reference • copyright 2023 • 419pp • H/C (ISBN: 9781668476840)
• US $325.00 (our price)

Neuromorphic Computing Systems for Industry 4.0
S. Dhanasekar (Department of ECE, Sri Eshwar College of Engineering, India) K. Martin
Sagayam (Karunya Institute of Technology and Sciences, India) Surbhi Vijh (ASET, Amity
University, Noida, India) Vipin Tyagi (Jaypee University of Engineering and Technology,
India) and Alex Norta (Tallinn University, Estonia)
Engineering Science Reference • copyright 2023 • 377pp • H/C (ISBN: 9781668465967)
• US $270.00 (our price)

Business Models and Strategies for Open Source Projects
Francisco José Monaco (Universidade de São Paulo, Brazil)
Business Science Reference • copyright 2023 • 339pp • H/C (ISBN: 9781668447857) •
US $270.00 (our price)

Advanced Applications of Python Data Structures and Algorithms
Mohammad Gouse Galety (Department of Computer Science, Samarkand International
University of Technology, Uzbekistan) Arul Kumar Natarajan (CHRIST University (Deemed),
India) and A. V. Sriharsha (MB University, India)
Engineering Science Reference • copyright 2023 • 298pp • H/C (ISBN: 9781668471005)
• US $270.00 (our price)

For an entire list of titles in this series, please visit:
http://www.igi-global.com/book-series/advances-systems-analysis-software-engineering/73689

701 East Chocolate Avenue, Hershey, PA 17033, USA
Tel: 717-533-8845 x100 • Fax: 717-533-8661
E-Mail: cust@igi-global.com • www.igi-global.com

Table of Contents

S. Deeksha, School of Computer Science and Engineering, Vellore
Institute of Technology, Chennai, India
Sannasi Ganapathy, Centre for Cyber-Physical Systems and School of
Computer Science and Engineering, Vellore Institute of Technology,
Chennai, India
V. Muthumanikandan, School of Computer Science and Engineering,
Vellore Institute of Technology, Chennai, India

S. S. Ramyadharshni, Vellore Institute of Technology, Chennai, India
A. Bhuvaneswari, Vellore Institute of Technology, Chennai, India

V. Pandiyaraju, School of Computer Science and Engineering (SCOPE),
Vellore Institute of Technology, Chennai, India
P. Shunmuga Perumal, Vellore Institute of Technology, Vellore, India
V. Muthumanikandan, School of Computer Science and Engineering
(SCOPE), Vellore Institute of Technology, Chennai, India

Detailed Table of Contents

Chapter 1

S. Deeksha, School of Computer Science and Engineering, Vellore
Institute of Technology, Chennai, India

Sannasi Ganapathy, Centre for Cyber-Physical Systems and School of
Computer Science and Engineering, Vellore Institute of Technology,
Chennai, India

V. Muthumanikandan, School of Computer Science and Engineering,
Vellore Institute of Technology, Chennai, India

In smart cities, road accidents are very serious and avoidable. In addition, road accidents are very common in India, and they are also becoming a serious issue all over the world. In this world, the people are not able to reach hospitals due to the traffic, lack of transport facility, and unavailability of hospitals after the accidents. To enrich the population of urban people, the "smart cities" are developed to enhance the sophistication in daily life through technological development. The proposed image classifier model has been tuned with different values of hyperparameters such as number of units, activation function, optimizer, learning rate, and number of epochs. The efficiency and accuracy of the model is duly considered while building the model for predictive analysis. The images were transformed and augmented before feeding them into the neural network to ensure proper training by blocking over-fitting of the model because of lack of data. The proposed model achieves 98.21% accuracy, which is greater than the existing works.

    S. S. Ramyadharshni, Vellore Institute of Technology, Chennai, India
    A. Bhuvaneswari, Vellore Institute of Technology, Chennai, India

Social networks play a dominant role in connecting communication devices, which play as essential role in exchanging a large amount of interpersonal data. As a result of exchange of messages, they leave behind some traces, which help in identifying the nature of the network. So, these are helpful in detecting crime users. The algorithms like SVM, Bayesian linear regression will not help in finding out the crime network. It also results in less accuracy for higher amounts of data. So, developing the trace learning system in GAN, which is a higher order of deep learning neural network, larger neural network dataset will be fed into the model, which has digital traces into the neural network done through proposed CrimedetGAN. A trained accuracy system model automatically identifies the digital traces which have been left in the crime natured social network. Experimenting with existing GAN frameworks, namely MaliGAN, seqGAN, LeakGAN, proposed CrimedetGAN came with a test score accuracy of 91.23% on the coherence NLP testing in tracing the relevant data fields for the given input datasets.

    V. Pandiyaraju, School of Computer Science and Engineering (SCOPE),
        Vellore Institute of Technology, Chennai, India
    P. Shunmuga Perumal, Vellore Institute of Technology, Vellore, India
    V. Muthumanikandan, School of Computer Science and Engineering
        (SCOPE), Vellore Institute of Technology, Chennai, India

Coal is one of the major natural sources of power production. It contributes to about 56% of the total production. Conventionally, coal is stored in stockpiles for production of electricity without any logs. Storage of coal for a longer time in the open type stockpile results in self-oxidation of coal, which leads to increased ignition temperature. Detection and prevention of spontaneous combustion and self-ignition stands to be major issues in stockpile. This chapter proposes an automated system using internet of things (IoT), which aids in detecting the fire at an earlier stage and to prevent it, thereby avoiding economic loss. Wireless sensor nodes are deployed to detect the parameters such as temperature, humidity, gases from the stockpile, and the data is transmitted to the server and to the ground station with the aid of GSM modules. Data is monitored in the ground station, and the critical values are evaluated to prevent fire by detecting it at its early stages. The system is implemented in an open rail coal stockpile, and the data is represented in the form of graph for evaluation.

Chapter 4

    P. Saranya, Vellore Institute of Technology, Chennai, India
    R. Maheswari, Vellore Institute of Technology, Chennai, India
    Ramesh Ragala, Vellore Institute of Technology, Chennai, India

Agri-food systems are continually evolving to feed an ever-growing population. However, several challenges such as quality products, inefficient supply chain, and excessive food wastage are needed to be faced in order to meet global demand. Among these constraints, supply chain traceability systems are one of the technology solutions that can identify and resolve the challenges of agri-food systems. The traditional supply chain lacks traceability, transparency, and information exchange. In this work, the blockchain projects utilizing the public and private blockchain platforms are discussed. Also, the product ownership management has been developed using Hyperledger composer for tracing the flow of agriculture products at every stage. It supports storing the supply chain activities as a ledger transaction in a permanent and immutable way. Agriculture products are mentioned as lots with a unique lot code provided for each batch of products. The chain of lot codes can be used to identify the product along the supply chain. This system ensures product ownership.

Chapter 5

    P. Renugadevi, Vellore Institute of Technology, Chennai, India
    R. Maheswari, Vellore Institute of Technology, Chennai, India
    V. Pattabiraman, Vellore Institute of Technology, Chennai, India
    R. Srimathi, Vellore Institute of Technology, Chennai, India

Electrification is a primary concern in the recent years because of new emerging technologies in day-to-day life. Therefore, to run a variety of devices, you need an uninterrupted power supply, and equipment that is powered as well. There are various reasons such as natural disasters, transmission, and distribution issues that prevent 30% of residents in rural and isolated areas from accessing basic electricity. This lack of electrification has an adverse effect on people's survival on radical level in many circumstances. It may be possible to reduce both current and future power constraints by improving the microgrid concept so that standalone microgrids in remote locations work well. Especially when isolated from main grids and unable to receive regular electricity, standalone microgrids present many difficulties and problems. Formerly, diesel generators were considered indispensable to off-grid microgrids, as they provide electricity for the entire system. Power losses can be reduced by employing power optimizers with a maximum power point tracking approach.

Chapter 6

Valentina Tomat, University of Murcia, Spain
Alfonso Pablo Ramallo-González, University of Murcia, Spain
Antonio Fernando Skarmeta-Gómez, University of Murcia, Spain

On the last EPBD, a new indicator to measure smart technologies in buildings has
been developed: the smart readiness indicator (SRI). The SRI framework evaluates
the smart services that the building could deliver, with the threefold purpose of
optimising energy efficiency, adapting to the needs of the occupants and responding
to the signals from the grid. The chapter analyses the increase of smart readiness
in eight real-world buildings, characterised by different climate conditions and
retrofitted with cost-effective interventions. On this study, the assessment was done
with two different methods, one using the same maximum obtainable score for all
the buildings and the other using a list of smart services adapted to each building.
The outcomes are compared to spot the potentialities of the new indicator, and its
usability has been tested through a questionnaire. Finally, the applicability to DLC
is discussed to support the role that the indicator can assume in enhancing the load
shifting potential in buildings, toward the energy transformation of the European
society.

Chapter 7

P. Saranya, Rohini College of Engineering and Technology, India
R. Rajesh, Rohini College of Engineering and Technology, India

The IoT is a rapidly emerging research area. It refers to an infrastructure network
that includes digital data, mechanical objects, computational devices, and sensors
that have unique identities. IoT delivers many solutions in various domains by
providing connection of devices through the internet. Recently electricity is very
important in our day-to-day lives. The consumption of electricity is also rapidly
increasing. It is necessary to improve the production of electricity and also reduce
the wastage of electricity in transmission lines. The energy grid refers to the next
generation power grids, with bi-directional or two-way flows of electricity through
the communication interface or protocols. The energy management in grid ensures
stability between the supply and demand, which is maintained for reducing the
wastage of electricity. In order to achieve this reduction, it is necessary to monitor
the parameters of the PV system by the IoT hardware. Specifically, the authors focus
on IoT technologies for monitoring the parameters of PV systems such as voltage
and current by sensors in IoT.

Chapter 8

Siddharth Chatterjee, Vellore Institute of Technology, India
Ishan Sagar Jogalekar, Vellore Institute of Technology, India
K. Lavanya, Vellore Institute of Technology, India

Biometric fingerprint devices used in electronic voting machines (EVMs) for voter verification and authentication eliminates two main threats towards present-day voting systems, which include illegal voting as well as repetition of votes. This application has extensive use in real world scenarios and helps to conduct fair and free elections. The person at the polling booth need not carry his ID, which contains his required details; only placing his finger on the device would allow the acquisition of an on-spot fingerprint from the voter – an authentic identification. The fingerprint reader would read details from the tag; the data is then passed onto the controlling unit for verification. The controller fetches the data from the reader and compares the data with pre-existing data stored during registration of voters using biometric. This prototype is based on IoT (internet of things), and the microprocessor platform uses Arduino Uno as the microchip and some TFT displays to successfully simulate the architecture for voting systems and consequently improve the traditional EVM-based voting.

Chapter 9

S. Muthurajkumar, Anna University, Chennai, India
R. Praveen, Anna University, Chennai, India
S. Yogeshwar, Anna University, Chennai, India
K. A. Muthukumaran, Anna University, Chennai, India
K. C. Abishek, Anna University, Chennai, India

The smart city is an evolution of a smart home. According to a report by ABI Research, almost 300 million smart homes have been installed around the world by 2022. The smart sensors of separate homes, various organizations are connected to make a city smart. The regular language encryption is privacy ensuring and at the same time proves to be secured against the keyword guessing attack (KGA). The authors propose a model in which they regulate the way the user wants to search and return results. They also provide privacy to the outsourced data by encrypting the content before being outsourced to the database server. The entire module is controlled by keyword generation center (KGC), which is responsible for approving the owners for uploading the files to the cloud server and the users for downloading the files from the same. In this work, the authors introduce a model to behave in a way where the approved user has the entire control over his data and also has the role of granting permission to the user who requests access for the particular data.

Preface

In an era defined by technological advancements and the relentless pursuit of innovation, the concept of smart cities has emerged as a beacon of hope and progress. These cities strive to leverage cutting-edge technologies, interconnected systems, and data-driven insights to enhance the quality of life for their citizens, drive sustainable development, and create a seamless integration between the physical and digital realms. This book aims to shed light on the transformative power of Cyber-Physical Systems (CPS) in the context of smart cities. CPS refers to the integration of computational elements with physical processes, enabling a symbiotic relationship between the virtual and physical worlds. It encompasses a diverse range of technologies, such as Internet of Things (IoT), artificial intelligence, cloud computing, big data analytics, and more, all working in harmony to drive innovation and efficiency in urban environments. In *Cyber-Physical System Solutions for Smart Cities*, we bring together a collection of insightful chapters contributed by experts and thought leaders from various domains, including academia, industry, and government. Each chapter delves into different facets of CPS and its applications in transforming urban spaces into smart cities of the future.

The book begins with a comprehensive introduction to the fundamental concepts of CPS and its role in smart cities. We explore the underlying principles and key technologies that form the foundation of these systems, setting the stage for a deeper exploration of their real-world applications. Throughout the subsequent chapters, we delve into various domains where CPS can revolutionize the way cities function. From transportation and energy management to healthcare, governance, and environmental sustainability,

Furthermore, we address the critical challenges and considerations associated with implementing CPS in smart cities. We discuss issues such as data privacy and security, interoperability, scalability, and the ethical implications of relying heavily on technology to govern urban spaces. It is imperative that we approach the development of smart cities with a keen awareness of the potential risks and ensure that these systems are designed and deployed in a manner that prioritizes inclusivity, fairness, and the well-being of all citizens.

As you embark on this exploration of *Cyber-Physical System Solutions for Smart Cities*, I encourage you to approach each chapter with an open mind, ready to absorb new knowledge, and envision the possibilities that lie ahead. Together, let us dive into the fascinating realm of smart cities, where the synergy between technology, infrastructure, and human ingenuity has the power to reshape our urban landscapes and pave the way for a more sustainable and prosperous future.

May this book serve as a source of inspiration, guidance, and collaboration as we navigate the intricate pathways towards the realization of truly smart cities.

Chapter 1: An IoT-Aware Road Accident Prevention System for Smart Cities Using Machine Learning Techniques

In this chapter the authors discuss about smart cities, the road accidents are very serious and avoidable. In addition, the road accidents are very common in India and it is also becoming a serious issue in all over the world and smart cities. The proposed image classifier model has been tuned with different values of hyperparameters such as number of units, activation function, optimizer, learning rate, and number of epochs. The efficiency and accuracy of the model is duly considered while building the model for predictive analysis. The images were transformed and augmented before feeding them into the neural network to ensure proper training by blocking over-fitting of the model because of lack of data. The proposed model achieves 98.21% as accuracy which is greater than the existing works.

Chapter 2: CrimedetGAN – A Novel Generative Digital Trace Learning System for Detecting Crime Natured Nodes in Social Networks

In this chapter the authors identified Social networks play a dominant role in connecting communication devices, which act as essential role in exchanging a large amount of interpersonal data as a result of exchange of messages, they leave behind some traces, which helps in identifying the nature of the network. So, these helpful in detecting crime users. The algorithms like SVM, Bayesian Linear regression will not help in finding out the crime network. It also results in less accuracy for higher amounts of data. So, developing the trace learning system in GAN, which is higher order of deep learning neural network, Larger neural network dataset will be feed into the model, which has digital traces into the neural network done through proposed CrimedetGAN. A trained accuracy system model which automatically identify the digital traces which have been left in the crime natured social network. Experimenting with existing GAN frameworks namely, MaliGAN, seqGAN, LeakGAN, Proposed CrimedetGAN came with a test score accuracy of 91.23% on the coherence NLP testing in tracing the relevant data fields for the given input datasets.

Chapter 3: Coal Fire Detection and Prevention System Using IoT

Coal is one of the major natural sources of power production which contributes for about 56% of the total production. Conventionally, coal is stored in stockpile for production of electricity without any logs. Storage of coal for a longer time in the open type stockpile results in self-oxidation of coal which leads to increased Ignition temperature. Detection and prevention of spontaneous combustion and self-ignition stands to be major issue in stockpile. This paper proposes an automated system using Internet of Things (IoT) which aids in detecting the fire at earlier stage and to prevent it, thereby avoiding economic loss. Wireless Sensor Nodes are deployed to detect the parameters such as temperature, humidity, gases from the stockpile and the data is transmitted to the server and to the ground station with the aid of GSM modules. Data is monitored in the ground station and the critical values are evaluated to prevent the fire by detecting it at its early stage. The system is implemented in a open rail coal stockpile and the data is represented in the form of graph for evaluation.

Chapter 4: Blockchain for Agri-Business – A Simulation for Assuring Product Ownership Using Hyperledger Composer

Agri-Food systems are continually evolving to feed an ever-growing population. However, several challenges such as quality products, inefficient supply chain, and excessive food wastage are needed to be faced in order to meet global demand. Among these constraints, Supply chain traceability systems are one of the technology solutions that can identify and resolve the challenges of Agri-Food systems. The traditional supply chain lacks traceability, transparency, and information exchange. In this work, the blockchain projects utilizing the public and private blockchain platforms are discussed. Also, the product ownership management has been developed using Hyperledger composer for tracing the flow of agriculture products at every stage. It supports to store the supply chain activities as a ledger transaction in a permanent and immutable way. Agriculture products are mentioned as lots with a unique lot code provided for each batch of products. The chain of lot codes can be used to identify the product along the supply chain. This system ensures product ownership.

Chapter 5: Difficult and Intriguing Performance of Standalone Microgrid and Diesel Generator With Big Data Analytics in Rural Electrification

Electrification is a primary concern in the recent years, because of new emerging technologies in day-to-day life. Therefore, to run a variety of devices, you need an uninterrupted power supply, Equipment that is powered as well. There are various reasons such as natural disasters, transmission, and distribution issues that prevent 30% of residents in rural and isolated areas from accessing basic electricity. This lack of electrification has an adverse effect on people's survival on radical level in many circumstances. It may be possible to reduce both current and future power constraints by improving the microgrid concept so that standalone microgrids in remote locations work well. Especially when isolated from main grids and unable to receive regular electricity, standalone microgrids present many difficulties and problems. Formerly, diesel generators were considered indispensable to off-grid microgrids, as they provide electricity for the entire system. Power losses can be reduced by employing power optimizers with a maximum power point tracking approach.

Chapter 6: Evaluation of Energy Flexibility Potential of Different Interventions Through the SRI Score – Evaluation Under the IoT Paradigm

On the last (EPBD), a new indicator to measure smart technologies in buildings has been developed: The Smart Readiness Indicator (SRI). The SRI framework evaluates the smart services that the building could deliver, with the threefold purpose of optimising energy efficiency, adapting to the needs of the occupants and responding to the signals from the grid. The chapter analyses the increase of smart readiness in eight real-world buildings, characterised by different climate conditions and retrofitted with cost-effective interventions. On this study, the assessment was done with two different methods, one using the same maximum obtainable score for all the buildings and the other using a list of smart services adapted to each building. The outcomes are compared to spot the potentialities of the new indicator; and its usability has been tested through a questionnaire. Finally, the applicability to DLC is discussed to support the role that the indicator can assume in enhancing the load shifting potential in buildings, toward the energy transformation of the European society.

Chapter 7: Evolution of Smart Energy Grid System Using IoT – Smart Grid, Online Power Monitoring in Buildings, Smart Sensors for Smart Grid Protection

The IoT is a rapidly emerging research area, refers to an infrastructure network that includes digital data, mechanical objects, computational devices, and sensors that has a unique identity. IOT delivers many solutions in various domains by providing connection of devices through the internet. Recently electricity is very important in our day-to-day life. The consumption of electricity is also rapidly increasing. It is necessary to improve the production of electricity also reduce the wastage of electricity in transmission lines. The energy grid refers to the next generation power grids, with bi-directional or two-way flows of electricity through the communication interface or protocols. The Energy management in grid ensures stability between the supply and demand which is maintained for reducing the wastage of electricity, and in order to achieve this reduction, it is necessary to monitor the parameters of the PV system by the IoT hardware. Specifically, we focus on IoT technologies for monitoring the parameters of PV systems such as Voltage, Current by sensors in IoT.

Chapter 8: E-Voting – Portable Fingerprint-Based Biometric Device for Elderly and Disabled People

Biometric finger print devices used in Electronic Voting Machines (EVMs) for voter verification and authentication eliminates two main threats towards present-day voting system which includes illegal voting as well as repetition of votes. This application has an extensive use in real world scenario and helps to conduct fair and free elections. The person at the polling booth need not carry his ID which contains his required details; only placing his finger on the device would allow the acquisition of an on-spot fingerprint from the voter - an authentic identification. The Finger Print reader would read details from the tag; the data then passing on to the controlling unit for verification. The controller fetches the data from the reader and compares the data with pre-existing data stored during registration of voters using biometric. This prototype based on IoT (Internet Of Things) and microprocessor platform uses Arduino Uno as the microchip and some TFT displays to successfully simulate the architecture for voting system and consequently improve the traditional EVM based voting.

Chapter 9: Regular Language Encryption for Secured Storage of Cloud Data in Smart Home-Based Cities

The smart city is an evolution of a smart home. According to a report by ABI Research, almost 300 million smart homes installed around the world by 2022. The smart sensors of a separate homes, various organizations are connected to make a city smart. The regular language encryption that is privacy ensuring and at the same time, proves to be secured against the keyword guessing attack (KGA). We propose a model in which we regulate the way the user wants to search and return results. We also provide privacy to the outsourced data by encrypting the content before being outsourced to the database server. The entire module is controlled by Keyword Generation Center (KGC) which is responsible for approving the owners for uploading the files to the cloud server, and the users for downloading the files from the same. In this work, we introduce a model to behave in a way where the approved user has the entire control over his data and also has the role of granting permission to the user who requests access for the particular data.

Vanamoorthy Muthumanikandan
Vellore Institute of Technology, Chennai, India

Anbalagan Bhuvaneswari
Vellore Institute of Technology, Chennai, India

Balamurugan Easwaran
University of Africa, Toru-Orua, Nigeria

Sudarson Rama Perumal
Rohini College of Engineering and Technology, India

Acknowledgment

We would like to express our heartfelt gratitude to the reviewers who dedicated their time and expertise to provide valuable feedback and insights during the development of this book, *Cyber-Physical System Solutions for Smart Cities*. Their meticulous review process and constructive criticism played a pivotal role in ensuring the quality and accuracy of the content presented within these pages. Their commitment to excellence and their dedication to advancing knowledge in the field of Cyber-Physical Systems and smart cities are truly commendable. We are grateful for their expertise and grateful for the time and effort they invested in reviewing the chapters and providing their valuable suggestions and recommendations.

Additionally, we would like to express our deepest gratitude to all the contributors who shared their expertise and insights in this book. Their knowledge and passion have enriched this collection and have contributed to a comprehensive exploration of Cyber-Physical System Solutions for Smart Cities. Their commitment to advancing the field of smart cities and their willingness to share their experiences and research are greatly appreciated.

The collective efforts of the reviewers, contributors, and the entire publishing team have made this book possible. We are grateful for their contributions and honored to have worked alongside such talented individuals. Our hope is that this book will serve as a valuable resource for researchers, practitioners, and policymakers who strive to create smarter, more sustainable cities for the benefit of future generations.

Chapter 1

An IoT aware Road Accident Prevention System for Smart Cities Using Machine Learning Techniques

S. Deeksha
School of Computer Science and Engineering, Vellore Institute of Technology, Chennai, India

Sannasi Ganapathy
Centre for Cyber-Physical Systems and School of Computer Science and Engineering, Vellore Institute of Technology, Chennai, India

V. Muthumanikandan
School of Computer Science and Engineering, Vellore Institute of Technology, Chennai, India

ABSTRACT

In smart cities, road accidents are very serious and avoidable. In addition, road accidents are very common in India, and they are also becoming a serious issue all over the world. In this world, the people are not able to reach hospitals due to the traffic, lack of transport facility, and unavailability of hospitals after the accidents. To enrich the population of urban people, the "smart cities" are developed to enhance the sophistication in daily life through technological development. The proposed image classifier model has been tuned with different values of hyperparameters such as number of units, activation function, optimizer, learning rate, and number of epochs. The efficiency and accuracy of the model is duly considered while building the model for predictive analysis. The images were transformed and augmented before feeding them into the neural network to ensure proper training by blocking over-fitting of the model because of lack of data. The proposed model achieves 98.21% accuracy, which is greater than the existing works.

DOI: 10.4018/978-1-6684-7756-4.ch001

INTRODUCTION

Rapid growth of technological development, many intelligent and autonomous systems have been introduced by various researchers in the last decade. Recently, the people are more dependent on technologies that works automatically for making things to be easier and also comfortable. Moreover, the various smart systems are available to supply a better and sophisticated life with the incorporation of technological solutions for facing accidental issues. In addition, there is no recent technology is available as a completely for accidents that is used to predict the accident time and place accurately.

This work focuses on solving these problems. A well trained automated model can be trusted to make fewer mistakes as it can have the capacity to produce results with a near perfect accuracy. This paper focuses on solving the problem of accident detection by building a Convolutional Neural Network (CNN) model which can predict if an accident has occurred in the nearby proximity of any vehicle traveling by that lane or nearby with the help of a dashboard camera installed on the dashboards of on road vehicles.

Most of the existing papers in this have analysed what factors caused the accident or use pressure, impact sensors to analyse if similar impact is experienced as in that of when an accident has occurred and some do not have an autonomous system in place to stop accidents. The suggested solution focuses on images taken from a dashboard camera which is cheap and quick and can give instant updates on any accident faced by the user or in the nearby locality. Papers related to image classification help analyze and come out with the best image classification algorithms for this paper.

The algorithm preferred has the ability to extract features from image data on its own rather than requiring explicit data points to be given for every feature which makes CNN ideal for image classification. An exhaustive testing on different hyperparameters has been done to give a fair data analysis on the effects varying different parameters have on the model. The model uses the best values of parameters for the learning process of the model in order to create a model which can give precise predictions on the products fabricated. A data set containing multiple images of accident and on-accident based on dashboard camera images of cars taken from YouTube through scrapping of videos has been used to perform the training process and testing process. Section 2 states the relevant works that are available in this direction. Section 3 provides a detailed system architecture of the proposed system. Section 4 determines the results and discussion. Section 5 states the conclusion and future work.

LITERATURE SURVEY

Many accident prediction systems are available for predicting the accidental area in the various regions of the world. Among them, Kinoshita et al. (2022) paper deals with a dataset which shows certain regions in Japan with heavy snow conditions which lead to traffic congestion. A laser-based method and depth map based on snow piled in the corners. The benefits of this solution include that piled snow on road shoulders is taken into account, with the capacity of detecting 3 levels of snow conditions. However, it is only useful in snowy conditions and is unidirectional. Abramowski et al. (2018) paper identifies the cause of accidents based upon DVRs and surveillance cameras. This helps identify formulas devised for speed, acceleration and energy of vehicles. The solution proposed is kind of a black box solution to know the cause of accidents and not completely avert them, guidelines can be enforced based on outcomes of research. Rajendran et al. (2022) use ESP and USB camera together with the help of cNN detect potholes on highways and roads and send the information to the highway department this help detect potholes with a notification service for the ministry of road transport and highways to increase the efficiency of their functioning.

Wu et al. (2012) analyze the effect of a surveillance camera's angle to calculate parameters relating to road accidents. This is done using coordinate transformation. The effects of this research have no impact on controlling or stopping accidents but helps find correct camera position angles to place the camera in regards to the future prospect of installing it to run ML models for prediction and aversion. Sabry et al. (2021) predict if road accidents have occurred or can occur based on the CCTV footage from cameras installed on roads. This helps send immediate notification for detection of accidents but installing and operating CCTV cameras incurs huge costs on the infrastructure of roads.

Mallidi et al. (2018) have used impact sensors to detect accidents and notify thereafter. As simple as the solution seems to be it is difficult to know if every impact caused is only because of the accident results may not always be accurate. Aishwarya et al. (2015) propose a prevention of accidents based on analyzing blinking movement with the help of IR sensors and accelerometer fixed onto the forehead to measure the angles by the mounted device. Although the forehead angle is perfect for correct predictions it might be uncomfortable for the driver. Sandeep et al. (2017) developed a new technological solution to predict the accidents early by analysing the datasets. End of the analysis, the majority accidents are happened due to the drivers who drunk and drive. These kinds of drivers can be alerted by using the alcohol sensor.

Shetgaonkar et al. (2015) detect flame or smoke in the car's engine followed by user notification. The prediction systems are capable of monitoring the car abnormality and it detects the car accidents by predicting them early. Sane et al. (2016) develop a new accident detection system that is used to predict the accidents when fit into the car. On sensing any obstacles, the user needs to push a switch which leads to immediately turning on the buzzer. The biggest disadvantage here is that the system is non-autonomous. Schultz et al. (1996) have based their research on analysing images which are extracted from moving videos inter-coupled with each other. Finally, to come up with the best algorithms for extracting images from inter-coupled moving videos which is a novel solution for sampling videos using subsampling.

Wong et al. (2006) analyse the effect different types of SVM and ANN algorithms have on image classification i.e. analysis and retrieval. The findings of the research focus on how CNN has a better effect on image classification papers because it has better feature extraction.

Kim et al. (2019) analyse how different dimensions of feature extractions lead to better and more accurate results. In 3D CNN preservation of temporal information leads to better and more accurate results as compared to 2D CNN. This although requires more processing power hence is time consuming. Perumal et al. (2018) SVM, CNN, KNN, Deep CNN and RF among various others are the algorithms which are analysed extensively to find which has better accuracy with respect to image classification. The results show that CNN has better accuracy compared to others. Parsania et al. (2014) image classification algorithms have different effects and they have analysed non-adaptive and adaptive techniques of which adaptive prove to be lighter on the CPU. This research is based on interpolation techniques for image scaling and analysing for scaling to different resolution, aspect ratio or size. All the available works are not able to predict the accidents accurately. For this purpose, this work is used to predict the accidents accurately and detect them. Moreover, it provides necessary details to the people and prevents the accidents and also helpful for reaching the hospitals quickly and safeguard the people on time.

PROBLEM STATEMENT

The paper explores the domain of image classification using Convolutional Neural Network for practical use in professional large-scale activities. Now, to address the issue of accident detection with help of cheap infrastructure and immediate results for self-car accidents and of those nearby, we have come up with a solution where we shall detect if an accident has occurred or not using an appropriate Deep Learning model and ML algorithms. Initially, this work starts by creating our own database from scratch by scrapping accident videos recorded from dashboard cameras on vehicles, available on YouTube and other online sources. Then we shall use the Binary Classification algorithm for building the image classifier model and as far as the optimizer is concerned, we shall be using the Adam optimizer in order to reduce the losses so that we achieve a better accuracy. The proposed model predicts whether an accident has occurred or not from an unknown set of images of the items using Image Classification. For this purpose, this paper addresses this issue by presenting an efficient approach for classification of accidents based on immediate analysis of images recorded from the dashboard camera.

PROPOSED WORK

This work proposes a new accident prediction system that considers the newly generated dataset and also applies deep classifier, augmentation and hyperparameter tuning process.

Proposed Work Introduction

Detection of a required image being that of accident or not will be done by using a deep learning model which will be trained using an image dataset. At first the dataset is completely created from scratch using scrapping of videos available on YouTube and other online sources all images are insured to be of 720p resolution and converted to greyscale for better building of the model. The dataset is split into training and test set and then the images are rescaled and normalized by a factor of 1/255. Creation of binary classes called "accident" and "no-accident" is done. The model is initialized and alternate convolution and pooling layers are added to the model with some dropout layers in between them. Rectifier activation function has been used in the convolution layers. The fully connected layers are then added and in the last layer, i.e., the output layer, sigmoid has been used as the activation function as it is a binary classification problem. The model is compiled using Adam as the optimizer and binary cross-entropy as the loss function. The model is trained against the training set and evaluated against the test set and then a function is defined for making predictions against an unknown set of images.

Creating Dataset

From YouTube videos, google archives and newspaper articles high resolution(720p) images are scrapped and converted to Gray scale and of similar size to create a dataset of accident and no-accident images which are captured from the front dashboard of vehicles where the camera is placed.

Image Augmentation

Image Augmentation is applied to transform the images in the training set without affecting the class to which the image belongs in the original dataset. The transformations include horizontal and vertical flips, rotations, zoom, horizontal and vertical shifts and many other techniques for image manipulation. Keras provides an ImageDataGenerator class to facilitate image augmentation. Horizontal and Vertical Shift is applied to shift all the pixels of the images either horizontally or vertically without changing the dimensions of the images. The images are flipped horizontally and vertically using the horizontal flip and vertical flip respectively. A rotation augmentation is used to rotate an image by 360 degrees in clockwise direction. The images can also be zoomed in and out using the zoom augmentation.

The Hyperparameters

There are several hyperparameters we need to consider when building a deep learning model. We shall see later how by changing the values of the hyperparameters is leading to change in the performance of the model. Some of the hyperparameters we are going to consider for our image classifier model include number of epochs, learning rate of the model, number of neurons in the fully connected layers, etc. Epochs refers to the number of iterations a model undergoes to get trained on batches of images. Learning rate is initialized when we create the optimizer and it denotes how fast the weights will get adjusted, i.e., lower the learning rate the more time the model takes to get trained. Each fully connected layer in the neural network has some neurons which get activated when a particular feature of the image data gets extracted pertaining to that neuron. We can tune the model by changing the number of neurons in each dense or fully connected layer of the network.

Keras Sequential Model

This work uses the Sequential model of Keras to create own image classifier model. The sequential class is used to create deep learning models layer by layer having a single input and output tensor. In order to create the CNN model we add alternate convolution and pooling layers to the sequential model with some dropout layers in between them. After adding the convolution layers we add the fully connected layers and a final output layer to the network.

Convolution Layers

Each image is represented as a matrix having pixel values ranging from 0 to 255. This image matrix is converted to a feature map by the feature detector. Generally, the feature detector is a matrix of size 3x3 which extracts the features from the matrix representing the image and maps them into a feature map.

Back Propagation and Gradient Descent

The model gets trained by back propagation, i.e., when the model propagates in forward direction and gives an output which becomes the predicted value. The loss function or cost function is calculated and the aim is to minimize the loss function. The model back propagates to adjust the weights on the basis of learning rate. After adjusting the weights the model propagates in forward direction and makes the prediction. This process continues and this is how gradient descent is used as an optimizing algorithm to minimize the loss function, thereby ensuring a higher accuracy.

Proposed Work Architecture

The model will be trained and then implemented in a flow as given in Figure 1. Initially, we start with creating and finalizing an image dataset for the training of the dataset. This is one of the most important steps as a perfect dataset with pre-processing is very important. The role of data in machine learning is bigger than it appears and thus, this is the initial, yet one of the most important stages of the flow of the paper. Now, then we move on to the rescaling and normalizing the dataset. Since we know how important dataset is, we need to be aware that the dataset should be normalized before use, i.e., under-sampling or over sampling of the data should be done along with other required pre-processing techniques so as to ensure enhancement of the quality of data which in turn will improve the quality of the trained model. The selected image dataset is then divided into training and testing dataset. Training dataset is the part of the data that the model learns and trains on. This is basically the food that the model gets and builds itself upon. Then is testing data which is important in ensuring proper working and estimating the accuracy of the trained model. This is used after the model is ready so as to test the metrics of the trained model. Now we start implementing the CNN procedures to the dataset to train our model. We start with creating binary classes from the data attributes so that it is easier to classify accident and no accident images with 0s and 1s.

Then we move on to implementing keras sequential model. Under this, we add convolution layers and pooling layers slowly and observe the changes in accuracy to

Figure 1. Proposed system architecture

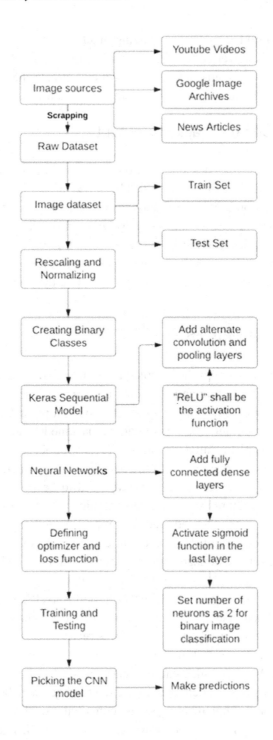

identify the optimum number of layers. This is the main task here that we identify the exact number of layers that will give the best possible result. Also, 'relu' will be the activation function being used here because of binary classification being our primary focus. Then we go towards the implementation of neural networks. This includes adding dense layers (fully connected dense layers) followed by activating the sigmoid function in the last layer. We will also set the number of neurons as two as we are doing binary classification in order to predict from 2 classes. Now after the creation of the neural network, the next important step is to define the optimizer and loss function followed by final training of the model. After the training is complete, the model is tested on the training data and the accuracy metrics of the model are noted and analysed. Now we go back to the training of the model and change the hyperparameters (here, the number of layers, epochs, and the train-test data split) and then perform all the operations again. The best possible hyperparameter tuning values' model shall be selected as the one for prediction. This is the penultimate step where we pick the final CNN model for further prediction and result of the paper. Finally, we create the pickle file of the model so that it can be used in any website or app for predictive analysis or for giving a graphical user interface to the model.

Algorithm

Image Augmentation is applied to transform the images in the training set without affecting the class to which the image belongs in the original dataset. The transformations include horizontal and vertical flips, rotations, zoom, horizontal and vertical shifts and many other techniques for image manipulation. Keras provides an ImageDataGenerator class to facilitate image augmentation. Horizontal and Vertical Shift is applied to shift all the pixels of the images either horizontally or vertically without changing the dimensions of the images. The images are flipped horizontally and vertically using the horizontal flip and vertical flip respectively. A rotation augmentation is used to rotate an image by 360 degrees in a clockwise direction. The images can also be zoomed in and out using the zoom augmentation.

$$\delta v_{i_1 \dots i_g} = \frac{\sum_{c=1}^{N_\Omega} \cdot \left(\frac{\partial \xi}{\partial x}\right)_c \prod_{j=1}^{d} \cdot B_{i_f}\left(x_j^c\right) \prod_{j=1}^{d} B_{t_j}^2\left(c_j^c\right)}{\left(\sum_{c=1}^{N_\Omega} \cdot \prod_{j=1}^{d} \cdot B_{t_j}^2\left(x_j^c\right)\right)\left(\sum_{k_1=1}^{y+1} \sum_{k_d=1}^{y+1} \cdot \prod_{j=1}^{d} \cdot B_{k_i}^2\left(x_j^e\right)\right)} \tag{1}$$

There are several hyperparameters we need to consider when building a deep learning model. We shall see later how by changing the values of the hyperparameters is leading to change in the performance of the model. Some of the hyperparameters we are going to consider for our image classifier model include number of epochs, learning rate of the model, number of neurons in the fully connected layers, etc. Epochs refers to the number of iterations a model undergoes to get trained on batches of images. Learning rate is initialized when we create the optimizer and it denotes how fast the weights will get adjusted, i.e., lower the learning rate the more time the model takes to get trained. Each fully connected layer in the neural network has some neurons which get activated when a particular feature of the image data gets extracted pertaining to that neuron. We can tune the model by changing the number of neurons in each dense or fully connected layer of the network. We calculate the learning rate and regularization parameter by the given parameters respectively

We use the Sequential model of Keras to create our image classifier model. The sequential class is used to create deep learning models layer by layer having a single input and output tensor. In order to create the CNN model, we add alternate convolution and pooling layers to the sequential model with some dropout layers in between them. After adding the convolution layers we add the fully connected layers and a final output layer to the network. The number of parameters in 2D convolution layers is calculated by using the formula given in equation (2).

$$Parameter\_No. = (output\_Channel\_Number * Kernel\_Height * Kernel\_Width + 1)$$
(2)

The parameter number when we use 2 dense layers is calculated by the formula given in equation (3).

$$Parameter\_No. = Output\_Channel\_No. * (Input\_Channel\_No. + 1)$$
(3)

Each image is represented as a matrix having pixel values ranging from 0 to 255. This image matrix is converted to a feature map by the feature detector. Generally, the feature detector is a matrix of size 3x3 which extracts the features from the matrix representing the image and maps them into a feature map. This work calculates the pre-nonlinearity input by the give formula in equation (4).

$$x_{ij}^{\ell} = \sum_{a=0}^{m-1} \cdot \sum_{b=0}^{m-1} \omega_{ab} y_{(i+a)(j+b)}^{\ell-1}$$
(4)

To calculate error while applying convolution layers, following formulae given in equation (5) and (6).

$$\frac{\partial E}{\partial y_{ij}^{\ell-1}} = \sum_{a=0}^{m-1} \cdot \sum_{b=0}^{m-1} \cdot \frac{\partial E}{\partial x_{(i-a)(j-b)}^{\ell}} \frac{\partial x_{(i-a)(j-b)}^{\ell}}{\partial y_{ij}^{\ell-1}} = \sum_{a=0}^{m-1} \cdot \sum_{b=0}^{m-1} \cdot \frac{\partial E}{\partial x_{(i-a)(j-b)}^{\ell}} \omega_{ai} \tag{5}$$

$$\frac{\partial E}{\partial \omega_{ab}} = \sum_{i=0}^{N-m} \cdot \sum_{j=0}^{N-m} \cdot \frac{\partial E}{\partial x_{ij}^{\ell}} \frac{\partial x_{ij}^{\ell}}{\partial \omega_{ab}} = \sum_{i=0}^{N-m} \cdot \sum_{j=0}^{N-m} \cdot \frac{\partial E}{\partial x_{ij}^{\ell}} y_{(i+a)(j+b)}^{\ell-1} \tag{6}$$

$$\frac{\partial E}{\partial x_{ij}^{\ell}} = \frac{\partial E}{\partial y_{ij}^{\ell}} \frac{\partial y_{ij}^{\ell}}{\partial x_{ij}^{\ell}} = \frac{\partial E}{\partial y_{ij}^{\ell}} \frac{\partial}{\partial x_{ij}^{\ell}} \left(\sigma(x_{ij}^{\ell}) \right) = \frac{\partial E}{\partial y_{ij}^{\ell}} \sigma'(x_{ij}^{\ell}) \tag{7}$$

The above formulae are useful for making effective decision over the input that are provided in the form of input dataset.

EXPERIMENTAL SETUP AND RESULT

This work has been created the data from scratch by scraping YouTube videos, google archives and newspaper articles all of which have been normalized to a resolution of 720p and converted to grayscale for better analysis and research. The observations have been carried out with different split sizes of the dataset which are 0.7 (70% training data and 30% test data), 0.8 (80% training data and 20% test data) and 0.9 (90% training data and 10% test data). The accuracy varies for different split sizes on CNN models. The CNN model with 90-10 train-test split ratio is giving the best results. Figure 2 shows the accuracy analysis with respect to model specification.

Figure 2. Model specification vs. accuracy

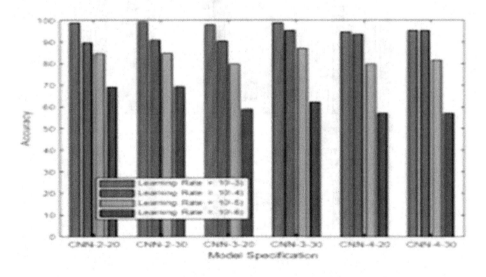

In Figure 2 it is observed that CNN with 2 convolution layers and the CNN with 3 convolution layers are providing decent accuracies which are quite similar. While for CNN with 4 convolution layers it is seen that the accuracy obtained is quite less than that of the former models. Such behaviour is caused by over-fitting of the image classifier model with 4 convolution layers, which is caused due to the small size of the dataset. Thus, any further increase in the number of convolution layers after 3 will lead the model to get over-fitted on the training set, creating room for erroneous predictions.

Figure 3 illustrates the accuracy with different learning rates for models with 2,3 and 4 convolution layers with 20 epochs and 30 epochs each. This graph contrasts the extensive observations against each other to give a fair idea of the accuracy trends in the whole flow consisting of the 3 most important factors of the model. For learning rate 0.001, CNN with convolution and 30 epochs performs the best while CNN with 4 convolution layers and 20 epochs gives the least accuracy of all. General trend for learning rate 0.001 is that the accuracy is going down with an increase in the number of convolution layers. Also, models with 30 epochs are performing better than the models with 20 epochs. For learning rate 0.0001, unlike learning rate 0.001, the accuracy increases with increase in the number of convolution layers. Though, the trend for number of epochs is same as in learning rate 0.001, i.e., accuracy increases with increase in number of epochs. For the learning rate

Figure 3. Learning rate vs. accuracy

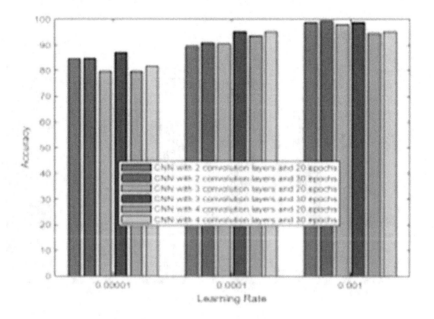

0.00001, there is no general trend that can be figured out directly. Overall, it can be observed clearly that the accuracy increases when we increase epochs from 20 to 30 while keeping the number of convolution layers, and the learning rate same. This indicates that the suitable number of epochs for creation of the proposed model in order to achieve the best possible results is 30.

CONCLUSION AND FUTURE WORK

An efficient image classification technique has been proposed for predicting the accidents early in this paper for avoiding the accidents in smart cities. Simulation results demonstrate that the proposed model achieves a maximum accuracy of 98.34% using a convolutional neural network of 2 layers with a learning rate of 0.001 and 30 epochs; the activation function used is ReLU, thereby ensuring correct predictions in almost all the cases. This algorithm should also be capable of working with live stream data as the dataset is capable of being scrapped from videos and so is the testing data. Therefore, a solution is established which is cheap and feasible. With this setup of the dashboard camera in vehicles accidents can be instantaneously detected and lives can be saved. In future a notification after detection mechanism can be set in place to convert this research into a functional paper. Furthermore, if we increase the from 2 class prediction that is accidents and no-accident to a 3 class prediction being accident, no-accident and almost accident this solution would be a phenomenal breakthrough that would help avert or reduce fatalities caused by accidents. This includes an almost accident case if detected, the vehicle can be made to apply instant brakes or airbags can be popped out; provision can also be made to cushion the outer surface of the vehicles to reduce impact immensely.

REFERENCES

Abramowski, M. (2018, April). Application of data video recorder in reconstruction of road accidents. In *2018 XI International Science-Technical Conference Automotive Safety* (pp. 1-6). IEEE. 10.1109/AUTOSAFE.2018.8373327

Aishwarya, A. R., Rai, A., Charitha, Prasanth, M. A., & Savitha, S. C. (2015). An IoT Based Accident Prevention & Tracking System for Night Drivers. *International Journal of Innovative Research in Computer and Communication Engineering, 3*(4).

Kim, S. Y., Lim, J., Na, T., & Kim, M. (2019). Video Super-Resolution Based on 3D-CNNS with Consideration of Scene Change. *2019 IEEE International Conference on Image Processing (ICIP),* 2831-2835. 10.1109/ICIP.2019.8803297

Kinoshita, H., Yagi, M., Takahashi, S., & Hagiwara, T. (2022, July). A Method for Classifying Road Narrowing Conditions Based on Features of Surrounding Vehicles and Piled Snow in In-vehicle Camera Videos. In *2022 IEEE International Conference on Consumer Electronics-Taiwan* (pp. 299-300). IEEE. 10.1109/ICCE-Taiwan55306.2022.9868980

Mallidi, S. K. R., & Vineela, V. V. (2018). IoT based smart vehicle monitoring system. *Int. J. Adv. Res. Comput. Sci*, 9(2), 738–741. doi:10.26483/ijarcs.v9i2.5870

Parsania, P. S., & Virparia, D. P. V. (2014). A review: Image interpolation techniques for image scaling. *International Journal of Innovative Research in Computer and CNommunication Engineering*, 2(12), 7409–7414.

Perumal, S., & Velmurugan, T. (2018). Preprocessing by contrast enhancement techniques for medical images. *International Journal of Pure and Applied Mathematics*, 118(18), 3681–3688.

Rajendran, T. (2022, January). Road Obstacles Detection using Convolution Neural Network and Report using IoT. In *2022 4th International Conference on Smart Systems and Inventive Technology (ICSSIT)* (pp. 22-26). IEEE. 10.1109/ICSSIT53264.2022.9716337

Sabry, K., & Emad, M. (2021, December). Road Traffic Accidents Detection Based On Crash Estimation. In *2021 17th International Computer Engineering Conference (ICENCO)* (pp. 63-68). IEEE. 10.1109/ICENCO49852.2021.9698968

Sandeep, K., Ravikumar, P., & Ranjith, S. (2017, July). Novel drunken driving detection and prevention models using Internet of things. In *2017 International Conference on Recent Trends in Electrical, Electronics and Computing Technologies (ICRTEECT)* (pp. 145-149). IEEE. 10.1109/ICRTEECT.2017.38

Sane, N. H., Patil, D. S., Thakare, S. D., & Rokade, A. V. (2016). Real time vehicle accident detection and tracking using GPS and GSM. *International Journal on Recent and Innovation Trends in Computing and Communication*, 4(4), 479–482.

Schultz, R. R., & Stevenson, R. L. (1996, June). Extraction of high-resolution frames from video sequences. *IEEE Transactions on Image Processing*, 5(6), 996–1011. doi:10.1109/83.503915 PMID:18285187

Shetgaonkar, P. R., & NaikPawar, VGauns, R. (2015). Proposed Model for the Smart Accident Detection System for Smart Vehicles using Arduino board, Smart Sensors, GPS and GSM. *Int. J. Emerg. Trends Technol. Comput. Sci*, 4, 172–176.

Wong, W.-T., & Hsu, S.-H. (2006). Application of SVM and ANN for image retrieval. *European Journal of Operational Research*, *173*(3), 938–950. doi:10.1016/j. ejor.2005.08.002

Wu, J., Xue, C., Zhao, Z., & Liu, B. (2012, July). Effect of camera angle on precision of parameters for traffic accident in video detection. In *2012 Third International Conference on Digital Manufacturing & Automation* (pp. 347-350). IEEE. 10.1109/ ICDMA.2012.84

Chapter 2
CrimedetGAN:
A Novel Generative Digital Trace Learning System for Detecting Crime-Natured Nodes in Social Networks

S. S. Ramyadharshni
Vellore Institute of Technology, Chennai, India

A. Bhuvaneswari
iD https://orcid.org/0000-0001-6651-2031
Vellore Institute of Technology, Chennai, India

ABSTRACT

Social networks play a dominant role in connecting communication devices, which play as essential role in exchanging a large amount of interpersonal data. As a result of exchange of messages, they leave behind some traces, which help in identifying the nature of the network. So, these are helpful in detecting crime users. The algorithms like SVM, Bayesian linear regression will not help in finding out the crime network. It also results in less accuracy for higher amounts of data. So, developing the trace learning system in GAN, which is a higher order of deep learning neural network, larger neural network dataset will be fed into the model, which has digital traces into the neural network done through proposed CrimedetGAN. A trained accuracy system model automatically identifies the digital traces which have been left in the crime natured social network. Experimenting with existing GAN frameworks, namely MaliGAN, seqGAN, LeakGAN, proposed CrimedetGAN came with a test score accuracy of 91.23% on the coherence NLP testing in tracing the relevant data fields for the given input datasets.

DOI: 10.4018/978-1-6684-7756-4.ch002

INTRODUCTION

Crime occurrences reported to law enforcement include the event date and time, the geographical location, and a brief narrative description of the event. Recently, crime theme models (Kuang, Brantingham, & Bertozzi, 2017) for crime report narratives were established to help categories occurrences into more detailed and accurate categories. These models are more coherent than human-defined categories and may result in more accurate geographic risk estimations (Pandey & Mohler, 2018). Crime event text data also appears on social media, such as Twitter (Wang, Gerber, & Brown, 2012), and machine learning algorithms have been developed to recognize, categories, and integrate such events in spatiotemporal forecasts. Recently, neural network-based representations in the form of restricted Boltzmann machines (RBM) for crime report data have been developed (Zhu & Xie, 2019).

Crime detection in social networks using Generative Adversarial Networks (GANs) is an emerging research area that utilizes the power of GANs to identify and predict criminal activities in online platforms. GANs offer a unique approach by generating synthetic criminal data that closely resembles real criminal behaviors, enabling more accurate and comprehensive training of crime detection models.

One application of GANs in crime detection is the generation of synthetic criminal profiles or posts that mimic the characteristics of actual criminal activities. These synthetic data points can be used to train machine learning models to recognize patterns, anomalies, and indicators of criminal behavior. By leveraging GANs, crime detection systems can capture the diversity and complexity of criminal activities, including fraud, cyberbullying, hate speech, and illicit activities, among others. The use of GANs in crime detection has several advantages. GANs can capture the underlying structure and dynamics of social networks, allowing for the detection of subtle and evolving criminal behaviors that may go unnoticed by traditional methods. They can also adapt and learn from unlabeled data, enabling the identification of emerging criminal patterns. Moreover, GAN-based crime detection models can improve their performance over time as they receive feedback and learn from real-time data.

However, there are challenges associated with using GANs for crime detection in social networks. Acquiring labeled criminal data for training GANs can be challenging, as it requires access to real criminal activities and may raise privacy concerns. Additionally, the scalability of GAN-based models in handling the vast amount of data generated in social networks is a significant consideration. Model performance, interpretability, and ethical considerations also need to be addressed to ensure the reliable and responsible use of GANs in crime detection.

Overall, crime detection in social networks using GANs has the potential to enhance the accuracy and effectiveness of identifying and preventing criminal activities in online platforms. By leveraging the power of GANs, researchers and practitioners aim to develop advanced crime detection systems that can contribute to creating safer and more secure online environments.

GANs are composed of two networks: one network that converts random Gaussian vectors from a latent space to artificial observations (such as artificial pictures or text reports), and another network that learns to discriminate between real and artificial data. The GAN learns an accurate representation of the data after successful (adversarial) training, and artificial and genuine instances may become unrecognisable. In this study, we aim to assess various approaches for generative modelling of crime text data.

This renowned action has a negative impact on society since it causes psychological disorders such as sadness, anxiety, and post-traumatic stress disorder in both those who experienced it and those who observed it (Krug et al., 2002). According to the official United States (U.S.) definition of domestic terrorism, violence is a component of terrorism (Jones, 2022). Interpersonal violence, intimate partner violence, and sexual violence that hinders economic growth harm millions of Americans (Sumner et al., 2015). The use of violence includes murder, robbery, and kidnapping. To ensure the security of the populace, a government must be aware of violent actions in real time. Recently, social media sites like Twitter and Facebook have been utilised as platforms to identify violence or keep an eye on violence-related activity from individuals who publish suspiciously relevant messages at specific times. Social media contains a variety of violent material and subjects. Prediction mechanism of

Figure 1. Model prediction mechanism of GAN

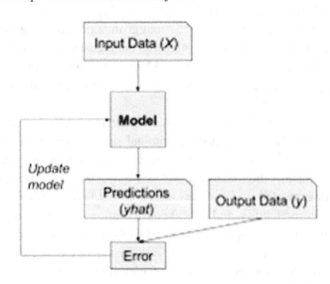

GAN is represented through Figure 1. Violent detection methods are able to extract violent subjects from social media and recognise sentences that are connected to violent content (Cano Basave et al., 2013).

Overview of Crime Detection Techniques in Social Networks

Crime detection in social networks is a critical task due to the increasing prevalence of criminal activities in online platforms. Traditional techniques for crime detection often involve rule-based systems, keyword matching, or manual inspection, which may be limited in their ability to handle the dynamic and complex nature of criminal behaviors in social networks. However, with the advent of advanced technologies and machine learning algorithms, there has been a growing interest in employing data-driven approaches, such as network analysis, text mining, and machine learning, to detect and analyze criminal activities in social networks.

Limitations of Traditional Methods and the Need for Advanced Approaches

Traditional methods of crime detection in social networks face several limitations. Firstly, they often rely on predefined rules or heuristics, which may fail to capture emerging or sophisticated criminal behaviors. Secondly, the sheer volume and complexity of data generated on social networks make it challenging for traditional methods to effectively process and analyze the data for detecting criminal activities. Moreover, the imbalanced distribution of criminal events poses a challenge, as rare criminal activities are often overshadowed by the overwhelming amount of normal user behavior. These limitations highlight the need for advanced approaches that can overcome these challenges and provide more accurate and robust crime detection in social networks.

Potential Advantages of Gans in Crime Detection on Social Networks

Generative Adversarial Networks (GANs) offer several potential advantages in crime detection on social networks. GANs can generate synthetic data that closely resembles the patterns and characteristics of criminal activities, enabling more comprehensive training of crime detection models. They can learn and capture the complex relationships and dynamics within social networks, allowing for the detection of subtle anomalies and patterns that may signify criminal behavior. GANs also have the ability to adapt and learn from unlabeled data, which is particularly beneficial in identifying new and evolving criminal behaviors. These advantages make GANs a promising approach for enhancing the accuracy and effectiveness of crime detection in social networks.

RELATED WORK

A lot of research have concentrated on using machine learning techniques for anticipating crime in space. Space-time clustering (Sumner et al., 2015), gun violence patterns on social networks (Cano Basave et al., 2013), and other phenomena are modelled using point process models (Osorio & Beltran, 2020). Applied to space-time crime predicting more recently, deep learning (Mensa et al., 2020; Ni et al., 2020), and learning to rank (Botelle et al., 2022; Khalifeh et al., 2015) techniques have demonstrated increased accuracy. From Google Street View photos, deep learning algorithms have also been used to infer crime rates (Byun et al., 2014). It has been demonstrated that auxiliary data, such as location data (Wang, Gerber, & Brown, 2012) and geolocated Twitter data (Wang, Gerber, & Brown, 2012), may enhance space-time models.

Text data has been the focus of other recent study in machine learning and crime. Latent Dirichlet Allocation (LDA) is used by Wang et al. (2012) to extract subjects from Twitter postings, and a generic linear model is then used to predict Hit And Run incidents. Kuang et al. (2017) take into account latent behavioural and situational factors that contribute to crimes before using latent distributions using topic modelling to cluster and categorise different types of crimes. An automated approach to extract information from unstructured text data, such as emails, chat logs, blogs, web pages, and text documents, was proposed by AlZaidy et al. (2012). to identify criminal gangs. Recently, gang offences have been categorised using text reports using partly generative neural networks (PGNNs) (Seo et al., 2018). The resulting criminal text data's quality was not assessed in that study, though.

The implementation of cutting-edge strategies like Generative Adversarial Networks (GANs) has become necessary due to the shortcomings of traditional methods for crime detection in social networks. Traditional approaches frequently find it difficult to keep up with how quickly criminal activity on online platforms is developing. These techniques frequently rely on predetermined criteria, heuristics, or manual examination, which may not be adequate for spotting new or complex criminal behaviours. Additionally, traditional approaches have substantial difficulties in successfully analysing and identifying nodes with criminal intent due to the sheer volume and complexity of data collected on social networks. The problem is made worse by the uneven distribution of illegal activity since it makes it challenging to identify uncommon occurrences within the massive volume of typical user behavior (Brock et al., 2021). Promising answers to these restrictions are provided by cutting-edge methodologies like GANs. GANs have the ability to provide synthetic data that more accurately captures the dynamic and complex character of criminal activity in social networks, allowing for more thorough training of crime detection algorithms. GANs can adapt to new and changing criminal behaviours without explicit labels by utilising unsupervised learning. GANs' adversarial training method makes it possible to find minute patterns and anomalies that might indicate illicit activity. The shortcomings of conventional approaches in detecting crimes on social networks highlight the need for cutting-edge methods like GANs, which can handle data difficulties, adapt to changing behaviours, and offer more precise and robust detection capabilities (Romano et al., 2021).

Unsupervised deep learning models in the Generative Adversarial Networks (GANs) class (Karazeev, 2017; Sornsoontorn, n.d.). A Generator Neural Network (G) and a Discriminator Neural Network are the two main parts of each GAN (D). The generator G(z) creates bogus data by taking an input, z, and a sample from the probability distribution p(z), which is commonly Gaussian. The discriminator uses binary classification to identify whether the input is real or artificial by using either an actual observation, in this case a criminal report, or synthetic output from the generator. The two networks are trained jointly using alternating gradient descent steps to I train the generator by freezing the weights of the discriminator and ii) train the discriminator to accurately distinguish between real and fake data. The generator is trained by initially freezing the weights of the discriminator. After a successful training, the two networks come to a minimax game-like equilibrium (Adford et al., 2015). GANs have mostly been successful when used to continuous data, such as photos (Che et al., 2017), while using GAN to discrete data, such as text, is difficult.

When used as a language model for text production, generative adversarial networks can be difficult to use GANs for generative modelling of discrete data (Jones, 2022), and GANs frequently lack consistency in long-term syntactic creation (Gretton et al., 2012). In order to address these issues, Zhang et al. (2016) developed new designs for each GAN network, namely using convolutional neural networks (CNNs) for the discriminator and long short-term memory (LSTM) cells as the generator. The discriminator then learns the sentence structure using a confusion training technique. Zhang et al. use feature distribution matching rather than data distribution matching. The training objective in this instance that represents feature mapping is as follows.

$$\min L_D = -E_{.s} \sim S^{\log D(s)} - E_z \sim P_{z(z)}^{\log[1-D(z)]} \qquad [1]$$

$$minL_G = tr(\sum_S^{-1} \Sigma r + \sum_r^{-1} \Sigma s + \left(\mu_s - \mu_r\right)^T \left(\sum_S^{-1} + \sum_r^{-1}\right)\left(\mu_s - \mu_r\right) \qquad [2]$$

Here Σs and Σr are the covariances of the real and fake feature vectors, and μs and μr are their means.

Another GAN-based model for generating text is TextGAN (Yu, Zhang, Wang, & Yu, 2017), which extends the standard objective function of GAN by two additional terms: the Euclidean distance between the recovered latent code and the original code, and the Maximum Mean Discrepancy (MMD), which is a distance on the space of probability measures (Zhang et al., 2017). Therefore, the discriminator must create the most demanding, representative, and discriminatory sentence characteristics. After then, the generator must match these qualities. The following provides the TextGAN's goal function:

$$maxL_D = L_{GAN} - »_r L_{recon} + »_m L_{MDD^2} \qquad [3]$$

$$minL_G = L_{MDD^2} \qquad [4]$$

$$L_{GAN} = E_S \sim S^{lodD(S)} - E_Z \sim P_{Z(Z)}{}^{\log[1-D(Z)]} \qquad [5]$$

$$L_{recon} = \left\| \hat{Z} - z \right\| \qquad [6]$$

Here, $\hat{Z}$ is the original latent code taken from the previous distribution $P_z(.)z$ is the reconstructed latent code, and L_{MDD^2} is the maximum mean discrepancy (MMD). Recurrent neural networks (RNN) in text production ultimately lead to exposure bias since the generated word is reliant on previous ones at each stage, according to Zhang et al. This mistake is proportional to the length of the sentence and is common in ordinary GANs. This issue is resolved by Lamb et al. (2012) proposal of a "professor forcing architecture," which makes use of a second discriminator trained to preserve stable long-term reliance within individual words in a sentence.

Various Applications of GANs in Real World Social Networks

The variations of Generative Adversarial Networks (GANs) commonly used in social network analysis encompass several notable models and techniques. In a literature review conducted on this topic, it was found that several GAN variants have been employed to address the challenges specific to social network analysis. One widely cited variant is the GraphGAN, proposed by Wang et al. (2018), which extends the traditional GAN framework to generate realistic graph structures that capture the relational information in social networks. Another significant variation is the SeqGAN model introduced by Yu et al. (2017), which utilizes the GAN architecture for sequential data generation. SeqGAN has been adapted in social network analysis to model and generate sequences of social network interactions or behaviors. Additionally, Adversarial Autoencoders (AAE), introduced by Makhzani et al. (2016), have been employed in social network analysis to learn latent representations that capture the underlying structure and dynamics of social networks. These variations of GANs, among others, have proven effective in addressing the unique challenges of social network analysis, offering valuable insights into network generation, sequence modeling, and latent representation learning.

Applications of GANs in Social Networks

Several studies have employed GANs for crime detection in social networks. These studies have explored various crime types, such as fraud, cyberbullying, hate speech, and illicit activities. GANs have been utilized to generate synthetic criminal data for training robust crime detection models. The generated data can capture the diverse characteristics and patterns of criminal activities, enabling more accurate identification and prediction of criminal behaviors in social networks. The application of GANs in social networks has shown promising results in enhancing crime detection capabilities and providing valuable insights into the nature and dynamics of criminal behaviors in online platforms.

CHALLENGES AND LIMITATIONS

While GANs hold promise for crime detection in social networks, they also present certain challenges and limitations. One challenge is the availability and quality of labeled training data, as obtaining labeled criminal data in social networks can be difficult and time-consuming. Ethical considerations, privacy concerns, and potential biases also arise when working with sensitive user data in crime detection. Scalability is another challenge, as GAN-based models may face computational complexities when dealing with large-scale social networks. Moreover, the dynamic nature of social networks requires continuous model adaptation and updating to stay effective in detecting emerging criminal behaviors. These challenges and limitations need to be carefully addressed to ensure the reliable and ethical use of GANs in crime detection on social networks.

Proposed Methodology: CrimedetGAN

"CrimedetGAN" refers to a hypothetical system or approach that combines the concept of crime detection with Generative Adversarial Networks (GANs). This term suggests the utilization of GANs in the context of crime detection in various domains, such as social networks, online platforms, or digital environments. CrimedetGAN could involve the development of a GAN-based model specifically designed for crime detection tasks. The GAN component would be responsible for generating synthetic criminal data that closely resembles real criminal activities, enabling more accurate training of crime detection models. The generated data could capture the diversity, complexity, and dynamics of criminal behaviors, thereby improving the detection and prediction of various types of crimes.

An Identification of Four GAN Models for Generating Crime Report Text

In this study, we examine SeqGAN (Lamb et al., 2016), MaliGAN (Zhang et al., 2016), LeakGAN, and CrimedetGAN as four GAN approaches for producing crime report text. We present a summary of the features of these four GAN models in Table 1. SeqGAN, which solves exposure bias in maximum likelihood inference and the difficulties of using GANs to generate discrete data, is the first method. The discriminator is a CNN, and the generator is a Recurrent Neural Network (RNN) with Long Short-Term Memory (LSTM) cells to handle vanishing gradients. When building a model, reinforcement learning (RL) is employed. The generated tokens are states, and the subsequent generated token is an action. Based on a complete sequence of tokens, the discriminator delivers prizes in this framework.

MaliGAN, the second technique, is based on an alternate objective function. MaliGAN's concept is to employ the discriminator's data as an extra training signal. The discriminator objective function is the same as the original GAN, but the generator is trained via significance sampling (Jones, 2022). The third model we consider is CrimedetGAN, where relative ranking information between phrases that were generated by a computer and those that were created by a person is used

Table 1. Comparison of utilized model

Model	Discriminator	Generator	Loss	Training
SeqGAN	CNN	RNN	MLE	Policy gradient
MaliGAN	CNN	RNN	D: MLE G: MLE importance sampling	Policy gradient
CrimedetGAN	CNN ranker regressor	LSTM	D: Ranking	Relative ranking information Policy gradient
LeakGAN	CNN	Hierarchical LSTM	MLE	Interleaved Training

to describe the learning process. The generator (LSTM network) is trained using the policy gradient approach, while the discriminator is a CNN rank regressor. The ranking scores of the ranker network are seen as rewards to learn for the language generator in the setting of policy gradients (Lin et al., 2017). A softmax operation is used to compare a sentence's ranking score to the relevance scores of all the other sentences in a comparison set. The Ranker (R) attempts to rank the produced data lower than the genuine data, and the generator is attempting to produce more realistic documents, simulating the min-max game of the original GAN.

The fourth model we take into account, LeakGAN, makes an effort to address semantic loss across lengthy phrases that has been noticed in SeqGAN, MaliGAN, and CrimedetGAN. Designing the discriminator for LeakGAN involves deviating from binary classification. The discriminator delivers extracted high-level characteristics to the generator in a reinforcement learning framework in addition to such a scalar reward represented in Figure 2. A Manager and Worker network-based hierarchical structure supports the generator. The latent vector is sent to the worker network by the manager network (LSTM) together with the high-level feature vector that was derived from the discriminator. The subsequent word is subsequently produced by the worker network using the latent vector of the previous word. LeakGAN therefore addresses the rewards' non-informativeness and sparsity problems. The parameters

Figure 2. The mechanism of CrimedetGAN architecture

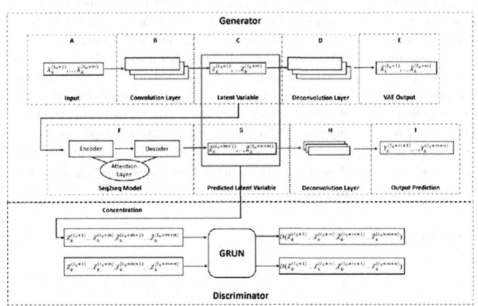

of LeakGAN are determined via interleaved training, which combines supervised learning (MLE) with adversarial learning (GAN).

Dataset Description

The text narratives from crime reports given by the Los Angeles County Sheriff's Department make up the dataset that we used in this study. Angeles Police Department (LAPD) between January 1, 2009, and July 19, 2014. The total number of crime reports in the data is 805556. In Table 3, we provide an example of an actual crime report text narrative.

The incomplete words in the data shown in Table 2 were restored as part of the preprocessing procedure. Our vocabulary size is 5000 words, and we create tokens of our narratives using the 'nltk' software package (Romano et al., 2021) to train GAN models.

PROPOSED METHODOLOGY

Evaluation

Three metrics—negative log likelihood, embedding similarity, and coherence—are used to assess the four GAN models. The average negative log-likelihood of each GAN model assessed using actual test data is known as the negative log-likelihood. BLEU (Wang et al., 2018), which assesses embedding similarity whether the model's produced n-grams can be found in a held-out corpus. Embedding similarity, or EmbSim, is a method of calculating text-similarity that was inspired by BLEU. EmbSim examines sentences' word embeddings rather than matching them word for word. The cosine distance between each word embedding for genuine text data and other words is calculated. The ith word's word embedding, e_i, is then used to create a matrix called W, where $w_{ij}=\cos(e_i,e_j)$ The similarity matrix of actual data is known as W. Similarity matrix W of a produced criminal text report is obtained after evaluating the word embedding of generated false data. In this case, $w_{ij}^0 = \cos(e_j^i, e_j^i), e_j^i$ is how the word I is embedded in the resulting data. Following is a definition of the EmbSim:

$$EmbSim = \log(\sum_{i=1}^{n} \cos\left(w_i^1, w_i\right) / N) \qquad [7]$$

Where W_i is the ith column of W (Yu, Zhang, Wang, & Yu, 2017). A sentence coherence score is the third statistic we take into account. First, we use topic modelling to extract the latent themes from both actual and produced tales. Topic modelling may be thought of as an adaptive categorization that, without human oversight, can adapt to newly developing criminal categories. To extract keywords for each latent topic in the data, we use Mallet's LDA as well as Latent Dirichlet Allocation (LDA). Table 4 lists the subjects and keywords that Mallet's LDA retrieved from our actual data. Then, using normalised point-wise mutual information (NPMI) and the cosinus similarity, we compare the coherence score Cv based on a sliding window, a one-set segmentation of the top words, and an indirect confirmation measure (Makhzani et al., 2016).

The sentence coherence score of a narrative entry determines how consistent the topic of a generated narrative is, such as whether it is obvious that the generated sentence is about a robbery or whether it contains inconsistent topics (for example, words associated with burglary mixed in with words associated with homicide). Equation 4 in our suggested sentence coherence score estimates how a story relates to the themes that are present in our actual data. A lower score indicates that the sentence has more subjects; a higher score indicates that the sentence has fewer topics.

$$Coherence_{narrative} = \left[\frac{count(W_u) - Count(W_c)}{Count(W_t)} \right] + \qquad [8]$$

Here $[.]^+ = \max(0,.)$ W_u is a term that appears in less than two topics, W_t is a word that appears anywhere in the narrative, and W_c is a topic keyword.

EXPERIMENTAL RESULTS

In this section, we contrast the three assessment metrics—SeqGAN, LeakGAN, MaliGAN, and CrimedetGAN—applied to the LAPD crime report narratives. Results for embedding similarity and negative log-likelihood are presented in Table 5. LeakGAN has the lowest (best) NLL and a reasonably high (better) embedding similarity based on these findings. For the purpose of constructing the sentence coherence score, we have used Mallet's LDA and Latent Dirichlet Allocation (LDA) to extract latent themes and associated keywords. Table 6, which displays the coherence scores, reveals that SeqGAN and LeakGAN have the best Mallet's LDA-coherence and LDA-coherence, respectively.

In Table 7, we show sample created narratives for each model along with a qualitative analysis of the test that was generated. We have listed our sentence

Table 2. LDA keywords in each topic

Topic ID	Keywords
0	victim, face, punch, time, verbal, strike, push, argument, dispute, hit
1	suspect, leave, lock, return, cut, bike, park, victim, secure, room
2	property, location, unknown, remove, flee, enter, victim, unsecured, unlocked
3	door, open, property, enter, remove, unknown, gain, entry, front, rear
4	victim, state, phone, call, suspect, kill, demand, threaten, order, fear
5	suspect, victim, flee, dog, attack, approach, screwdriver, vand, tie, res
6	suspect, item, store, pay, exit, location, business, walk, entered, purse
7	suspect, victim, flee, property, scene, removed, location, porch, package, unknown
8	victim, suspect, approach, grab, foot, approached, drive, fire, pull, hand
9	unknown, flee, direction, location, property, tool, remove, tire, type, slash
10	vehicle, window, unknown, smash, side, break, damage, hard, driver, pass
11	victim, suspect, make, card, money, permission, check, info, credit, personal

coherence score in the first column of Table 7. Though there are some samples that lack logic and occasionally contain misspelt words, we also find examples of realistically created statements like "suspect approach victim car inflict damage." We find that RankGAN and LeakGAN prefer creating lengthier tales than SeqGAN and MaliGAN by analysing the generated narratives from each model. The result, however, may not always be more realistic or meaningful storytelling.

In the context of split attention neural networks for sentence detection, the coherence score is a measure used to evaluate the alignment and coherence of the attended representations represented through Table 5. It quantifies how well the attended representations capture the relevant information for detecting sentences in a given input. The coherence score is typically computed based on the attention weights or similarity scores between the attended representations and the target sentence labels. The exact calculation may vary depending on the specific architecture

Table 4. Application of a method negative log likelihood and embedding similarity comparison

Method	NLL(epoch 180)	EmbedSim(epoch 180)
SeqGAN	$1.63E + 00$	$-1.13E - 02$
MaliGAN	$2.47E + 00$	$-9.96E - 3$
LeakGAN	$1.25E + 00$	$-1.21E - 02$
CrimedetGAN	**$2.85E + 00$**	**$-9.84E - 03$**

Table 5. LDA on real data coherence score performance is improved with a higher coherence score

Data Source	Model	C_v Coherence Score (Makhzani et al., 2016)
Real data	LDA	0.288 0.572
SeqGAN generated	LDA	0.462 0.423
MaliGAN generated	LDA	0.396 0.372
LeakGAN generated	LDA	0.475 0.411
CrimedetGAN generated	**LDA**	**0.426** **0.391**

and implementation of the split attention network. Here is a general overview of the process:

1.   Split Attention and Attended Representations:

In a split attention network, the input sequence is divided into multiple parts, and attention mechanisms are applied to each part independently. The attended representations for each part are obtained by combining the input features with the attention weights.

2.   Sentence Detection and Coherence Score Calculation:

After obtaining the attended representations, the sentence detection task aims to classify whether each part represents the start or end of a sentence.

To calculate the coherence score, the attended representations are compared with the ground truth sentence labels. The coherence score can be computed using metrics such as cosine similarity, cross-entropy loss, or accuracy.

The coherence score provides an indication of how well the split attention network attends to the relevant parts of the input and captures the coherence between the attended representations and the sentence labels.

During training, the CrimedetGAN model optimizes both the generator and discriminator simultaneously through an adversarial process represented through Table 7. The generator tries to minimize the generator loss, while the discriminator tries to minimize the discriminator loss. This adversarial competition drives the training process to a point where the generator generates increasingly realistic crime

Table 6. Methods, each of which generated two narratives. Our sentence coherence is measured by the score in this table. Score computed using LDA model and extracted topics.

Score	Narrative Sample
Real	
0.66	suspect continiously calls and text victim harrassing messages victim has repeatedly advised suspect to stop making contact
0.0	suspect approached victims vehicle punctured victims tires with an unknown sharp tool and fled location in unknown direction
SeqGAN	
0.38	a unknown suspect rmvs rent vehicle roll passenger door damage victim vehicle around vehicle cause deep dent
0.0	unknown suspect rmvs smash victims vehicle windows passenger windows vehicle
MaliGAN	
0.85	elm middle of former friends apt victim made unauthorized charge accounts in the secured her name without victim if he could not give anyone any one to defraud bank
0.2	elm mutual partner which occured suspect brother or care of victims suspect fled with victim property wo knowledge
LeakGAN	
0.0	suspect approach victims vehicle cause damage unknown suspect used his kindle carbon merchandis
0.33	suspect approach victim behind punch victim face victim and forcibly psych opcredit windows1 flee location
CrimedetGAN	
0.0	unknown suspect took victims property got to vehicle
0.5	unknown suspect t6ook victims vehicle victim was Brockton radiored stevely occs thnfled cummings mrcedes to unknown suspects akas v006 s1app forgets 1145 hrs and 242/243pc 30000usd merchandise failed in a automotivegarage

Table 7. Representation of learning rate in training

CrimedetGAN (Input Batch Size)	Accuracy	Loss (loss + val_loss)	Iteration (n)	Learning Rate
64	0	0	0	0.010
64	51.37	48.63	50	0.006
64	63.35	36.65	100	0.004
64	70.12	29.88	150	0.004
64	74.23	25.77	200	0.003
64	82.33	17.67	250	0.013
64	**95.70**	**4.30**	**300**	**0.002**

data, while the discriminator becomes more accurate in distinguishing between real and generated samples resulted with an accuracy of 95.70.

The specific mathematical equations and details of the loss function in CrimedetGAN can vary based on the implementation and specific modifications made to the GAN framework. It's essential to refer to the original research paper or the specific implementation's documentation to obtain the exact formulation and implementation details of the loss function used in CrimedetGAN.

CONCLUSION

Four of these techniques were used to create criminal tales using the most recent approach for GAN-based text creation. We discovered that LeakGAN and SeqGAN had the greatest (and comparable) LDA based coherence, whereas CrimedetGAN and SeqGAN fared the best in terms of negative loglikelihood and embedding similarity. The CrimedetGAN resulted in highest accuracy of possible feature generation of predicting the crime natured data from the nodes present within the networks turned out with a good accuracy test score in comparison with the existing GAN frameworks for crime detection. Future research may concentrate on enhancing GAN-based narrative production because our qualitative study reveals that GAN-generated crime reports fall short of human-quality standards. Future study might also focus on using GAN-based embeddings for particular purposes. For instance, Bidirection GANs may be applied to embed crime data in the latent space and invert the generator network. For crime connection analysis, anomaly detection, and criminal justice, such embeddings may be valuable.

As a future work, addressing the ethical considerations and privacy concerns associated with GAN-based crime detection is of utmost importance. Research efforts can focus on developing privacy-preserving GAN architectures or anonymization techniques to ensure that sensitive user information is protected while maintaining the effectiveness of crime detection systems. Lastly, scalability and efficiency are ongoing challenges in GAN-based crime detection systems. Advancements in parallel computing, distributed learning, and model compression techniques can enable the deployment of GAN-based models on large-scale social networks, making them more practical and accessible for real-time crime detection. By pursuing these research directions and advancements, GAN-based crime detection systems can become more accurate, interpretable, ethical, and scalable, contributing to the development of robust and reliable solutions for detecting and combating criminal activities in social networks.

REFERENCES

Adford, A., Metz, L., & Chintala, S. (2015). Unsupervised representation learning with deep convolutional generative adversarial networks. arXiv preprint arXiv:1511.06434.

Al-Zaidy, R., Fung, B. C., Youssef, A. M., & Fortin, F. (2012). Mining criminal networks from unstructured text documents. *Digital Investigation*, 8(3-4), 147–160. doi:10.1016/j.diin.2011.12.001

Botelle, R., Bhavsar, V., Kadra-Scalzo, G., Mascio, A., Williams, M. V., Roberts, A., Velupillai, S., & Stewart, R. (2022). Can natural language processing models extract and classify instances of interpersonal violence in mental healthcare electronic records: An applied evaluative study. *BMJ Open*, 12(2), e052911. doi:10.1136/bmjopen-2021-052911 PMID:35172999

Brock, A., Donahue, J., & Simonyan, K. (2021). BigGAN: Large Scale GAN Training for High Fidelity Natural Image Synthesis. *International Conference on Learning Representations*.

Byun, J. Y., Nasridinov, A., & Park, Y. H. (2014). Internet of things for smart crime detection. *Contemporary Engineering Sciences*, 7(15), 749–754. doi:10.12988/ces.2014.4685

Cano Basave, A. E., He, Y., Liu, K., & Zhao, J. (2013). *A weakly supervised bayesian model for violence detection in social media*. Academic Press.

Che, T., Li, Y., Zhang, R., Hjelm, R. D., Li, W., Song, Y., & Bengio, Y. (2017). Maximum-likelihood augmented discrete generative adversarial networks. arXiv preprint arXiv:1702.07983.

Gretton, A., Borgwardt, K. M., Rasch, M. J., Schölkopf, B., & Smola, A. (2012). A kernel two-sample test. *Journal of Machine Learning Research*, 13(1), 723–773.

Guo, J., Lu, S., Cai, H., Zhang, W., Yu, Y., & Wang, J. (2018, April). Long text generation via adversarial training with leaked information. *Proceedings of the AAAI Conference on Artificial Intelligence*, 32(1). doi:10.1609/aaai.v32i1.11957

Jones, S. G. (2022). *The evolution of domestic terrorism. Statement before the House Judiciary Subcommittee on Crime*. Terrorism, and Homeland Security CSIS-Center for Strategic and International Studies Washington.

Karazeev, A. (2017). *Generative adversarial networks (GANs): Engine and applications*. https://blog.statsbot.co/generativeadversarial-networks-gans-engine-and-applications-f96291965b47

Karras, T., Laine, S., Aittala, M., Hellsten, J., Lehtinen, J., & Aila, T. (2021). StyleGAN2: Analyzing and Improving the Image Quality of StyleGAN. In *Proceedings of the IEEE/CVF Conference on Computer Vision and Pattern Recognition (CVPR)* (pp. 10665-10675). Academic Press.

Khalifeh, H., Moran, P., Borschmann, R., Dean, K., Hart, C., Hogg, J., Osborn, D., Johnson, S., & Howard, L. M. (2015). Domestic and sexual violence against patients with severe mental illness. *Psychological Medicine, 45*(4), 875–886. doi:10.1017/S0033291714001962 PMID:25180908

Krug, E. G., Mercy, J. A., Dahlberg, L. L., & Zwi, A. B. (2002). The world report on violence and health. *Lancet, 360*(9339), 1083–1088. doi:10.1016/S0140-6736(02)11133-0 PMID:12384003

Kuang, D., Brantingham, P. J., & Bertozzi, A. L. (2017). Crime topic modeling. *Crime Science, 6*(1), 1–20. doi:10.118640163-017-0074-0

Kuang, D., Brantingham, P. J., & Bertozzi, A. L. (2017). Crime topic modeling. *Crime Science, 6*(1), 1–20. doi:10.118640163-017-0074-0

Lamb, A. M., Alias Parth Goyal, A. G., Zhang, Y., Zhang, S., Courville, A. C., & Bengio, Y. (2016). Professor forcing: A new algorithm for training recurrent networks. Advances in Neural Information Processing Systems, 29.

Lin, K., Li, D., He, X., Zhang, Z., & Sun, M. T. (2017). Adversarial ranking for language generation. *Advances in Neural Information Processing Systems*, 30.

Makhzani, A., Shlens, J., Jaitly, N., Goodfellow, I., & Frey, B. (2016). Adversarial Autoencoders. In *Proceedings of the 33rd International Conference on Machine Learning (ICML)* (pp. 1558-1566). Academic Press.

Mensa, E., Colla, D., Dalmasso, M., Giustini, M., Mamo, C., Pitidis, A., & Radicioni, D. P. (2020). Violence detection explanation via semantic roles embeddings. *BMC Medical Informatics and Decision Making, 20*(1), 1–13. doi:10.118612911-020-01237-4 PMID:33059690

Mohler, G., & Brantingham, P. J. (2018, April). Privacy preserving, crowd sourced crime Hawkes processes. In *2018 International Workshop on Social Sensing (SocialSens)* (pp. 14-19). IEEE. 10.1109/SocialSens.2018.00016

Ni, Y., Barzman, D., Bachtel, A., Griffey, M., Osborn, A., & Sorter, M. (2020). Finding warning markers: Leveraging natural language processing and machine learning technologies to detect risk of school violence. *International Journal of Medical Informatics, 139*, 104137. doi:10.1016/j.ijmedinf.2020.104137 PMID:32361146

Osorio, J., & Beltran, A. (2020, July). Enhancing the Detection of Criminal Organizations in Mexico using ML and NLP. In *2020 International Joint Conference on Neural Networks (IJCNN)* (pp. 1-7). IEEE. 10.1109/IJCNN48605.2020.9207039

Pandey, R., & Mohler, G. O. (2018, November). Evaluation of crime topic models: topic coherence vs spatial crime concentration. In *2018 IEEE International Conference on Intelligence and Security Informatics (ISI)* (pp. 76-78). IEEE. 10.1109/ISI.2018.8587384

Romano, Y., Elad, M., & Milanfar, P. (2021). ConSinGAN: Learning a Conditional SinGAN from a Single Natural Image. *International Conference on Machine Learning (ICML)*.

Seo, S., Chan, H., Brantingham, P. J., Leap, J., Vayanos, P., Tambe, M., & Liu, Y. (2018, December). Partially generative neural networks for gang crime classification with partial information. In *Proceedings of the 2018 AAAI/ACM Conference on AI, Ethics, and Society* (pp. 257-263). 10.1145/3278721.3278758

Sornsoontorn, C. (n.d.). *How do GANs intuitively work?* Available: https://hackernoon.com/how-do-gans-intuitively-work-2dda07f247a1

Sumner, S. A., Mercy, J. A., Dahlberg, L. L., Hillis, S. D., Klevens, J., & Houry, D. (2015). Violence in the United States: Status, challenges, and opportunities. *Journal of the American Medical Association, 314*(5), 478–488. doi:10.1001/jama.2015.8371 PMID:26241599

Wang, H., Wang, J., Wang, J., Zhao, M., & Yang, J. (2018). GraphGAN: Graph Representation Learning with Generative Adversarial Nets. In *Proceedings of the 27th International Joint Conference on Artificial Intelligence (IJCAI)* (pp. 4176-4182). 10.1609/aaai.v32i1.11872

Wang, X., Gerber, M. S., & Brown, D. E. (2012, April). Automatic crime prediction using events extracted from twitter posts. In *International conference on social computing, behavioral-cultural modeling, and prediction* (pp. 231-238). Springer. 10.1007/978-3-642-29047-3_28

Yu, L., Zhang, W., Wang, J., & Yu, Y. (2017, February). Seqgan: Sequence generative adversarial nets with policy gradient. *Proceedings of the AAAI Conference on Artificial Intelligence, 31*(1). doi:10.1609/aaai.v31i1.10804

Yu, L., Zhang, W., Wang, J., & Yu, Y. (2017). SeqGAN: Sequence Generative Adversarial Nets with Policy Gradient. In *Proceedings of the Thirty-First AAAI Conference on Artificial Intelligence (AAAI)* (pp. 2852-2858). 10.1609/aaai.v31i1.10804

Zhang, Y., Gan, Z., & Carin, L. (2016). Generating text via adversarial training. In NIPS workshop on Adversarial Training (Vol. 21, pp. 21-32). Academic Press.

Zhang, Y., Gan, Z., Fan, K., Chen, Z., Henao, R., Shen, D., & Carin, L. (2017, July). Adversarial feature matching for text generation. In *International Conference on Machine Learning* (pp. 4006-4015). PMLR.

Zhu, S., & Xie, Y. (2019, May). Crime event embedding with unsupervised feature selection. In *ICASSP 2019-2019 IEEE International Conference on Acoustics, Speech and Signal Processing (ICASSP)* (pp. 3922-3926). IEEE. 10.1109/ICASSP.2019.8682285

Chapter 3
Coal Fire Detection and Prevention System Using IoT

V. Pandiyaraju
School of Computer Science and Engineering (SCOPE), Vellore Institute of Technology, Chennai, India

P. Shunmuga Perumal
Vellore Institute of Technology, Vellore, India

V. Muthumanikandan
(iD) https://orcid.org/0000-0002-5863-5047
School of Computer Science and Engineering (SCOPE), Vellore Institute of Technology, Chennai, India

ABSTRACT

Coal is one of the major natural sources of power production. It contributes to about 56% of the total production. Conventionally, coal is stored in stockpiles for production of electricity without any logs. Storage of coal for a longer time in the open type stockpile results in self-oxidation of coal, which leads to increased ignition temperature. Detection and prevention of spontaneous combustion and self-ignition stands to be major issues in stockpile. This chapter proposes an automated system using internet of things (IoT), which aids in detecting the fire at an earlier stage and to prevent it, thereby avoiding economic loss. Wireless sensor nodes are deployed to detect the parameters such as temperature, humidity, gases from the stockpile, and the data is transmitted to the server and to the ground station with the aid of GSM modules. Data is monitored in the ground station, and the critical values are evaluated to prevent fire by detecting it at its early stages. The system is implemented in an open rail coal stockpile, and the data is represented in the form of graph for evaluation.

DOI: 10.4018/978-1-6684-7756-4.ch003

INTRODUCTION

Various process has been implemented and practised for the purpose of power production from the early ages. Thermal Energy conversion is one of the conventional method of electrical power production in which coal acts as a base energy. Coal has to be stored in a larger volume for continuous production of power without any periodical break. Open type stockpile formed by rail mounted stackers are implemented for the storage of coal and is stored for about 7-45 days based upon the possibility of transportation and amount of power production. Storage of coal in the stockpiles for a longer duration causes the coal to react with air to form coal-oxygen complexes which decomposes to yield complexes of carbon-dioxide and water. Increase in temperature further decomposes these groups into Carbon monoxide, Hydrogen and Hydrocarbon. Decomposition of these complexes generates heat, which causes the temperature of the stockpile to reach its critical level and also accelerates the rate of oxidation (Energybiz, n.d.). This results in the spontaneous combustion of coal, which gets ignited on its own without triggering any external source.

The outcome of spontaneous combustion results in decreased gross calorific value and coking property of the coal which reduces its efficiency in terms of power production leading to greater economic loss. The initiation of fire in stockpile has to be detected and prevented at its early stage to avoid economic loss. An automated system using Internet of Things (IoT) is approached and implemented in this work for the aforementioned problem.

The remainder of this paper is organized as follows: The review of spontaneous combustion, parameters and the various existing approaches that are used for detection are surveyed and detailed in Section 2. The systematic approach of the proposed model is presented in Section 3. In Section 4, the working of the model is discussed and the illustration of the data are formulated. The paper is closed in Section 5 with conclusion.

REVIEW OF EXISTING WORKS

Several approaches have been proposed by Researchers and Industrialist for the detection and prevention of fire in the coal stockpiles to avoid economic losses and to increase efficiency. This section aims to review the problem of spontaneous combustion, the various approaches and it's outcome that are proposed by the researchers in the past decade and also describes the research gap and motivation.

Literature Survey on Spontaneous Combustion of Coal

Adamus et al. investigated the factors that determines the spontaneous combustion of coal in the coal mines and classified the indicator gases into majority and minority gases for various analysis. They also tested the thermal oxidation of coal using chromatography laboratories and determined the deviation of spontaneous combustion gases (Adamus et al., 2011). Mao et al. experimentally investigated the spontaneous combustion of coal and illustrated the reaction of coal at different temperatures at different span of time and concluded that the coal that undergoes 39 days to reach a temperature of 158 $^{\circ}$C at which they began to combust spontaneously affecting the resources (Mao et al., 2013). Cunbao et al. studied the spontaneous combustion of coal and the various gas products formed by the combustion at various temperature using the FTI spectroscopic test and the reaction that occurs during the spontaneous combustion are explained using the tests. The results of the test indicates that in the reaction of coal oxidation and spontaneous combustion carbon dioxide and water are produced which increases the self-ignition temperature (Cunbao et al., 2010). Yang et al. analyzed the relationships between the Shortest Spontaneous Combustion Period(SSCP) and the judging indexes of the self-ignite tendency of different coals and established a calculating model of SSCP which shows that the SSCP non-linearly increases with the decrease of dynamic oxygen adsorption and increase of activation energy. They also stated that Heat release intensity of coal oxidation is a major parameter directly related to the coal spontaneous combustion (Yang et al., 2014). Zhu et al. investigated the relationship between oxygen consumption rate and temperature during coal spontaneous combustion. Coal samples were tested using coal heating and oxidation experiment and the result obtained from the experiment shows that the oxygen consumption rate and temperature of coal were linear relationships and it increases rapidly when coal temperature reaches a critical temperature of about 180 degree Celsius (Zhu et al., 2012).

Yuan and Smith investigated the emissions of Carbon monoxide (CO) and carbon dioxide (CO_2) during a spontaneous heating event in a coal mine under different airflow ventilation rate. The experiment was conducted at a coal mine by continuously monitoring the temperature at the centre of the coal sample and the CO, CO_2, and oxygen (O_2) concentrations of the exit gas and the results indicate that CO was generated immediately after the airflow passed through the coal whereas the CO_2 was generated in a late phase (Yuan & Smith, 2011). Singh explained the spontaneous combustion of coal and self-ignition and elaborated the causes, mechanism of spontaneous heating and technological advancement mainly development of chemical inhibitors for controlling and combating fire in coal mines (Singh, 2013). Kim and Sohn stated that coal exposed to air oxidizes slowly by oxygen, low-temperature oxidation of coal leads to spontaneous heating and if it continues in a stockpile for a long time, self-ignition can take place leading to combustion and also investigated the effect of wind barrier design and the flow of air in a stockpile (Kim & Sohn, 2016).

Nimaje and Tripathy collected forty-nine in-situ coal samples from different coalfields of India and the experimentation of the samples were carried out for various temperature and oxidation potential analysis to ascertain the proneness of coal to spontaneous combustion and the significant parameters are identified (Nimaje & Tripathy, 2016). Jun et al. studied the characteristic temperatures for prediction and prevention of coal spontaneous combustion and established the growth rate analysis to test index gases of CO and C_2H_4, CO/CO_2 and alkane ratio to determine the characteristic temperatures of different metamorphism degree of coal (Jun et al., 2014).

The above cited literatures aids to understand the spontaneous combustion, self-ignition of coal and the behaviour of the coal at different temperature and the parameters that are to be monitored to prevent the combustion at its early stage. The next section of the literature review deals with existing systems that are developed for the control of fire in the coal stockpile.

Literature Survey on Detection Methods

Various methods and solutions have been approached by the researchers and the industrialist to detect and prevent the fire in a stockpile at its early stage. This section of literature review surveys the various existing approaches that are used for the aforementioned problem.

Chen et al. proposed an early fire-alarm raising method using video processing based on the idea that RGB (red, green, blue) model based chromatic and disorder measurement is implemented for extracting fire-pixels and smoke-pixels extracted. The fire-pixels is verified as real fire by both dynamics of growth and disorder and iterative checking on the growing ratio of flames is done to give a fire-alarm when the alarm-raising condition is met (Chen et al., 2004). Zhao approached a prediction model based on artificial neural network model for spontaneous combustion using the nonlinear relations between coal spontaneous combustion stage and velocity of oxygen consumption, CO production, and CO2 production which detects the combustion stage at the coal mines (Zhao, 2011). Wang et al. employed infrared thermal imager to monitor underground coal fires in the mining area and analysed the changes in the distribution to approximate the locations of the coal fires. Infrared thermal imager was used to map the thermal field distribution of areas and the results were analysed to identify the hot spot trend and the depth of the burning point (Wang et al., 2015). Avila et al. used petrographic characterization of coal as a tool to identify the spontaneous combustion potential (Avila et al., 2014).

Qain et al. approached a novel method to predict Spontaneous Combustion of Coal Seam (SCCS) by using Support Vector Machine (SVM) and is experimented. The experimental results show that the SVM model obtained highest classification accuracy and proposed a properly trained SVM classification model can be used as a strong predictor for SCCS (Qian et al., 2008). Xie et al. developed an ethylene-enriching system based on the physical adsorption and desorption properties of coal to increase detection sensitivity of the ethylene concentration in mine air and successfully applied in underground coal mines to detect fire at its early stage (Xie et al., 2011). Wang et al. employed Wireless Sensor Network (WSN) technology in monitoring system to prevent the spontaneous combustion of coal gangue which monitors the environment of gangue and collects the temperature in real-time to prevent the occurrence of spontaneous combustion through networking strategy (Wang et al., 2010). Zhuang and Ren studied the nature of the indicator gases to forecast and predict coal spontaneous combustion and approached several techniques that detect the indicator gases such as detecting the carbon monoxide concentration, chromatography the gas composition, detecting the coal temperature and infrared radiation detection analysis to detect and predict the spontaneous combustion of coal (Zhuang & Ji-Ren, 2011). Zhang et al. developed a model to predict the spontaneous heating of coal pile by computational fluid dynamics (CFD) and to prevent the coal pile from self-ignition. They implemented 2-Dimensional numerical model in FLUENT and the coal piles under different conditions were calculated and measured kinetic parameters for detection (Zhang et al., 2016). Bhattacharjee et al. proposed a system for detecting fire hazard in a Bord-and-Pillar coal mine which uses wireless sensor networks (WSNs) (Pandiyaraju et al., 2020; Pandiyaraju et al., 2017) to detect the exact fire location and spreading direction and also provides a fire prevention system (Bhattacharjee et al., 2012). A congestion free transient plane is proposed for the effective link handling approach. The temporary plane which is used in this scheme has also the possibility to be sued in the coal fire detection (Vanamoorthy & Chinnaiah, 2020). A hybrid link failure approach for improved link connectivity can be used to in the detection approach (Vanamoorthy et al., 2020).

Research Gap

The above cited literatures and reviews shows that the spontaneous combustion and self-ignition in the coal mines is one of the major problem that has to be addressed. Various methods and that has been implemented by the past researchers and inventors addressed the solution to the problem but not upto the desired level. The values and parameters obtained from the coal fields are not stored for future analytics in the existing systems which lacks to provide an appropriate solution. The approached system using Internet of Things collects data from the various regions of coal mines using Wireless Sensor Networks (WSN) and transmit it to the control station using the GSM modules and the data is monitored and stored to a database. All the data collected from the nodes are pre-processed and stored to a database. Fire can be detected at its early stage using the formulation of the collected parameters. Thus the approached system detects and prevents the fire at its early stage.

DESIGN OF COAL FIRE DETECTION AND PREVENTION SYSTEM

The overall system of the proposed model consists of three modules for the process of data collection, transmission and storing: (1) Data collection from stockpiles (2) Data collection and Processing (3) Detection and Prevention of Self-Ignition. The overall structure and architecture for the proposed system is shown in Figure 1.

The first module consist of Wireless Sensor Nodes that are deployed in the various region of the stockpile to collect the parameters such as temperature, humidity, CO_2 value and smoke from the coal fields which acts as a major factors for detection of fire. In the second module, the collected data from the coal fields are pre-processed and the required data from the fields are arranged and processed and is sent to the control station with the help of GSM network. The third module comprises of a control station in which the transmitted data are monitored and stored for future analytics. The stored data is monitored using a monitoring GUI in real

Figure 1. Overall system architecture of the proposed model

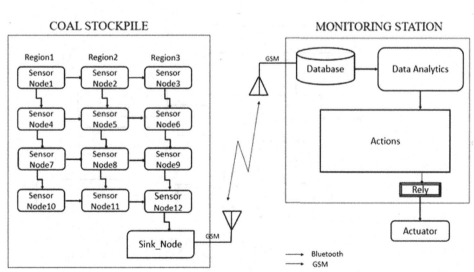

41

time. Condition are set on the monitoring station based on the critical value of the parameters to detect the fire and which when exceeded initiates preventive action to prevent and control the fire. The transmitted data are stored to a database which can be retrieved later for analytics and processing.

Data Collection From the Stockpiles

Stockpiles are usually a larger area of about 5-10 kilometers formed by stackers of open rail type. The height of the pile is about 20-35 metres based on the availability of coal and is stored for about 7-45 days. The entire stockpile is split into several regions based on the available sensor nodes and the sensor nodes are deployed in the regions to collect the data. The Wireless Sensor Networks consist of a Arduino UNO development board to which several sensors are connected to collect the parameters from the field. Based upon the parameters identified from the literature survey, the sensors such as DHT-11 sensor, MQ-2 Gas sensor and MQ-7 sensors are interfaced to the development board to measure the temperature, humidity, CO_2 content and smoke from the environment respectively.

DHT-11 sensor is used to measure the temperature and humidity value of the region as temperature is a major factor that determines spontaneous combustion. MQ-2 and MQ-7 sensors are deployed to measure the content of gases and smoke which gets emitted at the stage of spontaneous combustion. Several sensors are implemented in the nodes for efficient detection of heat at the early stage. A bluetooth device HC-05 which acts as a master is interfaced to the board to transmit the data

Figure 2. Architecture of wireless sensor node

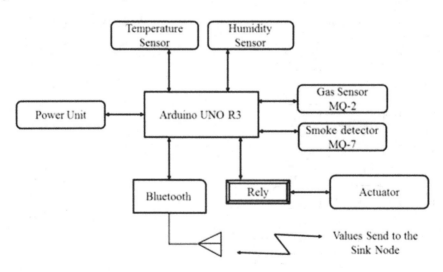

from one sensor node to the other node. The transmission of data between the nodes are done using multi-hop protocol. Figure 2 shows the architecture of WSN and the connection of sensors and actuators to the development board. Several sensor nodes are implemented at different regions to collect all the data at certain intervals of time. The collected data from the nodes are transmitted to the sink node placed at the end of one region which transmits the data to the control station. Actuators are connected to the noes to prevent the fire by monitoring the critical value. Fire detected at an area can be controlled by spraying inhibitors at the area which avoids the spreading of fire thereby saving the resources. The collected data are transmitted to the sink node for further transmission. Thus the necessary and required data are collected from the coal stockpile fields to detect the fire at its early stage.

Data Collection and Processing

The data from the sensor nodes collected using the bluetooth networks are transferred to the sink nodes placed at the end of the region. This module consist of a bluetooth network to receive the collected values from the sensor nodes.

The Bluetooth module connected to the sink node acts as a slave to receive the data.The collected data is aggregated in the sink node so that the unwanted periodical data collected are segregated from the useful data. The processed data are stored in the SD card placed at the sink node. GSM transceiver is interfaced at the sink node to transmit the processed the data to the control station. GSM is used to transmit the data as the GSM can transmit data to a longer distance than the other

Figure 3. Architecture of sink node

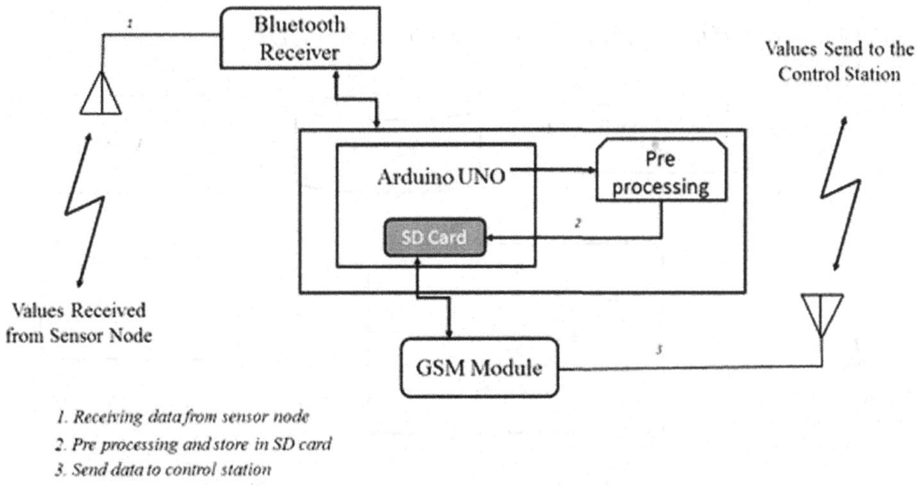

1. Receiving data from sensor node
2. Pre processing and store in SD card
3. Send data to control station

communication modules. Figure 3 shows the architecture diagram of the module. The data is transferred to the control station for monitoring and storing.

3.3 Detection and Prevention of Self-Ignition

Data transmitted from the sink node through the GSM transmitter is received by the GSM receiver placed at the control station. Data received by the GSM consist of the parameter values from the coal stockpiles that has to be monitored for detection and prevention of fire. The parameter values are stored to the database through MYSQL at definite intervals of time. The time is given to the server using the Real Time Clock (RTC) and the values are stored for the given time. Figure 4 layouts a control station which receives, stores and monitors the data.

A monitoring GUI is placed at the control station which interacts with the human at the control station. Monitoring GUI is designed using HTML to which fields can be customized based on the user requirements. The values are monitored in real time and is also stored to the database. Database is designed using PHP scripting language to store the data periodically. Various options are provided at the monitoring GUI to filter and view the data based upon the user requirements. Conditions are set at the monitoring GUI which checks the parameter value at regular intervals of time and if a parameter value exceeds the threshold value a signal is sent to the development board and to the user to initiate the actions to prevent the fire. The parameter values stored in the database can be retrieved for further analysis to identify the characteristic and initiation of fire at the various regions and the data are used to prevent the storage of the coal at the regions at which the fire occurs frequently. Preventive action is carried out by the spraying of inhibitors and other complexes,

Figure 4. Layout of the control station and monitoring GUI

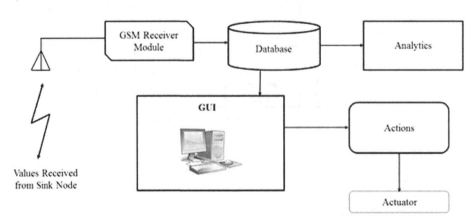

by exposing the correct amount of water and other procedures. Signal can be send to the Unmanned Aerial Vehicles to spray the inhibitors to the fire affected regions which reduces human loss and damages.

DATA FLOW MODEL

The data flow model of the proposed system is charted in Figure 5 which clearly depicts the flow of data from the collection to storage and monitoring. The Wireless Sensor Network is deployed in the coal stockpile region to collect the data from the coal fields. Various parameter values are collected from the field and the loop is repeated continuously as long as the coal is available in the stockpile. Data collected from the sensor nodes are transmitted to the sink node based on Ad-hoc routing for processing and aggregation. The processed data is transmitted to the control station through the GSM network and if the message that comprises of the values from the field are identified, it is stored to a database for analytics. Applications and MYSQL are used to store the value to the database. The data is then pulled to the monitoring GUI for real time monitoring with the user. If the value measured in the monitoring station exceeds the threshold value based on the set conditions, then the preventive actions are initiated to control and prevent the fire. If the values are under control, then it gets stored and monitored for future analytics.

EXPERIMENTAL SETUP

The proposed system is experimented by deploying the sensors to the development mode and measuring the values from an environment similar to the coal stockpile. The WSN is deployed in the environment and the values measured are transmitted to a control station at regular intervals of time. Figure 6 depicts the prototype of the proposed Wireless Sensor Node and the Sink Node from which the data is transferred to the control station. The control station in the testing module resembles a monitoring GUI developed on a computer. The values obtained from the environment are communicated between two bluetooth modules placed in the sensor nodes which acts as master and slave. The master module transmits the data to the slave module and the data is communicated to the monitoring GUI using GSM 900A module. The control station can be located at larger distance as the GSM can communicate data to greater distances. Another GSM 900A module receives the data at the control station from which the data is transferred to Microsoft Access Database through a windows application. Then the data is collected and stored to the cloud from which it can be retrieved and analysed further.

Figure 5. Flow chart

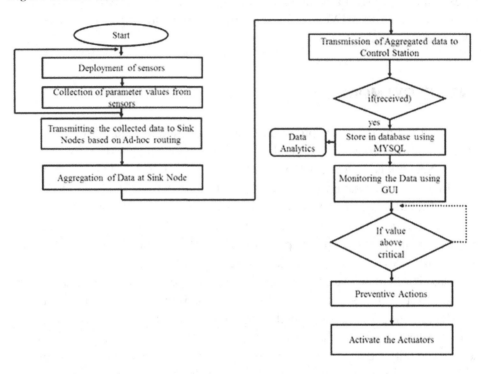

Figure 6. Prototype model of the proposed system

The data that is stored to a database is pulled from it to monitor the data in real time. Monitoring GUI is designed based on HTML and PHP scripting languages and the monitoring station is designed to filter and analyse the data based on the user requirements. The monitoring GUI and the data that is being monitored in real time is shown. Data is collected by varying the environment factors and the environment to monitor the detection of fire. Various factors are drastically varied up to the threshold level to monitor the proper working of the sensor nodes. The data transmission is verified based on the storage of data to the database at regular intervals of time. The preventive actions are initiated and tested by varying the environmental factors above the threshold level. The working of the entire setup is tested and monitored for its efficiency and reliability in detecting and preventing the fire in the coal stockpiles at its early age.

RESULTS AND DISCUSSION

The developed system is implemented in a coal stockpile like environment and the values are obtained and stored to a database. Sensors are deployed in the environment to measure the various parameters The stored value are graphed to identify the behaviour of the coal oxidation at different environment and different times. Figure 8a and 8b depicts the graphical relation between the time and the parameters that occurs during the changes in the environment. The stored values of the parameters are related to the time using the graphs. The X-coordinate of the graph depicts the time and the y axis depicts the values of the parameters and the values are graphed for a particular period of time. The graph explains the behaviour of the coal environment and the parameter value with respect to time. The graph of time interval versus temperature clearly shows that the temperature rises with respect to the time interval for the given five days of time. The values of temperature at different intervals for five days are aggregated to plot the graphs. The second graph of temperature versus CO_2 value shows that the value of carbon dioxide increases exponentially with respect to temperature. The data stored in the database is verified using the monitoring GUI at regular intervals. The accuracy of the proposed system is verified by the plotted graphs.

CONCLUSION

The proposed system is modelled, prototyped and tested in an environment that resembles the environment of a stockpile. Sensors and bluetooth are interfaced with the development board to form a Wireless Sensor Nodes. The sink node is also

Figure 7. Coal fire detection of time interval vs. temperature

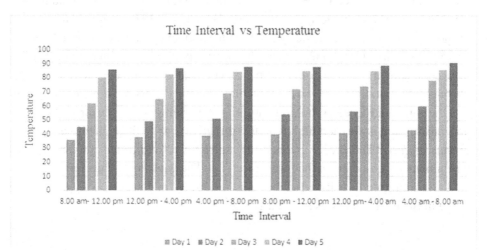

Figure 8. Coal fire detection CO_2 value vs. temperature

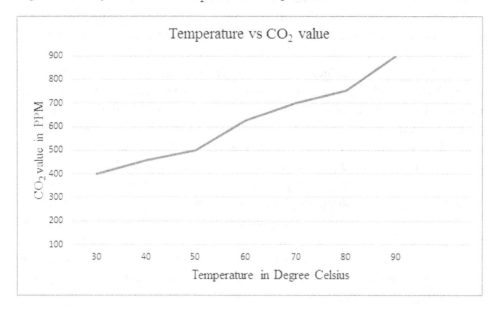

created to collect the data from the sensor nodes. GSM is interfaced with the sink node to transmit the data to the control station. The monitoring GUI is designed based on the user requirements. The data appears in the monitoring station can be searched, refined and filtered for a given period based on the user need. The periodical data can be analysed by retrieving the data from the database. Changes in the environment is made to check the reliability of the model to be used in the stockpile. Data processing is used to eliminate the unwanted data from the coal fields. Initiation of preventive measures at the time of extreme value shows that the system is efficient in determining the fire in the coal stockpiles at its early stage.

The work can be extended further by normalization of the sensor values to increase its efficiency and classifying the data based on algorithms for accurate measurements. Several other actions can be included for the prevention of fire such as using UAV to spray the inhibitors, ventilating the stockpile to a certain limit and initiating water hydrants at various points in the pile.

REFERENCES

Adamus, A., Šancer, J., Guřanová, P., & Zubíček, V. (2011). An investigation of the factors associated with interpretation of mine atmosphere for spontaneous combustion in coal mines. *Fuel Processing Technology, 92*(3), 663–670. doi:10.1016/j. fuproc.2010.11.025

Avila, C., Wu, T., & Lester, E. (2014). Petrographic characterization of coals as a tool to detect spontaneous combustion potential. *Fuel, 125*, 173–182. doi:10.1016/j. fuel.2014.01.042

Bhattacharjee, S., Roy, P., Ghosh, S., Misra, S., & Obaidat, M. S. (2012). Wireless sensor network-based fire detection, alarming, monitoring and prevention system for Bord-and-Pillar coal mines. *Journal of Systems and Software, 85*(3), 571–581. doi:10.1016/j.jss.2011.09.015

Chen, T.-H., Wu, P.-H., & Chiou, Y.-C. (2004). An early fire-detection method based on image processing. *Image Processing. ICIP'04. 2004 International Conference on*, 1707-1710.

Cunbao, D., Jiren, W., Xuefeng, W., & Hanzhong, D. (2010). Spontaneous coal combustion producing carbon dioxide and water. *Mining Science and Technology (China), 20*(1), 82–87. doi:10.1016/S1674-5264(09)60165-4

Energybiz. (n.d.). http://www.energybiz.com/article/11/11/prevention-and-control-module-spontaneous-combustion-coal-coal-yards

Jun, D., Jingyu, Z., Yanni, Z., & Ruilin, G. (2014). Study on Coal Spontaneous Combustion Characteristic Temperature of Growth Rate Analysis. *Procedia Engineering, 84*, 796–805. doi:10.1016/j.proeng.2014.10.498

Kim, C. J., & Sohn, C. H. (2016). Effects of wind barrier design and closed coal storage on spontaneous ignition of coal stockpiles. *Journal of Loss Prevention in the Process Industries, 40,* 529–536. doi:10.1016/j.jlp.2016.02.009

Mao, Z., Zhu, H., Zhao, X., Sun, J., & Wang, Q. (2013). Experimental study on characteristic parameters of coal spontaneous combustion. *Procedia Engineering, 62,* 1081–1086. doi:10.1016/j.proeng.2013.08.164

Nimaje, D., & Tripathy, D. (2016). Characterization of some Indian coals to assess their liability to spontaneous combustion. *Fuel, 163,* 139–147. doi:10.1016/j. fuel.2015.09.041

Pandiyaraju, V., Logambigai, R., Ganapathy, S., & Kannan, A. (2020). An energy efficient routing algorithm for WSNs using intelligent fuzzy rules in precision agriculture. *Wireless Personal Communications, 112*(1), 243–259. doi:10.100711277-020-07024-8

Pandiyaraju, V., Perumal, P. S., Kannan, A., & Ramesh, L. S. (2017). Smart terrace gardening with intelligent roof control algorithm for water conservation. *Pakistan Journal of Agricultural Sciences, 54*(2), 451–455. doi:10.21162/PAKJAS/17.4903

Qian, M., Hongquan, W., Yongsheng, W., & Yan, Z. (2008). SVM Based Prediction of Spontaneous Combustion in Coal Seam. *Computational Intelligence and Design. ISCID'08. International Symposium on,* 254-257. 10.1109/ISCID.2008.193

Singh, R. V. K. (2013). Spontaneous heating and fire in coal mines. *Procedia Engineering, 62,* 78–90. doi:10.1016/j.proeng.2013.08.046

Vanamoorthy, M., & Chinnaiah, V. (2020). Congestion-free transient plane (CFTP) using bandwidth sharing during link failures in SDN. *The Computer Journal, 63*(6), 832–843. doi:10.1093/comjnl/bxz137

Vanamoorthy, M., Chinnaiah, V., & Sekar, H. (2020). A hybrid approach for providing improved link connectivity in SDN. *The International Arab Journal of Information Technology, 17*(2), 250–256. doi:10.34028/iajit/17/2/13

Wang, Y., Sun, Y.-M., Yan, Y., & Ma, Y. (2010). Design of Wireless Sensor Networks in prevention of combustion on coal gangue based on pseudo-parallel genetic algorithms. *Advanced Computational Intelligence (IWACI), Third International Workshop on, 2010,* 294-298. 10.1109/IWACI.2010.5585211

Wang, Y., Tian, F., Huang, Y., Wang, J., & Wei, C. (2015). Monitoring coal fires in Datong coalfield using multi-source remote sensing data. *Transactions of Nonferrous Metals Society of China, 25*(10), 3421–3428. doi:10.1016/S1003-6326(15)63977-2

Xie, J., Xue, S., Cheng, W., & Wang, G. (2011). Early detection of spontaneous combustion of coal in underground coal mines with development of an ethylene enriching system. *International Journal of Coal Geology, 85*(1), 123–127. doi:10.1016/j.coal.2010.10.007

Yang, Y., Li, Z., Hou, S., Gu, F., Gao, S., & Tang, Y. (2014). The shortest period of coal spontaneous combustion on the basis of oxidative heat release intensity. *International Journal of Mining Science and Technology, 24*(1), 99–103. doi:10.1016/j.ijmst.2013.12.017

Yuan, L., & Smith, A. C. (2011). CO and CO 2 emissions from spontaneous heating of coal under different ventilation rates. *International Journal of Coal Geology, 88*(1), 24–30. doi:10.1016/j.coal.2011.07.004

Zhang, J., Choi, W., Ito, T., Takahashi, K., & Fujita, M. (2016). Modelling and parametric investigations on spontaneous heating in coal pile. *Fuel, 176*, 181–189. doi:10.1016/j.fuel.2016.02.059

Zhao, G. (2011). Predictions for coal spontaneous combustion stage based on an artificial neural network. *Computational Intelligence and Security (CIS), Seventh International Conference on*, 386-389. 10.1109/CIS.2011.92

Zhu, J., He, N., & Li, D. (2012). The relationship between oxygen consumption rate and temperature during coal spontaneous combustion. *Safety Science, 50*(4), 842–845. doi:10.1016/j.ssci.2011.08.023

Zhuang, L., & Ji-Ren, W. (2011). The Technology of Forecasting and Predicting the Hidden Danger of Underground Coal Spontaneous Combustion. *Procedia Engineering, 26*, 2301–2305. doi:10.1016/j.proeng.2011.11.2438

Chapter 4
Blockchain for Agri–Business:
A Simulation for Assuring Product Ownership Using Hyperledger Composer

P. Saranya
Vellore Institute of Technology, Chennai, India

R. Maheswari
Vellore Institute of Technology, Chennai, India

Ramesh Ragala
Vellore Institute of Technology, Chennai, India

ABSTRACT

Agri-food systems are continually evolving to feed an ever-growing population. However, several challenges such as quality products, inefficient supply chain, and excessive food wastage are needed to be faced in order to meet global demand. Among these constraints, supply chain traceability systems are one of the technology solutions that can identify and resolve the challenges of agri-food systems. The traditional supply chain lacks traceability, transparency, and information exchange. In this work, the blockchain projects utilizing the public and private blockchain platforms are discussed. Also, the product ownership management has been developed using Hyperledger composer for tracing the flow of agriculture products at every stage. It supports storing the supply chain activities as a ledger transaction in a permanent and immutable way. Agriculture products are mentioned as lots with a unique lot code provided for each batch of products. The chain of lot codes can be used to identify the product along the supply chain. This system ensures product ownership.

DOI: 10.4018/978-1-6684-7756-4.ch004

INTRODUCTION

Blockchain for business is the combination of a shared and immutable ledger that can open opportunities for blockchain innovation in businesses. A consensus among network members is provided to eliminate risk and efficient management of assets throughout the business network. These blockchain platforms ensure to activate and manage a secured, automated business network across multiple stages in an organization. Hyperledger is an open-source, not-for-profit blockchain platform, that accelerates the adoption of business technologies. Many business requirements trust Hyperledger because of its hosting organization, LINUX foundation. It paves way for enterprises to design a customized business network in terms of writing consensus algorithms, block data structure, and multi-language options which is an added advantage over other blockchain platforms. In China, the Yijian Blockchain Technology Application System is a Hyperledger Fabric-based blockchain, a permissioned platform. It is in production with Hejia a pharma chemical industry, to eliminate some of the financial challenges in it. The system is designed to reduce the turnover time of funds on the supply chain and inform banks about the process and allow to grant early funds to the pharmaceutical manufacturers and retailers (QuillHash, 2019). The retailer giant Walmart has successfully completed two pilot projects using Hyperledger Fabric: Pork in China and Mangoes in America (IBM., 2017).

Another blockchain solution using a permissioned fabric network is for Borsa Italiana, the Italian Stock Exchange Group. The shareholder data is managed to expand credit access at the same time. The blockchain solution is developed to replace the paper trading certificates with a digital streamlined process for a transparent process of trading among various parties (FinExtra., 2017). TenneT Energy Community is utilizing blockchain solutions for the efficient management of energy supply. It analyses the integration of energy supplied in electric cars and household batteries into the electric grid. TenneT is currently involved in two pilot projects such as collaboration of Vandebron in the Netherlands for efficient supply of electricity according to the demand, the second project by Sonnet services in Germany (the energy group of the Sonen group) integrates the use of solar batteries with wind energy in order to effectively use the renewable energy sources with this joint venture. SAP, (Systems, Applications, and Products in Data Processing) a multinational software giant has launched a cloud platform dedicated to corporate blockchain application development. The solution provides a framework to build business applications on top of Hyperledger Fabric given in Table 1.

A simple overview of Blockchain technology is needed to understand how Blockchain came into the spotlight for supply chain systems. Blockchain technology is originated from Bitcoin meant for storing cryptographically secured transactions in a centralized database (Nakamoto., 2008). Bitcoin is a public blockchain platform, where anyone can involve in it without any trusted third party. Bitcoin itself emerges as a trusted service to many domains other than finance (Yuan et al., 2016). Later Blockchain emerged as a breakthrough technology that can be adopted for various domains. Based on the criteria of authorization Blockchain can be divided into two types. They are permissioned and permissionless Blockchain. While Bitcoin, Ethereum comes under Permissionless Blockchain (Wood, 2014), Hyperledger Fabric comes under the Permissioned category (Cachin, 2016).

The main objectives of this work are to compare and analyze the suitable blockchain platform to develop a supply chain traceability system based on the business requirements. This work also aims to overcome the supply chain traceability issues like the information gap that arise among the stakeholders, achieving trust and trackability. The contributions of this paper are listed below.

1. A comparative study has been made to analyze the commonly used blockchain platforms for business solutions
2. Based on the study, a traceable supply chain application has been prototyped using Hyperledger composer playground.
3. The different layers of the prototype have been explained.

RELATED WORK

Various domains are adopting Blockchain technology for their applications. Among them, commodity applications are widely utilizing Blockchain in recent times

Table 1. List of pilot projects using blockchain by the well-known companies worldwide

Company	Country	Blockchain Platform	Type	Solutions
Hejia	China	Yijian blockchain solution	Permissioned	Pharmaceutical
Walmart	China	Hyperledger fabric	Permissioned	Food supply chain for Pork
Borsa Italiana	Italy	Fabric Groups	Permissioned	Stock Exchange
TenneT Energy Community	Vandebron / Netherland	Hyperledger fabric	Private network	Electric Grid
Sonnet services	Germany	Ethereum	Permissioned	Renewable energy sources
SAP	USA	Fabric	Permissioned	Software application development
Walmart	USA	Hyperledger fabric	Permissioned	Mangoes supply chain

(Kamilaris et al., 2019). Transparency, traceability, and immutable transaction records provide a meaningful solution to the supply chain and logistics community. The overall structure of the food and agriculture supply chain is vast and complex, as various participants are involved in it starting from producers, processors, transporters, retailers, and consumers (Cooper et al., 1997). Hence there is a need to develop a traceability framework that can trace from sourcing to consuming benefitting all the participants across the supply chain network.

A double chain storage structure is proposed by Xie et al. (2017) where the chained data structure is used to store the transaction hash along with the blockchain main-chain to ensure double layered safety for the agricultural product data. Caro et al. (2018) proposed a fully decentralized Agri-Food traceability solution using blockchain. They have designed a use case from farm to fork, then developed and deployed it with Ethereum and Hyperledger sawtooth platforms. This work experiments with Go-Ethereum 1.9 as a blockchain platform.

Lin et al. (2018) proposed a food traceability system with EPS information Service (records the data and transaction event with a unique global identity). It has developed a prototype system with on-chain and off-chain data to reduce the data explosion problem in blockchain for IoT. The proposed solution was implemented in Ethereum. As Ethereum is a public platform in terms of financial considerations it can be avoided for user-defined traceability systems. Since the single language data structure of an Ethereum network could be a barrier for developing sophisticated business networks, multiple languages supported platform is preferred. Finally, the consensus algorithm of Ethereum is CPU- intensive, it will not be suitable for tiny devices such as IoT sensors and communication gateways due to its limited computation power (Miguel et al., 2018).

Salah et al. (2019) proposed a soybean traceability solution utilizing smart contracts and the Ethereum framework to perform business transactions without centralized authority by providing integrity, scalability, and security. Yang et al. (2021) proposed a trusted Traceability System using Blockchain technology for Fruit and Vegetable Agricultural Products focusing on reducing the storage burden of the system. A dual storage structure of on-chain and off-chain data structure for information database and Blockchain respectively had been discussed. He also proposed reputation-based smart contracts for uploading traceability data by network nodes.

Some other traceability solutions discussed the combination of blockchain with other technologies such as RFID and IoT. Tian (2016) proposed a system combining Blockchain technology with RFID while a traceability system was proposed with IoT and Blockchain by Kim et al. (2018). Boehm et al. (2017) provided a Blockchain-based traceability system with NFC (Near Field Communication).

Based on the literature review and the need of our system, it is feasible to utilize RFID tags over agriculture products to communicate product information

Table 2. The state-of-the-art blockchain solutions for agri business

Journal/Year	Aim of the Work	Features	Blockchain Use
Springer/2019	To build a system that traces the real food source along the supply chain	Integrating blockchain with CouchDB, RESTful APIs & HTTP server	Using Hyperledger fabric with three smart contracts: storage, trading, and traceable
IEEE Access/2020	To sustain the trustworthiness of the supply chain entities & the quality of the food products	Developed using blockchain & IPFS to maintain transactions	Smart contracts: Registration Contract, Add to Lot Contract & Add Transaction Contract, deployed on Ethereum testnet "Rinkeyby"
Sustainability/2020	Perform real-time monitoring of food supply chain	Implemented using blockchain as a base layer, IPFS file system & AWS for testing	Smart contracts based on Ethereum and Istanbul Byzantine Fault-Tolerant algorithm
IEEE Access/2020	Propose a solution for an economy post-COVID-19	Integrating blockchain with machine learning methods and AI for sales prediction	Smart contracts for uploading retailer and customer data
Operations Management Research/2021	Propose a solution for supply chain management	Increases the robustness, Achieves a high global desirability index	it cannot perform the upstream and downstream.
Cluster computing/2022	Proposes a sustainable solution	higher traceability, scalability enhances	applicable only for the system having less transaction time, confines the performance with the symmetric key
IEEE /2018		RandHound and Verifiable Random Function (VRF), Assigning and rotating validators	,gossip protocol to consensus, Limited to cryptocurrency applications
IEEE Access/2016	Proposed three block structure	zyzyvva protocol	sharding, Cosi consensus to improve scalability
ACM / 2018		Fast Cross-Shard Verification,Decentralized Bootstrapping	scaled well, limited to crytpcurrency applications
ACM / 2016	First sharding protocol	random assignment of nodes	cannot process cross-shard transactions

externally while storing data in Blockchain database applications internally (Toyoda et al., 2017). Also, the comparison of the Blockchain system's performance obtained by Miguel et al. (2018), enable us to conclude that Hyperledger Fabric can provide a better environment for developing customized traceability applications. Additionally, the latency of the permissionless blockchains is higher and it affects the flexibility of the system (Pearson et al., 2019). Hence, the proposed system utilizes the Hyperledger composer playground tool to design and simulate the traceability system. The deployment and testing of agriculture commodity trading are carried out in this work (Saranya et al., 2023). The recent literature of blockchain based solutions for agriculture and food supply chain businesses are listed in Table 2.

System Implementation

The proposed system has used a unique product identifier for the rice product used. A lot is the bulk production of the same item and its ID can be a combination of letters or a combination of number-letter. Here, the product lot is meant to identify a rice product. Additionally, the product name, quantity, origin, time, description of the product is mentioned and captured by an RFID tag in order to ensure the ownership of the product at the current state.

The simulation of the agriculture traceability system goes through various layers shown in Figure 1.

Business Layer

Here it has been identified that the actors and products in lot. name the lot package with a global product identifier code so as to identify the product along the supply chain. In our system, the participants utilized are buyer, seller, main Exchange (point of distribution) and business network, admin. Buyer and seller are involved in supply chain participants where business network admin are meant to provide certificate ID to authenticate the users in the business network.

Communication Layer

In this layer RFID tag is utilized, an Information Communication Technology (ICT) to read the unique product lot codes automatically at the supply chain networks and store the product information into the application. The lot information such as product name, quantity, owner of the current state, main Exchange point will be saved and transferred via RFID tags to the various supply chain layers.

Blockchain Application Layer

The application layer is designed using Hyperledger fabric and simulated via composer playground tool to deploy and test the traceability system in a business network. This layer requires creating a unique ID for creating the network. The user ID ensures the authenticity of the involved actors/participants by the network admin. The network requires to create a model framework for the sample participants, sample assets, and set of access control rules. After deploying it, the network will

Figure 1. The architecture of a blockchain traceability system

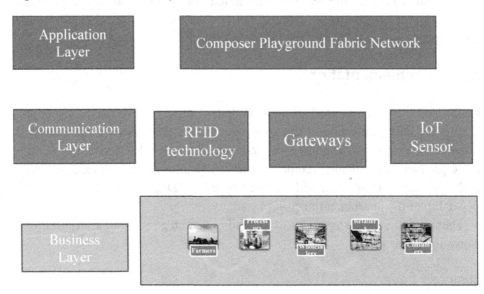

be tested by giving the real participants details and product assets for transactions. All the transactions are monitored by the network participants allowing a transparent traceable reliable network.

Development Environment

Composer playground allows to simulate organization blockchain networks, create blockchain applications quickly, and continue work with the supplied examples. It deploys and tests the business network with minimum cost and time.

System Configuration

Composer playground needs some prerequisites (prerequisites 1) to be installed system and required to set up a development environment. This work utilised Hyperledger fabric in Ubuntu 16.04 LTS installed in Oracle virtual box. The system configuration is an i5 processor, 8GB RAM installed with the 64-bit operating system.

Application Requirement

There are a few important files to be added and modified for designing the business network in composer.

- Model file
- Script file
- Access control file, and
- Query file.

SYSTEM ANALYSIS

Performance: Performance is the priority in any simulation. In this work, the performance will be based on the transaction throughput for given parameters.

Safety: The system is designed in modules where errors can be detected and fixed easily. This makes it easier to update new functionality.

Reliability: The system runs parallel processing which eases the workload, making the performance better and more reliable.

Maintainability: After deployment of the system, any error can be corrected and maintained by the developer.

Testability: The system will be tested considering all the aspects.

Usability: The system is not a GUI application, the output generated is on the terminal and represented through the graph.

After designing the network, it has to be tested with the user-defined participants and assets allocated with the access control by the admin. The architecture of the composer playground is shown in Figure 2.

The steps utilized to create the supply chain business network are explained. The supply–chain business network has been deployed first under the web profile to get started. Then, the empty business network file has been chosen to start our implementation from scratch.

There are two main steps involved while deploying a business network using Hyperledger fabric. They are Connecting to the business network requires creating an ID for the business network. In our case it is supply chain. Making a business network definition requires adding/modifying three important files. 1. Model file 2. The script file and 3. Access control file shown in Figure 3 and 4.

The business network needs to be defined with a participant, asset and the access control files to define the rules for different participants to access various assets provided by the business network.

Figure 2. The architecture of a composer playground in Hyperledger fabric

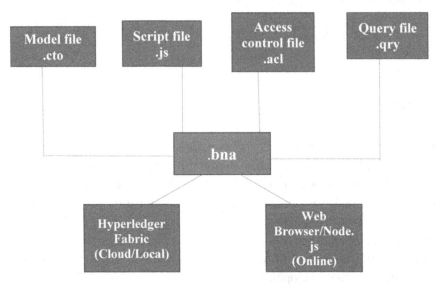

Figure 3. The structure of a blockchain business network to create participants and assets

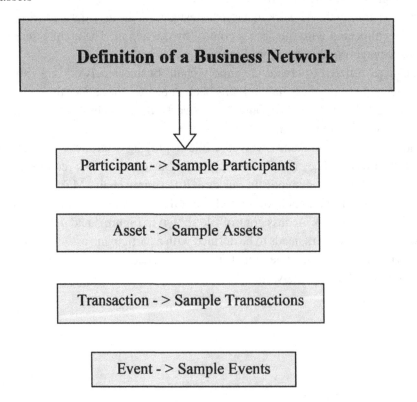

Figure 4. The various files required to define the sample network

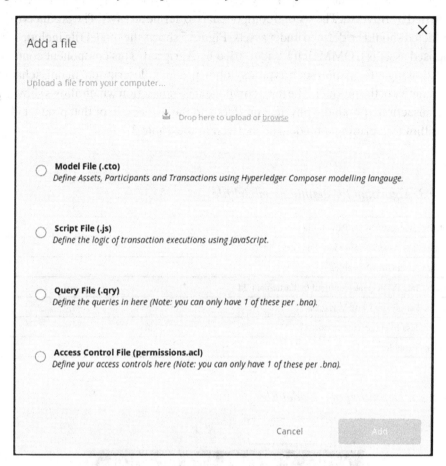

RESULT ANALYSIS

Model File

The model file consists of three main elements such as:

1. A single namespace
2. Resource definitions for participants, assets, transactions, and events
3. Optionally an import file.

The system namespace need not have values for assets and participants. But the events and transactions are identified by an eventid, transactionid and a timestamp. The namespace also contains the historian records, system transactions and registries.

The proposed business network 'mynetwork' have defined a participant 'TRADER' identified by BuyerId. The second component is to define an asset. The products to be transacted should be defined under assets. Figure 5 shows the model file includes the proposed asset is COMMODITY identified by Agriprod. This component contains the following information such as prodsymbol, product_description, mainExchange and quantity of the product. The third component is transaction which allows showing the transaction of both the physical product and the ownership of that product. The algorithm for defining a model file in given in the Table 3.

Table 3. Algorithm for defining a model file

Define Namespace by Its Parent File
Create Class Asset Identified by The Asset_Id
Declare Asset Class Variables
Create Class Participant Identified by Participant_Id
Declare Participant Class Variables
Create Class Event or Transaction
Declare Variables

Figure 5. Definition of a model file

```
Model File  models/model.cto

1   /**
2    * My commodity trading network
3    */
4   namespace org.acme.mynetwork
5   asset Agriprod identified by prodSymbol {
6     o String prodSymbol
7     o String description
8     o String mainExchange
9     o Double quantity
10    --> Trader owner
11  }
12  participant Trader identified by BuyerId {
13    o String BuyerId
14    o String firstName
15    o String lastName
16  }
17  transaction Trade {
18    --> Agriprod agriprod
19    --> Trader newOwner
20  }
```

Script File

Every single transactional object in a model file must be associated in a script file. There are two main parts are involved to invoke script file. First to specify the transaction and its parameters and second is to call the transaction. The algorithm for defining a script file is shown in the Table 4 and its definition is shown in the Figure 6.

The new assets can also be added or update the existing asset by the participant. The new asset will then be added to the network. Figure 7 shows the new asset 'Rice' has been added with features such as quantity, owner, symbol and its exchange. The access control to view or add/update the assets are set by the access control file. The sample code of our default access control file is given in Figure 8.

Table 4. Algorithm for defining a script file

Function Sample_Trade
If Product Transferred from Owner to New_Owner
Get Asset Registry
Update Owner==New_Owner
Return Updated Asset Registry

Figure 6. Definition of a script file

Script File lib/script.js ✏

```
1   /**
2    * Track the trade of a commodity from one trader to another
3    * @param {org.acme.mynetwork.Trade} trade - the trade to be processed
4    * @transaction
5    */
6   function tradeAgriprod(trade) {
7   trade.agriprod.owner = trade.newOwner;
8   return getAssetRegistry('org.acme.mynetwork.Agriprod')
9   .then(function (assetRegistry) {
10  return assetRegistry.update(trade.agriprod);
11  });
12  }
```

Figure 7. Json code to add a new asset in the network

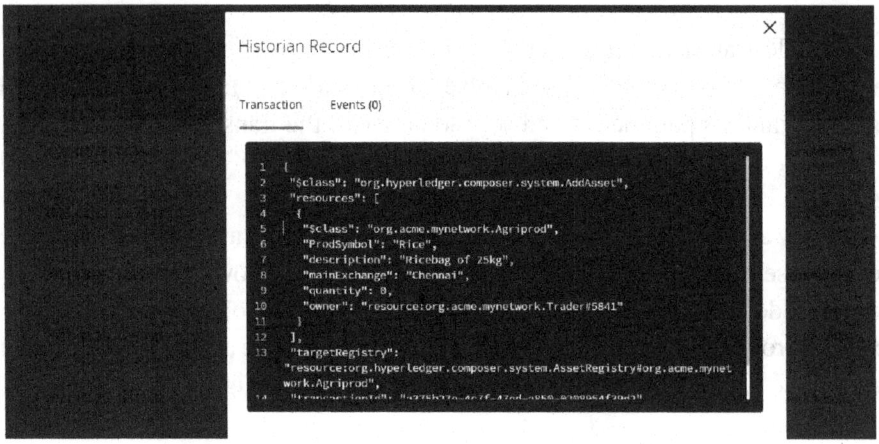

Access Control Files

The accessibility of participants on assets and transaction visibility are controlled by a set of rules included in an access control file. Figure 8 shows the rules given to access this network. Here participants have access to view and edit the assets and to view the transaction. After updating all the files, we deployed the network successfully. Then this network has to be tested by creating participants for our designed model. Here we created two participants under sample participants' tag. There is no event file required for this application as it is intended for checking current ownership of the product.

Figure 8. Defining the access control file for defining roles to the user

```
ACL File permissions.acl

1    /** * Access control rules for mynetwork */
2    rule Default {
3    description: "Allow all participants access to all resources"
4    participant: "ANY" operation: ALL resource: "org.acme.mynetwork.*"
5    action: ALLOW
6    }
7    rule SystemACL {
8    description: "System ACL to permit all access"
9    participant: "org.hyperledger.composer.system.Participant"
10   operation: ALL
11   resource: "org.hyperledger.composer.system.**"
12   action: ALLOW
13   }
```

PRODUCT OWNERSHIP MANAGEMENT

If the product has been transferred successfully from a trader to another trader, the ownership will be updated with the historical records of timestamped transactions. The external tracing of products will be read by the implemented RFID tags on the agriculture products. Internally, system utilizes the transaction id to trace back the products along the entire supply chain. The Figures 8 and 9 shows the change in ownership of the product in the blockchain model. The initial owner of the product can be seen as seller. After making the transaction, the ownership has been changed to buyer which is shown and highlighted in Figure 9 and 10.

CONCLUSION

This paper introduces the need for blockchain technology for business applications. Then through the thorough analysis of supply chain demands this paper designed and simulated an agriculture supply chain network model using Linux's Hyperledger fabric- Composer playground. Registered supply chain participants and assets are only allowed in this network for ensuring authenticity. Then to identify the products,

Figure 9. Status of a product ownership before making transaction

Figure 10. Ownership of a product changes after transaction

a unique lot number has been assigned for each batch of products. Products are traced physically with the use of RFID tags linked to the blockchain application, by the transactional records being stored in the blockchain ledger. Since, traceability systems need to be designed upon the requirement of the application, Hyperledger fabric composer has been chosen as a convenient platform for supply chain systems in both technical and monetary friendly as well. Additionally, the secured and scalable nature of Hyperledger framework allows business organizations to develop a private business network across the globe with low latency and high throughput solutions. The timestamped high transactions ensure the origin and current state of the product along the supply chain flow. This application also allows all the nodes/ stakeholders to have a local copy of the transactional ledger which in turn reduces the internal data tampering happens in the traditional supply chain.

REFERENCES

Boehm, V. A., Kim, J., & Hong, J. W. K. (2018). Holistic tracking of products on the blockchain using NFC and verified users. In *Information Security Applications: 18th International Conference, WISA 2017, Jeju Island, Korea, August 24-26, 2017, Revised Selected Papers 18* (pp. 184-195). Springer International Publishing. 10.1007/978-3-319-93563-8_16

Cachin, C. (2016, July). *Architecture of the hyperledger blockchain fabric* [Workshop session]. Distributed cryptocurrencies and consensus ledgers, IBM Research – Zurich, CH-8803 Ruschlikon, Switzerland. https://theblockchaintest.com/uploads/resources/IBM%20Resear ch%20-%20Architecture%20of%20the%20Hyperledger%20Blockchain% 20Fabric%20-%202016%20-%20July.pdf

Caro, M. P., Ali, M. S., Vecchio, M., & Giaffreda, R. (2018, May). Blockchain-based traceability in Agri-Food supply chain management: A practical implementation. In *2018 IoT Vertical and Topical Summit on Agriculture-Tuscany (IOT Tuscany)* (pp. 1-4). IEEE. doi:10.1109/IOT-TUSCANY.2018.8373021

Cooper, M. C., Lambert, D. M., & Pagh, J. D. (1997). Supply chain management: More than a new name for logistics. *International Journal of Logistics Management*, *8*(1), 1–14. doi:10.1108/09574099710805556

FinExtra. (2017, July 19). *Borsa Italiana partners IBM on securities data blockchain system for SMEs*. The finextra blog. https://www.finextra.com/newsarticle/30848/ borsa-italiana-partners-ibm-on-securities-data-blockchain-system-for-smes

IBM. (2017). *Maersk and IBM unveil first industry-wide cross border supply chain solution on blockchain* [Press release]. www-03.ibm.com/press/us/en/pressrelease/51712.wss

Kamilaris, A., Fonts, A., & Prenafeta-Boldú, F. X. (2019). The rise of blockchain technology in agriculture and food supply chains. *Trends in Food Science & Technology*, *91*, 640–652. doi:10.1016/j.tifs.2019.07.034

Kim, M., Hilton, B., Burks, Z., & Reyes, J. (2018, November). Integrating blockchain, smart contract-tokens, and IoT to design a food traceability solution. In *2018 IEEE 9th annual information technology, electronics and mobile communication conference (IEMCON)* (pp. 335-340). IEEE. https://doi: 10.1109/IEMCON.2018.8615007

Lin, Q., Wang, H., Pei, X., & Wang, J. (2019). Food safety traceability system based on blockchain and EPCIS. *IEEE Access : Practical Innovations, Open Solutions*, *7*, 20698–20707. doi:10.1109/ACCESS.2019.2897792

Nakamoto, S. (2008). *Bitcoin: A Peer-to-Peer Electronic Cash System*. www.bitcoin.org

Pearson, S., May, D., Leontidis, G., Swainson, M., Brewer, S., Bidaut, L., Frey, J. G., Parr, G., Maull, R., & Zisman, A. (2019). Are distributed ledger technologies the panacea for food traceability? *Global Food Security*, *20*, 145–149. doi:10.1016/j.gfs.2019.02.002

QuillHash Team. (2019). Will Hyperledger be the Platform that Successfully Brings Blockchain into the Enterprises? *The Medium Blog*. https://medium.com/quillhash/will-hyperledger-be-the-platform-that-successfully-brings-blockchain-into-the-enterprises-c7759e38cc61

Salah, K., Nizamuddin, N., Jayaraman, R., & Omar, M. (2019). Blockchain-based soybean traceability in agricultural supply chain. *IEEE Access : Practical Innovations, Open Solutions*, *7*, 73295–73305. doi:10.1109/ACCESS.2019.2918000

Saranya, P., & Maheswari, R. (2023). Proof of Transaction (PoTx) Based Traceability System for an Agriculture Supply Chain. *IEEE Access : Practical Innovations, Open Solutions*, *11*, 10623–10638. doi:10.1109/ACCESS.2023.3240772

Tian, F. (2016, June). An agri-food supply chain traceability system for China based on RFID & blockchain technology. In *2016 13th international conference on service systems and service management (ICSSSM)* (pp. 1-6). IEEE. 10.1109/ICSSSM.2016.7538424

Toyoda, K., Mathiopoulos, P. T., Sasase, I., & Ohtsuki, T. (2017). A novel blockchain-based product ownership management system (POMS) for anti-counterfeits in the post supply chain. *IEEE Access : Practical Innovations, Open Solutions*, *5*, 17465–17477. doi:10.1109/ACCESS.2017.2720760

Wood, G. (2014). *Ethereum: a secure decentralised generalised transaction ledger* (Vol. 151). Ethereum Project Yellow Paper. https://files.gitter.im/ethereum/yellowpaper/VIyt/Paper.pdf

Xie, C., Sun, Y., & Luo, H. (2017, August). Secured data storage scheme based on block chain for agricultural products tracking. In *2017 3rd International Conference on Big Data Computing and Communications (BIGCOM)* (pp. 45-50). IEEE. 10.1109/BIGCOM.2017.43

Yang, X., Li, M., Yu, H., Wang, M., Xu, D., & Sun, C. (2021). A trusted blockchain-based traceability system for fruit and vegetable agricultural products. *IEEE Access : Practical Innovations, Open Solutions*, *9*, 36282–36293. doi:10.1109/ACCESS.2021.3062845

Yuan, Y., & Wang, F. Y. (2016). Blockchain: The state of the art and future trends. *Acta Automatica Sinica*, *42*(4), 481–494. doi:10.16383/j.aas.2016.c160158

Chapter 5

Difficult and Intriguing Performance of Standalone Microgrid and Diesel Generator With Big Data Analytics in Rural Electrification

P. Renugadevi
Vellore Institute of Technology, Chennai, India

R. Maheswari
Vellore Institute of Technology, Chennai, India

V. Pattabiraman
iD https://orcid.org/0000-0001-8734-2203
Vellore Institute of Technology, Chennai, India

R. Srimathi
Vellore Institute of Technology, Chennai, India

ABSTRACT

Electrification is a primary concern in the recent years because of new emerging technologies in day-to-day life. Therefore, to run a variety of devices, you need an uninterrupted power supply, and equipment that is powered as well. There are various reasons such as natural disasters, transmission, and distribution issues that prevent 30% of residents in rural and isolated areas from accessing basic electricity. This lack of electrification has an adverse effect on people's

DOI: 10.4018/978-1-6684-7756-4.ch005

survival on radical level in many circumstances. It may be possible to reduce both current and future power constraints by improving the microgrid concept so that standalone microgrids in remote locations work well. Especially when isolated from main grids and unable to receive regular electricity, standalone microgrids present many difficulties and problems. Formerly, diesel generators were considered indispensable to off-grid microgrids, as they provide electricity for the entire system. Power losses can be reduced by employing power optimizers with a maximum power point tracking approach.

INTRODUCTION

The importunity for power has dramatically increased over the past few years, because of the rising technology with lack of energy sources. Hence, more electricity needs to be generated in order to be utilized efficiently. Predominantly, the Energy sources can be divided into renewable and non- renewable categories. Renewable energy is the only source of energy that is clean and pollution-free. Today's rapidly rising global energy demand is largely met by the production of traditional fossil fuels. A conventional power generation system cannot meet this increased energy demand without causing an exponential increase in global warming and pollution levels. The use of Microgrids (MGs) to generate hybrid energy reduces the dependence on traditional fossil fuel power plants. MG uses a variety of distributed energy sources, including solar, wind, fuel cells, Microturbines (MTs), and diesel generators, to partially address these environmental issues and to fulfil the local rise in load demand (Arcos et al., 2021). Researchers are currently addressing the challenge of implementing microgrids with Bigdata technologies. Medical Electronic documents, CT scans, X-Ray, paperwork, machines, and other unstructured data sources are all common in healthcare facilities. The hospital community regularly works 24 hours a day, so a constant power supply is necessary along with various data collection methods. Big data aids in patient recording or analyzing, and identifying the patient's history with the help of a doctor's support. Also, Big data can be examined for attack analysis crime detection, and visualization in the fields of government and military. The insurance industry uses big data to improve customer satisfaction, increase revenues, and create forecasts based on call records, social media, and customer behavior data. The use of standalone Microgrids coupled with renewable energy has skyrocketed due to global electricity and environmental degradation. These sources offer numerous benefits to a wide range of economic sectors, including energy management, transportation, manufacturing, production, and agriculture. The Smart Microgrid idea has arisen in this situation and it is considered to be an acknowledgment of the electrical system demand process. By using concurrent technology, smart grid initiatives improve grid planning and maintenance for greater control over energy expenditures. The amount of electricity produced universally from renewable energy sources increased by 70%. The term microgrid refers to a group of electricity-generating units located in an area, usually powered by diesel generators that are integrated with an Energy Management System (EMS) (Araujo et al., 2017; Bhamidi et al., 2019). Table 1 outlines the following guidelines for implementing microgrids at homes, businesses, and government facilities. In Figure 1, you can see how solar energy is converted into thermal energy.

RENEWABLE ENERGY RESOURCES

The predominant category of solar energy that reaches Earth is electromagnetic waves. These dissimilarities extend in wavelength from extremely tiny to very lengthy. The range of radiation that reaches the planet consists of 46% visible light, 44% infrared radiation, and 7% ultraviolet radiation. The western part of the country acquires the most solar energy, while the north-eastern region of the country obtains the least. Solar energy plays a vital role in microgrid implementation and design and it has several challenges. Table 2 explains the various pros and cons of solar energy.

Standalone Microgrids

There are various ways in which smart microgrids can function, including isolated and grid-connected modes(macrogrids), which include renewable energy sources. Predominantly in Islanded type microgrids is not connected to the main utility grid and sources are going to be received by the systems. The EMS is responsible

Table 1. Guidelines for implementing microgrids

Low conversion losses can be achieved by using power optimizers (dc/dc converters).
Renewable energy sources that use thin films of Indium gallium copper sulphide (CiGs)
Everything should be looked at using an appropriate simulation technique.
In distribution network, management system with respect to energy and voltage should be considered while installing the microgrid.
RES, energy storage systems, and backup diesel generators can all be used for these control management tasks.
However, using a backup diesel generator presents the following issues: Using different natural sources may introduce irregular loading issues, such as a waiting time when the generator is starting, persistent ON/OFF (switching), and persistent load fluctuations

Figure 1. Solar thermal power generation

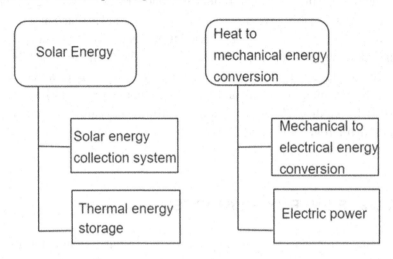

Table 2. Solar energy

Privileges	Drawbacks
It is a never-ending source of energy.	Earth receives solar energy, although it has a low power density that is1 KW/m2.
It is accessible all year long.	To rewarding capture an amount of energy, a big exterior is needed.
Secluded and rural locations can benefit from solar photovoltaic systems.	It experiences ongoing monitoring because it is irregular, cyclical, changes with the seasons, and the sun's orientation changes during the day.
The application of solar thermal power plants is possible in deserts, mountainous areas, etc.	There is a necessitate to store energy because the amount of solar energy obtained varies, which raises the cost.
There are gargantuan uses for it, including drying, cooking, heating, and producing power.	Solar energy has a high initial squandering cost for power consumption.

for maintaining to deliver an uninterruptible power supply to consumers, in spite of the fact that in Macrogrid mode. This type of grid controls the voltage as well as power generation/distribution in an effective way by reducing various losses in addition by giving and receiving power in the utility grid. Islanded microgrids play a vital role in rural and underdeveloped areas since these places require electricity to lead a normal life and it is considered to be the top research content in recent years (Bharathi et al., 2022). The outcome of simulations should be examined to reduce conversion losses and implement them in rural areas. The most important advantage of AC over DC is transferring power with various voltage levels can be possible by step-up and step-down transformers. Modern society uses DC power to power a large number of electrical loads, including PC systems, client electronics, various emitting diodes, and unsteady-speed motors. However, the above-mentioned DC provides the basis for distributed energy resources like solar panels and storage devices for batteries in particular for electric vehicles. Intricate inverters and controllers that can synchronize with ac harmonics are necessary to incorporate these technologies. Using Power optimizers for maximum power point tracking is the best approach to reduce these losses. For evaluating the performance of hybrid microgrids, PV and battery size are influential factors (Bhatt et al., 2022).

Challenges in Microgrids

Maintaining the microgrid bus voltage within the limits in a standalone microgrid depends heavily on control and management strategies using renewable energy sources, a backup diesel generator, and energy storage systems. When used in coexistence with RES, a backup diesel generator has distinctive difficulties, such as start-up delays, frequent switching, and uneven loading. In islanded mode, extreme frameworks such as DG failures, scheduled maintenance, low power generation, and battery charge are examined. Compared to AC microgrids, DC microgrids are gaining supremacy. It can be found in utility-linked mode and isolated/islanded mode. On the whole, standalone DC MGs are used to provide remote applications like telecommunications systems, data available markets, and residential consumers when a standard grid supply is not a practical option. Due to their low cost and high pliability, diesel generators utilized by fossil fuels are coupled with RES to address the problem. Utilizing non-renewable energy sources and loads can increase reliability even though efficiency can't be considered until fuel is well organized and power is managed efficiently (Bertheau et al., 2020). Figure 2 illustrates the different control measures used in Standalone Microgrids. The generation of energy and power must be located close to the demand location in order to cut back on lengthy transmission and distribution losses. To reduce these kinds of losses, various emissions, and also boost the affability and power quality. The trend in power systems is shifting away from integrated bulk generating and distributed energy resources (DER) as a result of DER development. One possibility and the solution for managing DERs is the use of Microgrids (Changliang et al., 2017).

Short Circuit Analysis

It is a critical component of the design and analysis of microgrid protection. Calculating the maximum fault current in a microgrid can be identified by IEC 60909 method also employed by the basic fault analysis technique. Also, IEC 60781 is examined to the other best assumption for short circuit analysis. Long-established copious circuit

Figure 2.

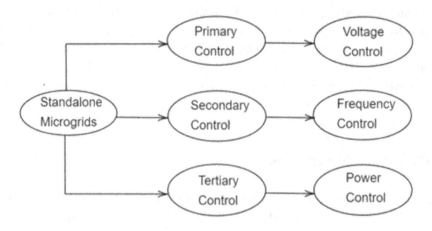

breakers and fuses concerning protection are used to safeguard the microgrid and one of the Relays suggested in this case is SEL751A. It is made up of distributed energy sources that produce electricity to power enough loads. Through the shared connection point is called as Point of Common connection (PCC), microgrids can function in both the grid-connected and islanded modes. To deliver power to particular loads, the electricity generated by several sources is a summation on a single DC bus and converted to AC form using a suitable inverter. During a breakdown or fault, the microgrid's failing area can be promptly isolated from the grid using circuit breakers (CB) situated on the output side of each energy source as well as in inverters. Small-scale freestanding or off-grid MGs, as well as grid-connected MGs, are frequently accustomed to rural electrification (Hofer et al., 2017).

Challenges in Supplying Power and Stability Problems

Off-grid community without connection to the national grid typically receive their power from standalone microgrids. Circuit breakers (CB), which are found in inverters and on the output side of each energy source, allow the failing part of the microgrid to be quickly cut off from the grid in the event of a breakdown or fault. As a result, it is important to clearly outline the issues with securing microgrids as well as an outstanding research domain. Traditional protective measures are useless for microgrids when it is connected to the grid. The model-driven microgrid controller offered by ETAP (Electrical Transient Analyzer program) is fully programmable and allows a great deal of flexibility to achieve desired control functionality. Testing can be done by physically interacting the physical controller with a model of the microgrid and its related devices after the controller logic has been appropriated to the hardware as well as software-in-the-loop of the Microgrid controller with ETAP. In a previous paper, it showed that standalone microgrids typically have a smaller capacity than traditional grids, which means only with fewer customers they can serve. In existing systems may not have as much backup extent as traditional grids, which can pose a problem for balancing demand and supply.

Distributed Generators Integration

The integration of distributed generation is a crucial component to take into account for microgrid protection. An intelligent or adaptive protection method was suggested and put to the test in this study to address these issues. This can be maintained and protected with the use of circuit breakers and fuses. For the effective working of MG, there is a need for investigation into the capacity of DG units. They are often installed by the community they serve, have low-voltage AC grids, and frequently run-on diesel generators. Microgrids increasingly use a variety of distributed energy sources, like solar hybrid power systems, which dramatically cut carbon emissions.

Microgrid faults

Microgrid fault types embrace line-to-line, single-to-ground, double-to-ground, three-phase unbalanced, balanced, and other faults. The network's design and the resistance of each component through which short circuit currents will flow, determine the microgrid's short circuit current. The largest fault current levels are produced by three-phase short circuits, which are utilized to choose the right protective Relay settings (Karim et al., 2019).

Enhancing the Operation of Diesel Generator With Bigdata Analytics

Many different types of enterprises constantly use diesel generator sets as a backup additional energy source. It is employable in a range of capabilities for the different industries they support, including manufacturing, mining, off-shore platforms, offices, and colleges. Typically, a small shop will use a 20 KVA single-phase DG set while a major factory will utilize a 2000 KVA DG set. The problem is that the ratio of energy produced to fuel used gets skewed until the DG set is run at its optimal load, which is consummately 75% of the maximum load. A sub-optimal load might result in revenue losses of up to 75%. Additionally, DG sets begin operating Many different types of enterprises constantly use diesel generator sets as a backup additional energy source. It is employable in a range of capabilities for the different industries they support, including manufacturing, mining, off-shore platforms, offices, and colleges. Typically, a small shop will use a 20 KVA single-phase DG set while a major factory will utilize a 2000 KVA DG set. The problem is that the ratio of energy produced to fuel used gets skewed until the DG set is run at its optimal load, which is consummately 75% of the maximum load. A sub-optimal load might result in revenue losses of up to 75%. Additionally, DG sets begin operating less efficiently when routine maintenance is neglected. The only method to determine is to examine the amount of energy produced to the amount of diesel consumed. To successfully upgrade the DG set performance, one duty is to put aside a watch on a variety of variables. In the modification of the DG set, each of these factors plays a distinct role. The parameters in Table 3 are one of the elements that must be watched over and supplied.

Graph of Fuel Used About Operational Hours

It is feasible to prosecute the DG set's overall efficiency by keeping attention to the fuel it uses, especially when compared to the energy it produces and the number of hours it is in use. Maintenance is required for a DG that uses more fuel and produces less electricity. The condition of DG over a specific period can be determined by comparing fuel used for energy consumption. A trend of rising fuel use for decreasing energy production will be seen over time. Instead of waiting for a breakdown to occur, the DG can be sent for precautionary maintenance when such a pattern appears. As an outcome, the DG's uptime and lifespan are everlastingly increased.

PATTERNS OF LOAD

Judging DG set patterns of the load helps handle DG set usage patterns. Replace a DG with a smaller rating if it is primarily underloaded. In contrast, a DG that is frequently overloaded should be either replaced by a single, greater capacity DG or

Table 3. An overview of household appliance wattages

Rating of Power in Watts	Appliances Used for Residential Areas
25-30	Ceiling fan
145-350	Computer
50-85	Television
60	Incandescent bulb
20	CFL light

by several, lower capacity DGs. In situations where numerous DGs are being used, load analysis is very helpful. The operator can decide when to engage a single DG and when to engage the other DGs, for instance, if the load is rising or falling at regular times throughout the day (Liu et al., 2021).

Distributed Energy Resources and Microgrid Technology

Microgrids with recent technologies help to mitigate the global energy crisis. It can encourage the advancement accompanying the adoption of current energy and replenishable energy sources while overcoming the randomness, intermittency, and dispersity brought on by distributed energy. In contrast to the aggregate grid, MG functions as a specific unit that can be controlled and concurrently fulfils the customers' demand to ensure the safety of power supplies and power quality. It is an amalgamated unit of power technology's distributed generation-based energy storage, protection, and control de- vices that can operate independently or in conjunction with the grid. Both independent networks and grid-connected networks can run MG. When undetermined goes wrong with the grid, the MG turns off the demarcation switch and severing the link with the main network and switching to an island-based network. When the system is connected to the grid network, it can either absorb or supply power to the grid network as part of its normal operation. Employed in an isolated network state not only reduces the length of time that consumers are without power but also aids in the bulk grid's restart, which is beneficial in the event of an unconventional calamity or conflict. Therefore, MG can function as its critical situation energy source, and it can be taken into account (Ma et al., 2018; Maheswari et al., 2020). This systematization combines the initial distributed energy, promotes the power supply, and possesses demand-supply balances as a result of energy storage and control protection. MG is able to connect to the bulk grid in a way that overcomes the uncertainty of distributed energy and the spasmodic distribution of energy. We must examine the particularities and performances of traditional grids and smart grids, as well as microgrids, because distributed power will have a consequence on both. On account of the microgrid's bidirectional trend, it is our main accountability to guarantee the system's stability and safety. For a distributed generation system using renewable energy, real-time, adaptable, advanced power controller intelligent system and central management unit. Various approaches to system prediction, wavelet analysis, gray theory including neural networks have been used in order to build the random model in load. Build an internal random flow control model for MG using intelligent control such as fuzzy control, artificial neural network, and modern control theory, based on the main network scheduling plan, the load capacity of the mg, and the power quality requirements. It will prevent the need for transmission and distribution infrastructure (Mishra et al., 2021; Ndwali et al., 2021). The storage of excess energy from renewable sources should be sustained by higher level battery storage systems. Meanwhile, is to provide electricity during periods when renewable energy is not being produced. Converters and various inverters can encourage the efficiency of transmission and conversion of energy by using developed power electronics.

Accordance of Big Data Analytics and Storage

Specifically designed to manage, store, and retrieve very large data sets, or big data, big data storage is a type of storage system. Big data may be stored and sorted, making it very easy to retrieve. Additionally, services and programs may process data and use information. Finally, large data storage is designed to be highly flexible and scalable. It enables Big Data Analytics and real-time Data processing. Typically, it is about volumes that expand exponentially to a terabyte or petabyte scales. Specific volume size and capacity are not formally specified due to the aforementioned reason. Since many businesses and organizations produce, store, and manipulate more data than ever, the demand for big data storage has skyrocketed. The necessity for Bigdata storage is strongly advised due to the growth of IoT and AI technologies. Based on how businesses collect data from millions and even billions of devices. Big data storage's primary objective is to fortify the data with organization and intelligence making it possible to properly analyze the data. Modern analytics systems can quickly process very large amounts of semi- structured or even unstructured data. High-speed big data storage must be influenced by Facebook, Twitter, and Google (Ndwali et al., 2020).

Microgrid Big Data Collection

The coordination and governance of transformers, cables, substations, and circuit breakers, switch gears, transmission lines generate a wide range of equipment data. Switch gear information, including discharge, moisture content, and dis- charge rate. Waveforms of electrical signals, frequency variations, swell and sag in voltage levels, and some major information on transmission lines network. Temperature, dis- charge, and circumvolution of present information for power cables. Findings on substations, name, location, type, id and contamination level. Together with nominal capacity, current, connection, voltage, manufacturer, cooling arrangement, non- functioning recorders, inoperative sources, additional information of a substation, tripping data, details of SF6, protective resistance, governing mechanisms, equipment data in productivity, corresponding circuit breakers with relays, a circuit breaker is made up of a number of parameters. The various equipment used in residential areas can be overviewed in the below table (Pazmino et al., 2022). A source of Bigdata is data from proper and consistent equipment monitoring in all aspects. Data from monitoring systems may contain information about the equipment's volt- age, current, power, frequency, etc., and energy management systems. The one of the main sources of load management information include smart meters. The widespread extensive source of Bigdata is the load-side management factor. One million Smart meters, for instance, generate more than 1.82 Tb of data. From information on energy usage, such as consumer trends, Bigdata can identify the sort of load. The information on the loads acquired may likewise be shared by customers (Rathore et al., 2020; Sanjeev et al., 2017). Big data sources also include generated data in load in particular just like data from electric powered vehicles. The information includes everything even the position of the car, any defects, pedal examinations, various drives in machines, rate of velocity, depression of car tire, etc. The extensive use of renewable energy sources that are unpredictable and intermittent calls for the implementation of a new data-based energy management system in the microgrid control system to prevent grid volatility. There is an abundance of data sources surrounding the Microgrid, such as measurements from solar energy, required smart meters, various SCADA systems, environmental conditions, and data entered in electronic sensors (High communication data rates are used in smart control to enhance the whole power grid's quality, dependability, efficiency, and regulation. Petabyte-scale data volumes must be evaluated within minimal tolerable time frames, exceeding the capabilities of conventional computer techniques (Sheikholeslami et al., 2020). It is still early days for Bigdata techniques to be used in the microgrid, which represents a large amount of data. Big data is being produced by electricity networks. When data is gathered every 15 minutes from 1.2 million smart meters, 2915 Terabytes are produced. To choose the ideal position for the wind turbine, IBM examined 4 heterogeneous Petabytes of data, such as weather, wind, and other environmental data (Simeon et al., 2020). The microgrid's data are being streamed at a faster and faster rate in a variety of forms and configurations. The US power outage costs 118 to 190 billion dollars, demonstrating the growing demand for Microgrid data processing. Compared to the ceremonial methods utilized in the power grid industry, as Bigdata becomes the norm, a new era begins offers far more benefits. A decentralized computing environment where analysis takes place close to the data can ensure parallel, processing in real time, rapid knowledge extraction, and discovery of value beneath the gathered data. It is being researched how much it will cost to use large volume of data in the smart microgrid system. A comprehensive economic and friendly environment can be achieved by powering huge data processing centers with renewable energy. Applications of Big data in the field of Microgrids are highly valuable, influential, and significant. A look at bigdata sources in the Microgrid, platform constraints for managing Bigdata in the Microgrid, and a summary of investigation reports are all articulated in this paper. An illustration of a standalone microgrid system in rural electrification can be found in Figure 3.

Tools for Huge Data

Hadoop recommend great reliability because of its ease of scaling to thousands of nodes, performance at a high level, and speedy operation, as well as the reality that it is open source and cost-free. It is an ecosystem rather than a single application and is made up of several different parts, the majority of which were developed using open source and by the Apache Software Foundation. The primary elements of the Hadoop ecosystem include Mahout, Hive, Drill, Pig, and Cascading (Syed et al., 2021).

Figure 3. Standalone microgrid system in rural electrification

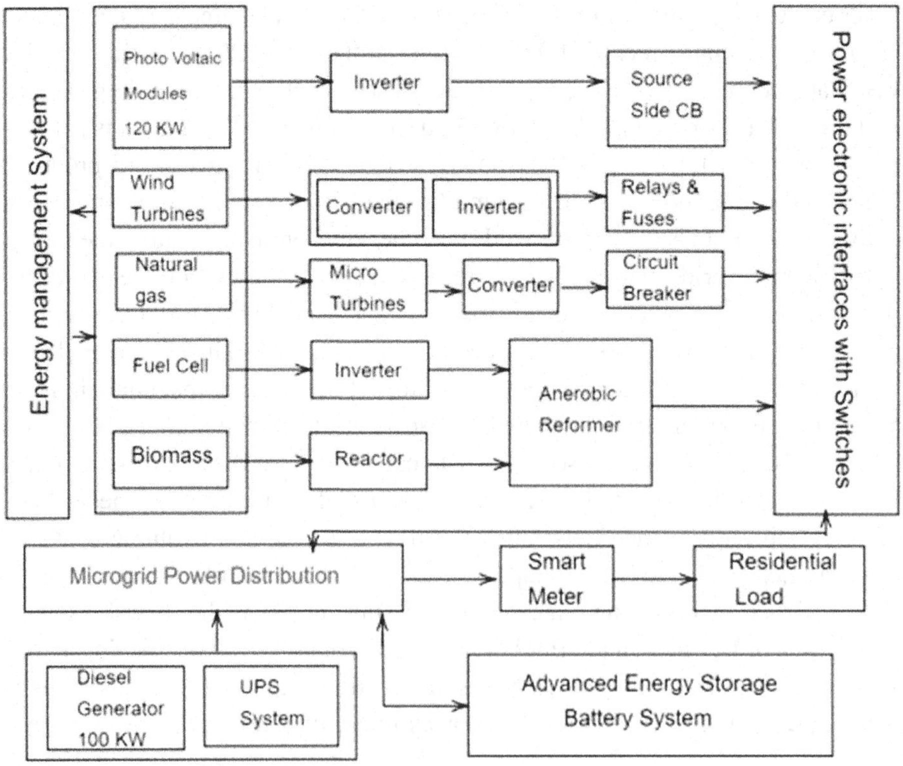

MapReduce

Google introduced this efficient distributed processing method. It carries out two steps of the process. Map tasks stipulate key-value pairs as input data. The algorithm trans- forms a few scalars. Outputs from the map are categorized by keys, subdivided into smaller tasks and sorted. Operation on arrays of values sets each key, and combinations of key matching can be applied after the map operation. Once the results have been collected, they are analyzed.

Apache Chukwa

Distributed system monitoring tool in Data storage and map- reduce with HDFS. It includes resources for showing and deciphering data outcomes (Umuhoza et al., 2019).

Machine Learning

It is provided via Apache Mahout.

Apache RHadoop

It is used for data visualization and mining.

Hive

A data warehouse built on top of Hadoop MapReduce for data storage. The two primary parts of it are WebHcat and Catalog. As a table, data can be simply entered into Hcatalog, and WebHcat's HTTP interface makes it possible to run Hive, Hadoop, Pig and MapReduce.

Apache Flume

A tool for HDFS streaming data gathering.

Apache HBase

HDFS is where data are kept. NoSQL data archiving. When the HDFS is insufficient or when data is updated by multiple applications, a Hadoop database is employed.

Cassandra

Open-source database administration

BUILDING BIGDATA IN A MICROGRID

Microgrids Can Be Built as Tiered Platforms for Bigdata

Layer for database collection: Data from sources such as load data, equipment data, generated data in various forms, numerous sensors are collected by it. Additionally, it delivers data wirelessly or across wires publicly accessible datasets.

Collection Description

Other data sources for Energy Plus include NREL, For the United States and some other regions, this site provides big datasets about energy sources like geothermal, marine power, biomass and wave power. There is an Open AMI Data Structured sample of five-minute data-based energy in the online repository that includes an accuracy, date, value, time, and accuracy. The platform for processing and analyzing Bigdata in the Microgrid (Vasluianu et al., 2019).

Sharing Information About the Analytics

Pre-processing of data: It is composed of subsystems that interface with HDFS and other data storage systems via SQOOP, FTP, and MQTT for database communication respectively. Transformation of data, detection, detailed evaluation and correction are the outcomes of this layer. Data management: Using Hive, HBase, and Impala, manage large amounts of structured and unstructured data. Additionally, MongoDB is a notable recent solution because it is compatible with MapReduce (Yu et al., 2017; Zhao et al., 2020).

RESULT ANALYSIS

Power Forecast

Microgrid planning utilizes a cloud-based platform with big data by matching the supply and the load suggests storing historical weather data, customer profiles, generating data, and load data in the Cassandra cloud. Data-driven predictions are made regarding the power generation. A MapReduce framework is used for data optimizing and prediction after redeeming the data from HDFS. Grolinger reported on a technique for foretelling energy consumption in large data sets using support vector regression (SVR) with local learning. Among the three methods used in the study to predict energy use, local SVR and H2O deep learning outperformed SVR, while SVR emerged as the most accurate proceedings. In Morocco, Daki et al suggested using Bigdata to balance energy production and consumption. The following examples illustrate some types of data sources: semi structured weather data, unstructured Kafka streaming data from real time sensors, and structured operational data such as proper planning and data equipment from logical databases utilizing HTTP protocol. MapReduce is a distributed computing system management tool for data processing. A high priority part of HBase's coordination is Zookeeper. Algorithms for machine learning are used to forecast how much electricity will be utilized. The result analysis in diesel generators utilization can be indicated in Table 4.

Homer Software

The simulation was conducted using HOMER software to determine the best arrangements for the batteries, diesel generator, and photovoltaic panels. As the industry standard for improving microgrid designs across all industries, HOMER Pro adds value to grid-connected campuses and military bases, as well as island utilities and villages. A hybrid optimization software known as HOMER (Hybrid Optimization of Multiple Energy Resources) can help you evaluate designs for grid-connected and off-grid power systems. Power systems are configured in a number of ways. Moreover, HOMER controls the transmission of power to the generators and the charging and discharging of batteries. Depending on the system con- figuration, HOMER runs the energy balance calculation for it. When a configuration is deemed feasible, it calculates the installation and maintenance costs during the project's life- cycle. Replacement costs, operations costs, capital costs fuel costs, and interest costs and maintenance costs are considered in calculating system costs.

CONCLUSION

The main issue in recent years is seen to be the electrification of rural areas. Because the primary utility system cannot provide basic electricity to 30% of the population. The supply of power is occasionally disrupted. The freestanding microgrids in remote places, especially in rural areas, play a crucial role in overcoming these erratic power supplies. This research focuses on the many issues related to the use of diesel generator-powered island microgrids. With the use of big data analytics

Table 4. Result analysis in diesel generators utilization

Load Factors	Operating Times (Hours)	Use of Fuel	Engine Heat, Coolant Pressure, and Lube Oil Pressure	Battery Condition
The amount of energy that a DG must provide is dependent on the load it is carrying.	One of the most crucial variables to deliberately track are how long the DG set has performing.	Utilization of fuel must be regularly tracked as well as determined.	Coolants are required to keep the engine at a constant temperature in order to prevent rusting of the engine.	Starting voltage, DG sets exploit batteries.
Running a DG at a lower than-optimal load causes the engine's inside to intensify carbon.	Given the range of uses for DG sets, operational hours are helpful in deciding how they are often employed.	Fuel theft is a major problem that will reduce the overall performance	If the decline in coolant particularly levels are not immediately fixed, DG overheats and can sustain the irreparable damage.	It becomes difficult to start the DG set because the batteries degrade over time.

tools, we should first analyze the problems and challenges before establishing the microgrid concept. In the microgrid community, we must gather relevant data, and this data is very helpful in identifying the main power quality flaws. Power losses can be reduced by employing power optimizers with a maximum power point tracking approach. By adopting renewable energy sources, 70% of the world's electricity has grown. keeping EMS in microgrids to maintain the voltage level. The IEC 60909 approach in this paper uses the SEL751A (Relay) to identify the maximum fault current. When it comes to managing the operation of the microgrid, ETAP (Electrical Transient Analyzer Program) is particularly adaptable. Diesel generator sets/units and capacity should be researched before establishing microgrid in a specific location. The operator should recognize the load patterns based on the load. Data can be collected in the microgrid system utilizing a variety of bigdata technologies. Last but not least, microgrid planning uses a cloud-based platform with bigdata to match supply and load, and it suggests large data sets with the use of map-reduce frameworks. Easily can assess ideas for grid-connected and off-grid power systems using HOMER, a hybrid optimization tool. Keeping the generator set examined and maintained most often will ensure its optimal performance. A fuel system promotes installing a fuel prefilter or fuel injector with higher level efficiency, can boost the performance of diesel generator sets. In order to increase the performance of the generator set, it may be necessary to replace the cooling system with an upgraded one. In my future work, the best option is to add a large radiator as well as cooling fan can lower the temperature during the operation of generator sets also it will increase the efficiency of whole system. The second option is to use a high-quality diesel fuel can enhance the potential of the generator set and increase its life expectancy.

REFERENCES

Araujo, J., Elson, R., & Anselmo, M. (2017). Assessment of the Impact of Microgrid Control Strategies in the Power Distribution Reliability Indices. *Journal of Control Automation and Electric System.* . doi:10.1007/s40313-017-0299-x

Arcos, A. (2021). An Energy Management System Design Using Fuzzy Logic Control: Smoothing the Grid Power Profile of a Residential Electro-Thermal Microgrid. *IEEE Access : Practical Innovations, Open Solutions*, *1*(17), 25172–25188. Advance online publication. doi:10.1109/ACCESS.2021.3056454

Bertheau, P., Hoffmann, M. M., Eras-Almeida, A., & Blechinger, P. (2020).*Assessment of Microgrid Potential in Southeast Asia Based on the Application of Geospatial and Microgrid Simulation and Planning Sustainable Energy Solutions for Remote Areas in the Tropics. In Green Energy and Technology*. Springer. doi:10.1007/978-3-030-41952-37

Bhamidi, L., & Sivasubramani, S. (2019). Optimal Planning and Operational Strategy of a Residential Microgrid with Demand Side Management. *IEEE Systems Journal*, *1*(9). . doi:10.1109/JSYST.2019.2918410

Bharathi, G., & Padmanabhan, T. S. (2022). Planning and Optimization of Energy Scheduling in Cohesive Renewable Energy Microgrid to Meet Electric Load Demand of an Educational Institution. *Journal of Electrical Engineering & Technology*, *17*(6), 3207–3221. doi:10.100742835-022-01138-8

Bhatt., N., Sondhi, R., Arora, S. (2022). Droop Control Strategies for Microgrid: A Review. In *Advances in Renewable Energy and Electric Vehicles*. Springer. https://doi.org//978-981-16-1642-612 doi:10.1007

Changliang, L., Yanqun, W., Kang, B., & Weiliang, L. (2017). Energy management strategy research for residential microgrid considering virtual energy storage system at demand side. *IEEE International Conference on Electronic Measurement Instruments (ICEMI)*, 273-280, 10.1109/ICEMI.2017.8265790

Effective Control Strategy in Microgrid. (n.d.). In *International Conference on Intelligent Computing and Smart Communication Algorithms for Intelligent Systems*. Springer. https://doi.org/10.1007/ 978-981-15-0633-8 94

Hofer, J., Svetozarevic, B., & Schlueter, A. (2017). Hybrid AC/DC building microgrid for solar PV and battery storage integration. *IEEE Second International Conference on DC Microgrids (ICDCM)*, 188-191. 10.1109/ICDCM.2017.8001042

Karim, M. (2019). State of the art in bigdata applications in microgrid: A review. *Advanced Engineering Informatics, 100945*. Advance online publication. doi:10.1016/j.aei.2019.100945

Liu, J., Wang, W., Zhang, Y., & Xu, X. (2019). Energy Management for Households Considering Uncertainty in Solar Irradiance with Various Probability Distribution. *Journal of Electrical Engineering & Technology, 14*(5), 1943–1956. doi:10.100742835-019-00243-5

Liu, Y., Guo, L., Wang, C., & Hou, R. (2021). Application of Optimization Techniques in the Design and Operation of Microgrid. In Design, Control, and Operation of Microgrids in Smart Grids Power Systems. Springer. 10.1007/978-3-030-64631-83

Ma, Y., Zhou, Y., Zhang, J., & Piao, C. (2018). Economic Dispatch of Islanded Microgrid Considering a Cooperative Strategy Between Diesel Generator and Battery Energy Storage System. *Journal of Shanghai Jiaotong University (Science), 23*(5), 593–599. doi:10.100712204-018-1988-8

Mishra, S., Kwasnik, T., Anderson, K., & Wood, R. (2021). *Microgrid's Role in Enhancing the Security and Flexibility of City Energy Systems. In Flexible Resources for Smart Cities.* Springer. doi:10.1007/978-3-030-82796-0 4

Ndwali, P.K., Njiri, J., & Wanjiru, E.M. (2021). Economic Model Predictive Control of Microgrid Connected Photovoltaic-Diesel Generator backup Energy System Considering Demand Side Management. *J. Electric Eng Technology*. https://doi.org/s42835-021-00801-w doi:10.1007/s

Ndwali, P. K., Njiri, J. G., & Wanjiru, E. M. (2020). Optimal Operation Control of Microgrid Connected Photovoltaic-Diesel Generator Backup System Under Time of Use Tariff. *J Control Autom Electric Syst, 31*(4), 1001–1014. doi:10.100740313-020-00585-w

Pazmin~o, I., Ochoa, D., Minaya, E. P., & Mera, H. P. (2022). Use of Battery Energy Storage Systems to Enhance the Frequency Stability of an Islanded Microgrid Based on Hybrid Photovoltaic-Diesel Generation. Sustainability, Energy and City. CSE City. Lecture Notes in Networks and Systems, 379. 10.1007/978-3-030-94262-55

Rathore, B., Srivastava, L., Gupta, N., Singh, S.P., & Sagwal, R. (2020). A Comprehensive Study on AC Microgrid Control Strategies at Primary Control Level. *Intelligent Computing Applications for Sustainable Real- World Systems. ICSISCET 2019. Proceedings in Adaptation, Learning and Optimization.* https://doi.org//978-3-030-44758-845 doi:10.1007

Sanjeev, P., Padhy, N. P., & Agarwal, P. (2017). Effective control and energy management of isolated DC microgrid. *IEEE Power Energy Society General Meeting*, 1-5. 10.1109/PESGM.2017.8273786

Sheikholeslami, M., Shahidehpour, M., Paaso, A., & Bahramirad, S. (2020). Challenges of Modeling and Simulation of Clustered Bronzeville Community Microgrid (BCM) and IIT Campus Microgrid (ICM) Using RTDS. *IEEE Power Energy Society General Meeting (PESGM)*, 1-5. 10.1109/PESGM41954.2020.9281885

Simeon, A., & Chowdhury, S. (2020). Protection Challenges in a Standalone Microgrid: Case Study of Tsumkwe Microgrid. *IEEE PES/IAS Power Africa*, 1-5. doi:.2020.9219972 doi:10.1109/PowerAfrica49420

Syed, D., Zainab, A., Ghrayeb, A., Refaat, S. S., Abu-Rub, H., & Bouhali, O. (2021). Smart Grid Big Data Analytics: Survey of Technologies, Techniques, and Applications. *IEEE Access : Practical Innovations, Open Solutions*, 9, 59564–59585. doi:10.1109/ACCESS.2020.3041178

Umuhoza, J., Zhang, Y., Zhao, S., & Mantooth, H. A. (2017). An adaptive control strategy for power balance and the intermittency mitigation in battery-PV energy system at residential DC microgrid level. *IEEE Applied Power Electronics Conference and Exposition*, *1341345*, 1341–1345. Advance online publication. doi:10.1109/APEC.2017.7930870

Vasluianu, O., Faida, C. N., Flangea, R., Giorgian, N., & Marinescu, M. (2019). Microgrid System for a Residential Ensemble. *22nd International Conference on Control Systems and Computer Science (CSCS)*, 375-379, 10.1109/CSCS.2019.00067

Yu, B., Guo, J., Zhou, C., Gan, Z., & Yu, Y. (2017). A Review on Microgrid Technology with Distributed Energy. *International Conference on Smart Grid and Electrical Automation (ICSGEA)*, 143-146. a.10.1109/ICSGEA.2017.152

Zhao, J., Li, C., & Wang, L. (2020). Hadoop-Based Power Grid Data Quality Verification and Monitoring Method. *Journal of Electrical Engineering & Technology*. Advance online publication. doi:10.100742835-022-01171-7

Chapter 6
Evaluation of Energy Flexibility Potential of Different Interventions Through the SRI Score:
Evaluation Under the IoT Paradigm

Valentina Tomat
University of Murcia, Spain

Alfonso Pablo Ramallo-González
University of Murcia, Spain

Antonio Fernando Skarmeta-Gómez
University of Murcia, Spain

ABSTRACT

On the last EPBD, a new indicator to measure smart technologies in buildings has been developed: the smart readiness indicator (SRI). The SRI framework evaluates the smart services that the building could deliver, with the threefold purpose of optimising energy efficiency, adapting to the needs of the occupants and responding to the signals from the grid. The chapter analyses the increase of smart readiness in eight real-world buildings, characterised by different climate conditions and retrofitted with cost-effective interventions. On this study, the assessment was done with two different methods, one using the same maximum obtainable score for all the buildings and the other using a list of smart services adapted to each building. The outcomes are compared to spot the potentialities of the new indicator, and its usability has been tested through a questionnaire. Finally, the applicability to DLC is discussed to support the role that the indicator can assume in enhancing the load shifting potential in buildings, toward the energy transformation of the European society.

DOI: 10.4018/978-1-6684-7756-4.ch006

INTRODUCTION AND BACKGROUND

The potential of smart technologies in the building energy sector has been a headline for the European Commission in the last decades (Directive 2002/91/EU, 2003). In line with the climate target of the Kyoto protocol (Kyoto Protocol, 1997), with the EU initiatives toward clean energy innovations (Communication 763, 2016; Communication 860, 2016) and with the expected reduction of the greenhouse gas emission by 2050 (Communication 112, 2011), the EU is doing a great effort to include the energy efficiency in buildings in its legislative framework. This effort resulted in guidelines for the building regulations, such as the Energy Efficiency Directive (Directive 2012/27/EU, 2012), the Renewable Energy Directive (Directive 2009/28/EC, 2009) and the European Performance of Building Directive (EPBD) (Directive 2010/31/EU, 2010). Currently, the energy efficiency of the European building stock is assessed by the Energy Performance Certificate (EPC). Nevertheless, a step forward was done in the third revision of the EPBD in 2018 (Directive (EU) 2018/844, 2018), since it is believed that emphasising the potential of smart technologies in the building sector will lead to an improvement in both energy efficiency and people's well-being. As a consequence, the concept of a Smart Readiness Indicator (SRI) was introduced, and it is proposed to be a common EU framework for rating the 'smartness' of a building. The introduction of the SRI should accelerate the transformation of the European building stock, a transformation that is more than urgent if considering that around 40% of it has been built prior the 1960s (Atanasiu et al., 2011).

The applicability of the SRI is discussed in several works, in particular with respect to the climate conditions. Janhunen et al. (2019) investigated the applicability of the SRI to Northern Europe countries undertaking a study that evaluated the assessment method for that specific region. After the study, they highlighted the need for methodological changes in the framework, also they do not consider that the SRI can be equally applicable to EU-wide energy efficiency interventions. The applicability of the SRI method for the Mediterranean climate has been evaluated by Ramezani et al. (2021), who proposed two case study buildings in Portugal. They considered that the framework worked correctly in describing the characteristics of the case study building for the Mediterranean climate conditions, but they noticed a weakness in predicting energy consumption with the proposed weighting factors, especially for non-residential buildings. Apostolopoulos et al. (2022), studied the applicability in five European countries, in residential buildings, and highlighted that low-cost retrofitting can significantly improve the SRI scores.

Some limitations in the methodology have been pointed out by some authors. Al Dakheel et al. (2020) analysed the concept of smartness in the built environment, with a special focus on smart retrofitting into smart buildings. They discussed the limitation of the SRI methodology, based particularly on the lack of possible ways to testing the real progress and the performances of smart technologies. Vigna et al. (2020) applied the methodology to a nearly zero-energy building located in Italy. It emerged from the analysis that the comparison among different buildings is possible only in presence of the same number of services, i.e., with comparable catalogue lists. Something remarkable that came up from their study, is the influence of subjective decisions, since the evaluation from two panels of experts gave slightly different outcomes. Also, Fokaides et al. (2020) analysed the method and found some critical points. First of all, as other studies also confirmed, they highlighted the element of subjectivity in the evaluation of the smartness of the buildings, since the assessment is based on the understanding of the designer. Then, they noticed that the SRI has a considerable gap, that is the non-applicability to historical buildings, that represent an important percentage of the European building stock. Finally, applying the method to a case study (the main wing of the Frederick University of Cyprus), they noticed e discrepancy between the rather good SRI score of the building (52%, considered a good score) and the considerable poor EPC of the building (class D, not considered a good score) what brings the question of the two indicators needing to be correlated. Hence, they suggested the development of a comprehensive methodology, by englobing the intelligence readiness in the energy class of the building linking the two together.

The introduction of the SRI is expected to give an impulse also to the concept of demand flexibility, in order to mitigate the stress that is currently suffered by the grid due to the massive increase in the buildings' energy demand, and the appearance of new peaks due to electro-mobility and extreme weather events (Church et al., 2011; Heinen et al., 2011). Future buildings could adapt their demand to the needs of the grid, changing their role from consumers to prosumers, and optimising the resources spent on infrastructure. The set of flexibility strategies is known in the literature as Demand Response (DR), englobing different programs that are aimed at shifting or shaving (or both) the peak power. In Annex 67 of the program Energy in Buildings and Communities of the International Energy Agency (IEA EBC Annex 67, 2015), it can be read that Energy Flexibility represents 'the capacity of a building to manage its demand and generation according to local climate conditions, user needs and grid requirements. Energy Flexibility of buildings will thus allow for demand side management/load control and thereby demand response based on the requirements of the surrounding grids'. This approach was englobed in the SRI framework in order to give a quantitative evaluation of the building flexibility as an output (ENER/C3/2016-554. 2020). For this aspect, new work needs to be done, as the demands and the potential attitudes of users towards them, needs to be identify. In Vigna et al. (2018), the analysis of the energy flexibility is done at a cluster approach, where a cluster is defined as a group to identify buildings interconnected to the same energy infrastructures. The interdependence between the new smartness indicator and the energy flexibility of a building is clear from their classification, since the categorisation of the clusters is strictly related to smart readiness. This relates with the way the SRI could be define, considering these groups of users, Märzinger and Österreicher (2019) proposed a quantitative assessment for the SRI, providing a numerical approach that classifies buildings according to their load shifting potential and their integration with the grid.

In the context of the Horizon 2020 Programme, the largest research and innovation programme of the European Union (Moseley, 2019), the European Project PHOENIX (PHOENIX, Horizon 2020) aims at studying the upgrade of smartness of existing buildings through the designing a portfolio of ICT (Information and Communications Technology) solutions among others. The project proposes user-friendly and cost-effective services to respond to the needs of the users, the grid and the building itself that are connected to each other by using a network of sensors and actuators integrated into an IoT platform. Such a connection has a significant impact on the smartness of the buildings, since it enables the report of information, the automatised control of several systems, the forecasting of data, predictive management, automatic fault detection and so forth. From the literature, it is clear the applicability of an IoT framework to the smart building sector, which is widely discussed and analysed from several perspectives: energy systems (Yaïci et al., 2021; Santos et al., 2019; Terroso-Saenz et al., 2019), occupants' comfort (Tomat et al., 2020), smart grid (Hafeez et al., 2020), predictive temperature control (Ramallo-González et al., 2020; Carli et al., 2020), and many others.

In particular, project PHOENIX has been the framework to realise the interventions in the eight buildings of the five pilots, with the aim of incrementing the SRI score shown on this paper. In fact, the SRI resulted to be a useful tool to quantify the effects of the connectivity's enhancement within the project what was one of the KPIs of the project. It was used in particular to evaluate the effectiveness of the ICT solutions proposed in the project, in terms of the smartness of legacy systems and appliances in the pilot buildings.

In this paper, the evolution of the SRI before and after the intervention for the five case studies within the project PHOENIX is presented. Furthermore, a questionnaire was created ad hoc to evaluate the usability of the SRI calculation tool an aspect that has also crucial importance for an assessment tool as the SRI. The rest of the paper is structured as follows. Section 2 explains the methodology used to calculate the SRI score. In the first subsection, five different real-world case studies are described, that are the pilots used to validate the PHOENIX solution; besides, the subsection contains a description of the interventions realised for each case study within the project PHOENIX. In the second subsection, it is explained the structure of the questionnaire that the pilot partners filled in after calculating the SRI. Section 3 collects the results: the SRI score is presented in terms of overall score and in terms of improvement for each domain. The results of the questionnaires are also presented in this section. Section 4 presents a practical discussion about the connection between the SRI and the evaluation of the building energy flexibility, with particular focus on the Direct Load Control strategy, a widely used strategy of demand response that has been applied to some of the pilots' buildings withing the project PHOENIX. Section 5 englobes the main conclusions of the work.

MAIN FOCUS OF THE CHAPTER

The SRI calculation is based on the evaluation of the capability of satisfying three key functionalities: optimising energy efficiency and overall in-use performance; adapting operation to the needs of the occupants and to adapt to signals from the grid. The three key smart-readiness functionalities are further detailed into seven impact criteria, namely energy-saving on-site, comfort, convenience, health and wellbeing, maintenance and fault prediction, information to occupants, grid flexibility and storage.

The methodology for calculating the SRI is based on the assessment of smart-ready services that the building has or could use. As explained in Verbeke et al. (2019), the calculation tool presents a list of pre-set smart services, and for each service, the assessor has to evaluate which is the level of smart readiness. To do so, the tool also proposes the functionality levels that can be assigned. The functionality level can vary from level 0, that is no automatisation, up to level 4. Depending on the level assigned, each one of the seven impact criteria receives a score. For further information about the scores' assignment, please refer to the official report on the technical support (Final report SRI, 2020). The smart services are grouped into nine technical domains, namely heating, cooling, domestic hot water, ventilation, lighting, dynamic envelope, electricity, electric vehicle and monitoring and control. For each domain, a weighting factor is assigned. The weighting factors, available in the SRI calculation tool or in the technical documentation (Final Report SRI, 2020), are obtained from the building stock observatory and then tailored according to the geographical context. Hence, they are automatically assigned according to the building type and geographical position. However, the assessors can use customised weighting factors, based on an energy balance, wherever deemed relevant.

Hence, the SRI framework is structured as follows: the assessment provides detailed scores by domain and impact criterion; then, the detailed scores are aggregated to obtain a score for each domain, as well as a score for each impact criterion; the aggregation is repeated to obtain a score for each key-functionality and, at the very end, the overall SRI score is obtained. Depending on the score, the SRI class will be assigned to the building.

The maximum obtainable score can be calculated in two main ways: (1) considering all the services of the selected service catalogue (detailed method with 54 services or simplified method with 27 services) or (2) considering just the services that are present in a building. The two approaches have different scopes. Approach (1) allows using the same maximum score for all the buildings, making easier the smart readiness comparison among different cases. Approach (2) provides a flexible method that can adapt to different circumstances, allowing to exclude from the calculation services that are not relevant, not applicable, or not desirable through a selection called the triage process.

The work shown on this paper wants to be as comprehensive as possible about the framework available. Considering that the triage process adds an extra level of flexibility to the assessor, it was decided to apply both approaches described in the previous subsection: the one with the complete list of services and the one with the specific services chosen by the assessors. Approach (1) will be used to have a common maximum score, so the level of smartness of the different pilots can be compared on the same basis, while approach (2) will be used to evaluate how each building's potentialities are exploited through the actuations. The calculations will be performed with the default weighting factors and the selected catalogue of services will be the detailed one (with a list of 54 services).

Case Studies

The framework described before has been applied to several different contexts, that are the five real-world pilots of the European project PHOENIX, with a total contribution of eight buildings. Within the project, the pilots are subjected to retrofitting interventions that aims to increase the smartness of the buildings among others. Hence, the SRI score can be calculated before and after the interventions proposed, to understand which are the effects of retrofitting on the indicator and which strategies can be considered more effective from a smart readiness perspective. The effect of the interventions is compared with other aspects of the actions such as cost to have a comprehensive view of the activities. The pilots are located in Spain, Greece, Ireland, and Sweden, characterised by different climate conditions. Moreover, among the buildings, there is a further differentiation between residential and non-residential. In this way, it is possible to spot the differences in the SRI calculations in very different scenarios, while exploring issues and suggestions that can derive from such different points of view.

Table 1. The five pilots in a nutshell. Summary of the study cases from the project PHOENIX (PHOENIX, Horizon 2020) and reasons for the selection

	Arden	KaMa	LTU	MIWenergía	UMU
Case Study					
Short Description	Community of RISEC to promote and deliver investment in sustainable energy in Dublin, Ireland.	Six-flat residential building for the Greek Army in Thessaloniki, Greece.	Three-floor building with 12 apartments and a commercial space in Skellefteå, Sweden.	Four-floor commercial building + residential building of four apartments in the Region of Murcia, Spain.	Five-floor building located in the Campus of the University of Murcia, Spain.
Why it was chosen	Representative sample of housing with a high potential for replication. The residents are engaged in emerging sustainable technologies.	The building is representative of the recent increasing number of renovations on the old Greek building stock	Chosen for both its characteristics and the wealth of data available from previous years	The buildings are representative of the Mediterranean building stock. The residents are engaged in energy management strategies.	The building was chosen since it has already been used for energy consumption prediction experiments and smart city scenarios.

Table 1 presents a summary of the study cases, to understand why they were chosen and which are the main characteristics. Then, for each pilot it will presented a brief description of the original state, a summary of the intervention within the project PHOENIX, and finally a list of equipment integrated into the buildings in order to have a more practical view of the interventions needed to increase the SRI score. Please notice that the calculation for each case study was managed by different assessors, who worked synergistically to obtain comparable outcomes.

Case Study: Arden

Arden proposes three testbeds for the project, located in the community of the Ringsend Irishtown Sustainable Energy Co-operative (RISEC), in Dublin, Ireland. Two of the buildings (that will be called Arden #1 and Arden #2) are residential, part of a social housing block, while the third one, the Rediscovery Commercial Centre, is commercial (Arden #3). The commercial building has a legacy BMS and it includes solar PV, CHP, heat pump and solar thermal. The residential pilot buildings dispose of EV charging, solar PV, electric heating and electric DHW.

The intervention in the residential buildings concerned several systems. The EV system has been included in the parking spaces of both buildings. The connection with the IoT platform through the installation of middleware enabled the flexible control of the HVAC system, the connection between the controllers and the BACS, and the possibility of storing historical data and forecasting data. In building Arden #1, the actuation concerned also the automatised control of the on-site energy storage system and the DHW storage system; besides, the appliances have been equipped with smart sockets, enabling real-time feedback.

In the commercial building, the interventions involved the installation of sensors to improve the ambient conditions, the installation of smart sockets for the appliances and the improvement of the communication with the occupants (e.g. performance evaluation and forecasting). The control of several systems has been improved as well, to achieve energy saving: for instance, the temperature control will depend on the outdoor temperature. The enhancement of the connectivity entails the possibility to respond to the signals from the grid, making possible the demand side management. The DHW installation has been improved through multi-sensor storage management, while the ventilation system through air quality sensors allows central demand control.

Equipment installed and upgraded to gain smartness:
Monitoring Devices for Energy Saving (Electrical Consumption/Generation):
    Three-phase smart meter on main incomer and 18 sub-metered loads
Monitoring Devices for Indoor Comfort and Energy Saving (Temperature):
    Temperature sensors connected to BMS, thermal boilers with differential thermostat
EV Equipment for Energy Saving: EV chargers
Gateway for Connectivity: Raspberry Pi + Z-Wave

Case Study: KaMa

Two-story residential building of six dwellings (around 80 m2 each) located in Thessaloniki, Greece. The building disposes of heat pumps for heating and cooling with individual room control for heat emission, demand-based control of the supply air flow (for heating), on-off control for the distribution pumps (both heating and cooling) and variable control for the generator capacity (both heating and cooling); besides, the interlock system avoids the simultaneous use of the heating and cooling systems. The DHW is managed by a single centralised solar water system with automatic control of storage charging and a supplementary heat generator (also automatised). Sequencing between the two systems is rated based on energy efficiency. Each flat is equipped with full LED lighting installations with manual control per room. A PV installation with battery storage and grid connection is present in the building: the generation data is available, and the consumption is optimised to prioritise the use of locally generated electricity. Finally, a charging point for the EVs is installed.

The intervention within PHOENIX aims to increase the energy efficiency and the use of renewable energy from PV and solar thermal, reducing the grid dependency and covering the building during eventual blackouts. For this scope, self-generation will be improved through the automated management based on the grid signals. The installation of an automatic shading system will improve the comfort of the occupants, and the communication with the end-users will be also improved by developing user interfaces. Several systems (namely, HVAC, DHW, EV and Lighting) will be equipped with sensors that enable automatic control.

Equipment installed and upgraded to gain smartness:
Monitoring Devices for Energy Saving (Electrical Consumption/Generation):
    Three-phase and single-phase smart meters
Monitoring Devices for Indoor Comfort and Energy Saving (Temperature):
    External/ internal ambient temperature, solar thermal boiler water temperature
Monitoring Devices for Visual Comfort and Energy Saving (Luminance):
    Luminance sensors
Monitoring Devices for Healthiness and Sustainability (Air Quality): CO_2 sensors
IoT Devices for Energy Saving: Smart lamps, smart plugs
Gateway for Connectivity: Raspberry Pi, ModEth modules + Z-wave USB

Case Study: MIWenergia

The pilot includes a commercial building (that will be called MIW #1) and a residential one (MIW #2), both located in the Region of Murcia, in the South-East part of Spain. The commercial building disposes of a central HVAC system for the common areas, that is an external machine on the rooftop of the building; the setpoint temperature can be controlled at floor level. Each office has an individual HVAC system, with a compressor located outside. DHW is served by an electric thermal system. The residential building disposes of split air conditioner systems in the apartments. Both pilot buildings are equipped with smart meters that provide hourly energy consumption data.

The intervention within the project consists of the insertion of sensors to measure the ambient conditions and to monitor the occupants' comfort, and of the installation of technical equipment to enhance the systems' control. Also in this case, the connection to the IoT platform will allow optimising the monitoring and control of several systems, enabling the possibility to share information with the occupants. Energy efficiency will be improved in both the HVAC system and lighting system in both buildings. In building MIW #1, the automatic control of the heating and cooling systems has been improved by enabling communication between the controllers and the BAC. The improved smartness of the building will enable the ability to adapt the operation mode in response to occupants and the grid's needs (flexible control). On the other hand, the actuation in the building MIW #2 will allow reporting real-time information on current performance and historical at an appliances level, because of the insertion of smart meters.

Equipment installed and upgraded to gain smartness:
Monitoring Devices for Energy Saving (Electrical Consumption): Three-phase smart meter and one phase smart meter; smart control devices (HVAC)
Monitoring Devices for Indoor Comfort and Energy Saving (Temperature and Humidity): Temperature and Humidity Z-wave sensors
Monitoring Devices for Healthiness and Sustainability (Air Quality): CO_2 Z-wave sensors
Gateway for Connectivity: Raspberry Pi + Z-Wave

Case Study: LTU

The pilot building is residential (although it includes also a commercial part) and it is located in Skellefteå, Sweden. Because of the cold winter, the building disposes of two heating systems: a metered district heating connection and an electric heating system. The building has an FDX system for ventilation with two fans (for supply and exhaust air), and 80% of the energy is sent back to the building. The parking places are equipped with heating points for cars.

The intervention within PHOENIX consists primarily of the insertion of sensors, for both air quality and the heating system. The gateways and the connection to the platform allow to report information about real-time and historical data and enable the communication with the BACS. Finally, a huge improvement has been done to the EV system, which was inexistent in the original state of the building and that has more than 50% of the parking space equipped with recharging points after the actuation.

Equipment installed and upgraded to gain smartness:
Monitoring Devices for Healthiness and Sustainability (Air Quality): CO_2 sensor
Monitoring Devices for Indoor Comfort and Energy Saving (Electrical Consumption): HVAC sensors
EV Equipment for Energy Saving: EV chargers
Gateway for Connectivity: Raspberry pi, Z-wave USB

Case Study: UMU

The building (four blocks, from 3 to 5 floors) forms part of the Campus of the University of Murcia, Spain. The building disposed already of smart meters and a legacy BMS to monitor the power consumption. Heating and cooling systems are managed through a centralised VRF with individual room control. The heat pumps dispose of an inverter with frequency control that allows having a variable control of the production depending on the load. DHW is managed through a double system of tanks, one with a solar collector and an additional one, without automatised control. The building has an air handling unit (AHU) with heat recovery, without automatised control, while several CO2 sensors allow air quality monitoring. The building already included a solar PV system and EV charging points.

Actuations within the project will concern mainly the way the systems communicate and connect. As mentioned in the Introduction, the IoT platform enhances the connection with the external signals from the grid (that allows also optimised control of the systems), whilst allowing to monitor and report information to the facility manager and to the occupants. Hence, the integration into the IoT platform involves several systems and, consequently, several domains and services. About the single domains, power meters have been added to three different circuits of the HVAC system, one for the AHU and two for the conditioning, enabling the communication between the controllers and the BACS. The DHW installation has been equipped with temperature reading points and a water consumption meter. The electricity domain has been improved through the insertion of WiFi power smart sockets and through the connection to the existing local electricity generation system (PV panels). A second electric control panel has been added to the EV charging installation, and meters and controllers have been added to connect to the platform.

Equipment installed and upgraded to gain smartness:
Monitoring Devices for Energy Saving (Electrical Consumption): Power meters monitored from IoT Gateways (HVAC & AHU)
Monitoring Devices for Indoor Comfort and Energy Saving (Temperature): Solar thermal boiler water temperature
Monitoring Devices for Healthiness and Sustainability (Air Quality): CO_2 sensors
IoT Devices for Energy Saving: WiFi Smart Sockets
EV Equipment for Energy Saving: Electric control panel
Gateways for Connectivity: Raspberry Pi + Z-wave

Questionnaire

To evaluate the usability of the tool, it was developed a questionnaire aimed for the people on the role of being the assessors, i.e., the participants in charge of calculating the SRI for each case study. The assessors are asked to perform a calculation with the detailed method, which consists in using the full list of services, and another calculation applying the triage process, by choosing the services that are applicable according to the specificities of the building. After using the two procedures, participants were asked to report their opinion in order to have feedback about the tool. The assessors were asked to use the same version of the calculation sheet, i.e., the fourth version released.

The questionnaire is composed of two main parts: general questions and technical questions, both mandatory. Each item is a sentence to which the respondents could assign a score on a Likert scale from strongly disagree to strongly agree (5-point scale). On the design of the questionnaire, the priority was to make it accessible and short, to make sure that the respondents were motivated so initial versions with a higher number of questions were changed into a final version with twelve items.

The general questions section is composed by six items and it aims to give feedback on the usefulness of the score. In particular, the authors tried to understand the respondents' opinion about the introduction of this novelty in the building world, by also comparing it conceptually with another major introduction, the Energy Performance Certificate. Besides, it was asked the respondents to give their opinion about how the general public will react to this change, focusing in particular on the possibility to give an impulse to smart technologies and smart buildings.

The technical section is composed of six items, and it investigates what respondents think about the calculation tool and the selection of the service catalogue. The usability of the calculation tool is analysed in order to understand if a non-technical person could easily calculate the SRI score, since the discussion about who should calculate it for simple dwellings is still open. The respondent's opinion about the triage process is the other main topic of this section, since it is not trivial to find a balance between its utility and the need to standardise the calculation basis. About this topic, Vigna et al. highlighted in their study that the triage process was one of the main issues in calculating the SRI score, so the authors wanted to verify this finding on the project's set.

Finally, an open question about who should assess the calculation was proposed.

SOLUTIONS AND RECOMMENDATIONS

For each pilot building, the calculation was performed referring to the original status of the building (prior to the retrofitting) and to the expected status after the intervention within the project PHOENIX.

As results, the first analysis concerns the improvements on the SRI itself, but taking into consideration the two approaches to tackle it. Besides the overall improvement, the effects of the interventions on both the domains and the impact scores have been evaluated. The outcomes have then been compared with the cost afforded for the interventions, in order to give an idea of which can be the most cost-effective solutions depending on the context considered. Finally, the usability of the methods considered has been evaluated by collecting the opinions of the SRI assessors.

As explained in the Methodology section, the interventions have been different for each case study, depending on the needs of the building and on the evaluation of which were the more cost-effective solutions for each case. Hence, in order to understand which systems have been improved within the project, the scores have been broken down by domain in Table 2. The calculations have been done using the full list of services, in order to avoid the influence of subjective parameters on the assessment. The reader is reminded that more information about the assigning scores is available in the SRI technical report.

From Table 3 it can be seen what aspects have been prioritised in each building. Some domains, such as Monitoring and Control, Heating and Electricity, have been improved in all the case studies, meaning that the solutions proposed for the

Table 2. Domain scores of each case study before and after the interventions, calculated with the full list of services

	Arden #1		Arden #2		Arden #3		KaMa		LTU		MIW #1		MIW #2		UMU	
	Bef.	After	Bef.	After	Bef.	After	Bef.	After	Bef.	After	Bef.	After	Bef.	After	Bef.	After
Heating	15%	52%	4%	17%	15%	45%	18%	35%	8%	28%	8%	48%	10%	21%	14%	65%
DHW	14%	46%	14%	32%	29%	53%	12%	37%	7%	25%	0%	0%	0%	0%	0%	33%
Cooling	0%	0%	0%	0%	0%	0%	9%	33%	0%	0%	6%	45%	13%	21%	13%	59%
Ventilation	0%	0%	0%	0%	0%	41%	0%	0%	11%	30%	5%	30%	0%	25%	19%	53%
Lighting	15%	15%	15%	15%	44%	51%	15%	43%	0%	0%	0%	0%	0%	0%	0%	0%
DE	0%	0%	0%	0%	24%	24%	0%	63%	0%	0%	0%	0%	0%	0%	0%	0%
Electricity	1%	50%	0%	5%	13%	22%	24%	82%	5%	5%	1%	5%	1%	12%	1%	19%
EV	0%	44%	0%	44%	0%	0%	0%	42%	0%	0%	0%	0%	0%	0%	0%	42%
MC	0%	41%	0%	23%	31%	41%	0%	20%	4%	15%	0%	27%	0%	22%	2%	30%

Table 3. Overall SRI score of each case study, before and after the actuation planned within the project PHOENIX. Calculations were performed with both the full catalogue of services and the triage process.

Case Study	Building Type	Climate Zone	Before the Intervention		After the Intervention	
			SRI - Full Catalogue	SRI - Triage Process	SRI - Full Catalogue	SRI - Triage Process
Arden #1	Residential	West Europe	6%	9%	37% (+31%)	48% (+39%)
Arden #2	Residential	West Europe	3%	6%	12% (+9%)	23% (+17%)
Arden #3	Non-Residential	West Europe	14%	21%	29% (+15%)	37% (+16%)
KaMa	Residential	South Europe	13%	15%	34% (+21%)	42% (+27%)
LTU	Residential	North Europe	7%	9%	15% (+8%)	22% (+13%)
MIW #1	Non-Residential	South Europe	3%	7%	32% (+29%)	45% (+38%)
MIW #2	Residential	South Europe	6%	16%	15% (+9%)	33% (+17%)
UMU	Non-Residential	South Europe	9%	13%	41% (+32%)	60% (+47%)

correspondent systems are effective regardless of the context or of the climate zone. Also, it can be seen from the table that some domains scored 0% both before and after the interventions, a sign that some domains are not applicable or not relevant for some buildings, as explained in the technical documentation. From the table, it appears that interventions on Lighting and Dynamic Envelope have been chosen only in a few cases, a sign that in the preliminary analysis they had not been considered the most cost-effective solutions for the examined buildings.

The final SRI scores are collected in Table 3, and the improvement due to the intervention is shown in brackets. In this case the calculations were performed with both the approaches discussed in the previous section: (1) full-service list and (2) triage process.

Taking into consideration the increase of the SRI percentage for each domain, it is natural to wonder how much the improvement would cost. Considering the cost needed for each increment, the future assessors will be able to make a more considered and informed choice when it comes to selecting the more cost-effective solutions, depending on the starting point of the building in terms of smart readiness and the climate context. Table 4 shows the investments made for each domain, as well as the total cost of the intervention. The reader should note that the investments are not necessarily founded only by the project PHOENIX.

Table 4. Investment in € for each building, broken down by domain. The total investment needed to increase the SRI is shown in the last row.

	Arden #1	Arden #2	Arden #3	KaMa	LTU	MIW #1	MIW #2	UMU
Heating	-	-	-	1 000 €	26 400 €	-	2 500 €	5 500 €
DHW	500 €	500 €	-	1 650 €	-	-	-	2 800 €
Cooling	-	-	-	1 000 €	-	-	2 500 €	5 500 €
Ventilation	-	-	-	-	3 300 €	400 €	1 700 €	5 500 €
Lighting	-	-	-	850 €	-	-	-	-
DE	-	-	-	1 000 €	-	-	-	-
Electricity	500 €	-	500 €	1 320 €	3 300 €	880 €	3 250 €	3 000 €
EV	1 200 €	500 €	-	710 €	30 000 €	-	-	1 500 €
MC	3 500 €	2 500 €	7 500 €	3 200 €	-	-	-	800 €
TOTAL	5 700 €	3 500 €	8 000 €	10 730 €	63 000 €	1 280 €	7 450 €	13 600 €

The most noteworthy information that can be deduced from the table concerns the EV. In this domain both KaMa and UMU with an affordable investment obtained an improvement of 42% in the SRI domain, while LTU, even with a rather large investment, did not manage to increase the score. That is because the functionality service 'EV Charging grid balance' gives a negative score if the charging is uncontrolled. Hence, from an SRI point of view, one could consider that an easy way to increase the EV score is by actuating on the way of charging, more than on the number of charging points, this could represent a loophole of the methodology on the long run. In general, most of the pilots decided not to invest in the domains of lighting and DE. However, the example of KaMa demonstrated that small funding can give very good results on this domain (respectively an increase of 28% and 53% on the domains' score). Analysing the relationship between improvements and investments in heating, cooling, ventilation, electricity and DHW, it appears that increasing the domain score is more expensive when the smartness of a domain has to be risen from scratch. For instance, the buildings of UMU and MIW #2 started with an almost null score for the electricity domain (1%) and the investment needed to increase the smartness of the domain to a modest percentage (respectively to 18% and 11%) was around 3000€; on the contrary, KaMa started scoring 24% in the electricity domain, and could rise that percentage of a 58% with an investment of just 1320€. The case of the non-residential building of MIW is particularly interesting from a cost-effective perspective, since they invested a small amount in smart meters that would affect the heating, cooling and electricity domains, obtaining a total increase of 29% on the final score with a more than affordable investment (1280€). Finally,

Figure 1. Comparison of increments of the relative scores broken down by impact criteria for each case study

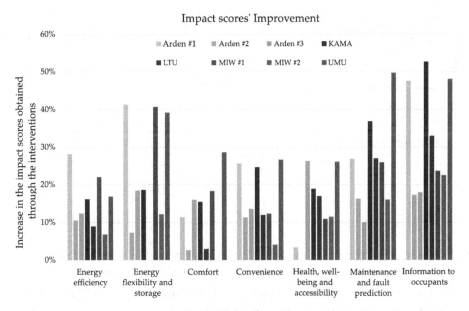

is deducible from the table that Monitoring and Control is the only domain that, in most cases, managed to increase indirectly, without a dedicated investment.

To have a more complete vision about the meaning of the final scores, Figure 1 shows the increment of the relative scores of the seven impact criteria that compose the SRI, i.e. the difference in the percentages before and after the intervention. Also in this case, the analysis represents the calculation concerning the full list of services.

It can be seen at a glance from the comparison that the most considerable improvements have concerned the information to occupants and the energy flexibility and storage, in line with the objective of using the SRI score to impulse the building capacity to respond to the need of the occupants and of the grid. Also, maintenance and fault prediction has been considerably incremented through the connection to the platform.

For what concerns the questionnaire, the results from the general questions are collected in Figure 2, while the outcomes from the technical questions are shown in Figure 3. Each colour represents a respondent, although there is no legend in the plots for privacy.

On Figure 2 one can see that the respondents agreed with the usefulness of the new indicator, with how the several aspects of the building are analysed and with

Figure 2. Outcomes from the questionnaire: General questions

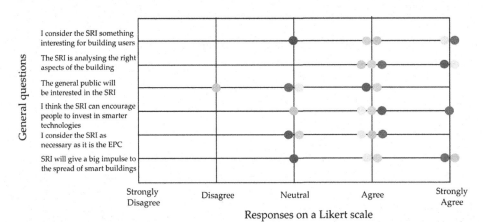

the influence that the indicator will have in improving the smart technologies in buildings. In particular, with the statement 'the SRI is analysing the right aspects of the buildings', no one disagreed among the respondents. This is in line with the literature, with respect to the capability of the method of recognising the characteristics of the building studied. Regarding the statements 'I consider the SRI something interesting for building users' and 'SRI will give a big impulse to the spread of smart buildings', one can see that four out of five respondents agreed, while one remained neutral on both questions.

It is slightly less clear whether or not the SRI will succeed in awakening the interest of the general public, according to the respondents: on the affirmation 'The general

Figure 3. Outcomes from the questionnaire: Technical questions

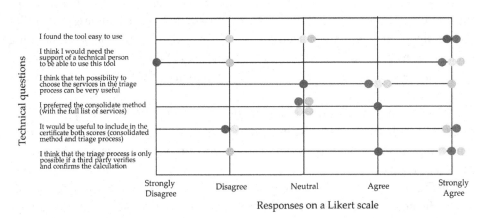

public will be interested on the SRI', the overall opinion according to the results was neither favourable nor unfavourable. No one strongly agreed with the sentence 'I consider the SRI as necessary as it s the EPC', although no one disagreed either.

When observing Figure 3 regarding the technical aspects of the tool, the respondents had more diverse views. In particular, the role of the technician to manage the assessment is not considered needful by all of them, as well as the proposal of including both scores on the certificate.

Analysing more in detail the answers, the statement 'I found the tool easy to use' had two respondents strongly agreeing, but two neutral and one disagreeing. The opinions are even more diverse for the statement 'I think I would need the support of a technical person to be able to use this tool', where one can see that one respondent even strongly disagreed. This can suggest the need for more detailed explanations of the method in general and of the smart services in particular, in order to allow a total understanding of the tool for everyone.

Regarding the statements 'It would be useful to include in the certificate both scores (consolidated method and the triage process' and 'I think that the triage process is only possible if a third party verifies and confirm the calculation', it is interesting that the respondents agreed with the usefulness of the triage process, but most of them are neutral when it comes to expressing a preference between the two methods.

About the open questions on who should assess the SRI calculation, not all the respondents had a suggestion to express. One respondent considered that the tool is easy enough to be used by the building owner itself, while according to the other two respondents a professional with experience in energy and buildings is needed to perform the assessment, i.e., an engineer or an architect.

FUTURE RESEARCH DIRECTIONS: SRI FOR FLEXIBILITY

The smartness of the building is a concept that could be related to the need for energy flexibility, which is one of the key functionalities of the framework. For this reason, an extra effort was dedicated to the understanding of the relationship between de SRI and the grid flexibility. In the SRI technical support study, about the category 'Energy flexibility and storage', it can be read: 'This impact category refers to the impacts of services on the energy flexibility potential of the building' (Verbeke et al., 2019; Final report SRI, 2020). The level of connection and interaction with the grid is fundamental to enable the response of the demand side. This concept is well explained by the terms 'grid-friendly building' and 'grid-responsive building' proposed in Wang et al. (2016). For the efficiency of the grid-building system, a building can just avoid creating additional stress on the power grid (grid-friendly) or can respond to the needs of the grid, helping with maintaining the power balance (grid-responsive). On this work, which level of smartness is 'required' in order to prepare the building for flexibility strategies was studied, with a special focus on one of the most common DR strategies, the Direct Load Control (DLC) (Siano, 2014; Palensky & Dietrich, 2011). The DLC consists in leaving the management of the energy consumption of the building to a third party, e.g., the grid, and it is explored within the PHOENIX project as a solution to enhance the energy flexibility of the buildings.

Table 5 summarizes the domains, services, and functionality levels necessary for the applicability of the DR strategies. Another column suggests improvements in the functionality levels that would allow a better effectiveness. Comments are collected in the last columns, where is explained the correlation between each SRI parameter and the topics discussed in this paper.

Table 5. Relationship between SRI and DR strategies

Domain	Service	Functionality Levels (for Basic Functioning)	Functionality Levels (to Improve Effectivity)	Comments
Heating	1a - Heat emission control	L1 - Central automatic control (e.g. central thermostat)	L4 - Individual room control with communication and occupancy detection	Without automatic control of the HVAC, DLC cannot work. The improvement would allow enabling events' design based on the typology of users and their actual presence (in particular in non-residential buildings)
Heating	2b - Heat generation control (for heat pump)	L0 - On/Off control of heat generator	L3 - Variable control of heat generator capacity depending on the load AND external signals from the grid	Although this service is not necessary for DLC, a level 4 would make the building 'grid-responding' and open the door for the ancillary service program.
Heating	4 - Flexibility and grid interaction	L3 - Heating system capable of flexible control through grid signals (e.g. DSM)	L4 - Optimized control of heating system based on local predictions and grid signals (e.g. through model predictive control)	Level 4 would give the possibility of designing specific events based on local predictions.
Cooling	1a - Cooling emission control	L1 - Central automatic control	L4 - Individual room control with communication and occupancy detection	Without automatic control of the HVAC, DLC cannot work. The improvement would allow enabling events' design based on the typology of users and their actual presence (in particular in non-residential buildings)

continued on following page

Table 5. Continued

Domain	Service	Functionality Levels (for Basic Functioning)	Functionality Levels (to Improve Effectivity)	Comments
Cooling	2a - Generation control for cooling	L0 - On/Off control of cooling production	L3 - Variable control of cooling production capacity depending on the load AND external signals from the grid	Although this service is not necessary for DLC, a level 4 would make the building 'grid-responding' and open the door for the ancillary service program.
Cooling	4 - Flexibility and grid interaction	L3 - Cooling system capable of flexible control through grid signals (e.g. DSM)	L4 - Optimized control of cooling system based on local predictions and grid signals (e.g. through model predictive control)	Level 4 would give the possibility of designing specific events based on local predictions.
DHW	1a/b - Control of the DHW storage charging	L0 - Automatic control on/off	L3 - Automatic charging control based on local availability of renewables or information from the electricity grid (DR, DSM)	This is related to the concept of peak shifting, since the charging can be left to non-peak hours.
Electricity	8 - Support of (micro) grid operation modes	L1 - Automated management of (building-level) electricity consumption based on grid signals	L3 - Automated management of (building-level) electricity consumption and supply, with the potential to continue limited off-grid operation (island mode)	Automated management of the electricity at a building level would be necessary for DLC that acts on appliances.
EV	16 - EV charging grid balancing	L1 - 1-way controlled charging (e.g. including desired departure time and grid signals for optimization)	L2 - 2-way controlled charging (e.g. including desired departure time and grid signals for optimization)	EV's diffusion obliges to question what can be done to avoid burdening the grid with the chargers. Controlling the charging according to the grid signal is a perfect way to achieve the aim. This service is not strictly necessary.
MC	3 - Run time management of the HVAC system	L3 - Heating and cooling plant on/off control based on predictive control or grid signals	-	Although this service is not strictly necessary for DLC, a level 3 would make the building 'grid-responding'.
MC	25 - Smart Grid Integration	L1 – Demand side management possible for (some) individual TBS, but not coordinated over various domains	L2 - Coordinated demand side management of multiple TBS	L1 is necessary since in L0 the building is operated independently from the grid load.
MC	29 - Override of DSM control	L1 - DSM control without the possibility to override this control by the building users (occupant or facility manager)	L2 - Manual override and reactivation by the building user	Overriding an event is not necessary for the functioning of the DR strategies, but it is highly recommended for the comfort and wellbeing of the occupants.

Table 6. Capacity of performing demand response events of the different pilots' buildings

Arden #1	Arden #2	Arden #3	KaMa	LTU	MIW #1	MIW #2	UMU
YES	YES	YES	YES	NO	YES	NO	YES

The last row opens also the path for a discussion about users' acceptance of these kinds of strategies. It has been demonstrated that occupants are more willing to accept to leave the control of their thermostat to a third party if they are given the possibility to override the event (Xu, 2018). Nevertheless, the manual override and reactivation by the building user can mine the effectiveness of the DR strategy (Tomat et al., 2022). Improving the communication with the occupants, as suggested in the SRI framework, will mark a striking difference in the success of the energy flexibility plan.

Considering this, the capacity of the pilots studied to perform DR events is shown in Table 6.

CONCLUSION

In this paper, the SRI score is studied as a meter to evaluate the performance of different interventions on eight real buildings in different contexts in which real interventions have been performed. The SRI resulted to be a good tool for all the scenarios considered, since the assessors were able to realise the evaluation of the score consistently. The tool for the calculation resulted to be easy to use according to the feedback of the assessors (only one in five respondents disagreed with the consideration), in particular the new version that is more automatised and helps to avoid the mistakes of a manual calculation seems to be more appealing. The presentation of the results in the SRI framework, i.e., with a total score and partial scores for each domain and each impact criterion, was found particularly functional since it opens the path to different kinds of analyses.

Regarding cost-effectiveness, it has to be said that the first investment on a domain that has to be improved from scratch is considerably larger compared to the one needed to improve a domain that has already a good level of smartness. Also, it seems to be a competitive investment the installation of meters that can work on more than one domain at a time, what happen to be many. There are a few functionality levels related to negative scores, and that is something important to consider when deciding where to invest: in the examples of the EV, it can be seen that investing a small amount on the way of charging is far more useful from an SRI perspective than investing on more charging points.

From the work, it can be deduced that the triage process would represent a useful way to express the potential of a building. The scores obtained with the triage process are quite higher than the score obtained with the full list of services, indicating that the score with the full catalogue is penalised by services that are not relevant for the building (example of the Cooling domain in cold countries), or directly not applicable (for example, it is not likely that the same building disposes of more than two different DHW systems).

Nevertheless, as underlined in other studies and confirmed by the questionnaire here carried out, it remains an issue according to this work's results to find a way to make the triage process objective, and this is one of the main gaps in the method. A solution proposed by the respondents would be a mandatory double-check performed by an accredited technician. The mandatory double-check is a widely used method when it comes to official technical certifications: the assessor proposes their evaluation to a technician that has been accredited by the certification institute, and that has the obligation to revise the validity of the assessment.

Another main gap that the authors can highlight is the difficulty of fully understanding some of the smart services included in the assessment. In the effort of working synergistically, the different assessors of the case studies exchanged their opinions and views about the score assignment: it emerged that in some cases the interpretation of how to evaluate the same service was slightly different. As a solution, the authors suggest adding more practical and detailed information about each smart service proposed in the SRI assessment package, to avoid interpretation bias.

With respect to the aspect of making buildings more active with respect to their relationship with the gird using the so-called demand response events, the considerations about SRI for flexibility show how the SRI can be used to encourage the spread of demand response strategies in buildings, in order to obtain a more efficient distribution of the consumption that will relieve the load from the grid.

To conclude, the authors believe the SRI calculation if mandatory can give an important impulse to the modern evolution of the building sector, in particular considering that some of the interventions proposed have a highly affordable cost. The people interviewed showed a good acceptance of the method, once it is assured the subjectivity needed for a fair comparison among different cases and conditions.

ACKNOWLEDGMENT

This project has been funded by Horizon 2020 Project PHOENIX (grant number 893079) and by the State Research Agency (PID2020-112675RB-C44 – Adaptation of computing and network resources from the could to the edge: exploiting smart orchestration and security – ONOFRE-3-UMU). The authors would like to thank for their contribution the other pilot partners of the project PHOENIX: Arden Energy, Kataskevastiki Makedonias, MIW Energía, Luleå University of Technology and Skebit.

REFERENCES

Al Dakheel, J., Del Pero, C., Aste, N., & Leonforte, F. (2020). Smart Buildings Features and Key Performance Indicators: A Review. *Sustainable Cities and Society*, *61*, 102328. doi:10.1016/j.scs.2020.102328

Apostolopoulos, V., Giorka, P., Martinopoulos, G., Angelakoglou, K., Kourtzanidis, K., & Nikolopoulos, N. (2022). Smart readiness indicator evaluation and cost estimation of smart retrofitting scenarios - A comparative case-study in European residential buildings. *Sustainable Cities and Society*, *82*, 103921. doi:10.1016/j.scs.2022.103921

Atanasiu, B., Despret, C., Economidou, M., Maio, J., Nolte, I., & Rapf, O. (2011). *Europe's Buildings under the Microscope, A Country-by-Country Review of the Energy Performance of Buildings, Buildings Performance Institute Europe*. BPIE.

Carli, R., Cavone, G., Ben Othman, S., & Dotoli, M. (2020). IoT Based Architecture for Model Predictive Control of HVAC Systems in Smart Buildings. *Sensors (Basel)*, *20*(3), 781. doi:10.339020030781 PMID:32023965

Church, C., Morsi, W. G., El-Hawary, M. E., Diduch, C. P., & Chang, L. C. (2011). Voltage collapse detection using Ant Colony Optimization for smart grid applications. *Electric Power Systems Research*, *81*(8), 1723–1730. doi:10.1016/j.epsr.2011.03.010

COM. (2011). *112 Final. A Roadmap for Moving to a Competitive Low Carbon Economy in 2050*. European Commission.

COM. (2016). *763 Final. Accelerating Clean Energy Innovation*. European Commission.

COM. (2016). *860 Final, Annex 1. Accelerating Clean Energy in Buildings*. European Commission.

Directive 2002/91/EU of the European Parliament and of the Council of 16 December 2002 on the Energy Performance of Buildings; L1/65; Official Journal of the European Union: Brussels, Belgium, 2003

Directive 2009/28/EC of the European Parliament and of the Council of 23 April 2009 on the Promotion of the Use of Energy from Renewable Sources; L140/16-62; Official Journal of the European Union: Brussels, Belgium, 2009.

Directive 2010/31/EU of the European Parliament and of the Council of 19 May 2010 on the energy performance of buildings; L153/13; Official Journal of the European Union: Brussels, Belgium, 2010

Directive 2012/27/EU of the European Parliament and of the Council of 25 October 2012 on Energy Efficiency; L315/1-56; Official Journal of the European Union: Brussels, Belgium, 2012.

Directive (EU) 2018/844 of the European Parliament and of the Council of 30 May 2018 Amending Directive2010/31/EU on the Energy Performance of Buildings Directive 2012/27/EU on Energy Efficiency; L156/75; Official Journal of the European Union: Brussels, Belgium, 2018

ENER/C3/2016-554. VITO. Support for Setting up a Smart Readiness Indicator for Buildings and Related Impact Assessment. (2020). Available online: https://smartreadinessindicator.eu/

Final Report, S. R. I. (2020). *European Commission, Final report on the technical support to the development of a smart readiness indicator for buildings.* Publications Office of the European Union.

Fokaides, P. A., Panteli, C., & Panayidou, A. (2020). How are the smart readiness indicators expected to affect the energy performance of buildings: First evidence and perspectives. *Sustainability (Basel)*, *12*(22), 9496. doi:10.3390u12229496

Hafeez, G., Wadud, Z., Khan, I., Khan, I., Shafiq, Z., Usman, M., & Khan, M. (2020). Efficient energy management of IoT-enabled smart homes under price-based demand response program in smart grid. *Sensors (Basel)*, *20*(11), 3155. doi:10.339020113155 PMID:32498402

Heinen, S., Elzinga, D., Kim, S. K., & Ikeda, Y. (2011). Impact of Smart grid technology on peak load to 2050. International Energy Agency.

IEA EBC Annex 67. (n.d.). Available online: http://www.annex67.org/

Janhunen, E., Pulkka, L., Säynäjoki, A., & Junnila, S. (2019). Applicability of the Smart Readiness Indicator for Cold Climate Countries. *Buildings*, *9*(4), 102. doi:10.3390/buildings9040102

Kyoto Protocol, United Nations Climate Change. (n.d.). *Kyoto Protocol—Targets for the First Commitment Period*. Available online: https://unfccc.int/process/the-kyoto-protocol

Märzinger, T., & Österreicher, D. (2019). Supporting the Smart Readiness Indicator—A Methodology to Integrate a Quantitative Assessment of the Load Shifting Potential of Smart Buildings. *Energies*, *12*(10), 1955. doi:10.3390/en12101955

Moseley, P. (2017). EU Support for Innovation and Market Uptake in Smart Buildings under the Horizon 2020 Framework Programme. *Buildings*, *7*(4), 105. doi:10.3390/buildings7040105

Palensky, P., & Dietrich, D. (2011). Demand side management: Demand response, intelligent energy systems, and smart loads. *IEEE Transactions on Industrial Informatics*, *7*(3), 381–388. doi:10.1109/TII.2011.2158841

PHOENIX. Horizon 2020 project. (n.d.). Available online: https://eu-phoenix.eu/

Ramallo-González, A. P., Tomat, V., Fernández-Ruiz, P. J., Zamora-Izquierdo, M. A., & Skarmeta-Gómez, A. F. (2020). Conceptualisation of an IoT Framework for Multi-Person Interaction with Conditioning Systems. *Energies*, *13*(12), 3094. doi:10.3390/en13123094

Ramezani, B., Silva, M. G. D., & Simões, N. (2021). Application of smart readiness indicator for Mediterranean buildings in retrofitting actions. *Energy and Building*, *249*, 111173. doi:10.1016/j.enbuild.2021.111173

Santos, D., & Ferreira, J. C. (2019). IoT Power Monitoring System for Smart Environments. *Sustainability (Basel)*, *11*(19), 5355. doi:10.3390u11195355

Siano, P. (2014). Demand response and smart-grids – A survey. *Renewable & Sustainable Energy Reviews*, *30*, 461–478. doi:10.1016/j.rser.2013.10.022

Terroso-Saenz, F., González-Vidal, A., Ramallo-González, A. P., & Skarmeta, A. F. (2019). An open IoT platform for the management and analysis of energy data. *Future Generation Computer Systems*, *92*, 1066–1079. doi:10.1016/j.future.2017.08.046

Tomat, V., Ramallo-González, A. P., & Skarmeta Gómez, A. F. (2020). A comprehensive survey about thermal comfort under the IoT paradigm: Is crowdsensing the new horizon? *Sensors (Basel)*, *20*(16), 4647. doi:10.339020164647 PMID:32824790

Tomat, V., Vellei, M., Ramallo-González, A. P., González-Vidal, A., Le Dréau, J., & Skarmeta-Gómez, A. (2022). Understanding patterns of thermostat overrides after demand response events. *Energy and Building*, *271*, 112312. doi:10.1016/j.enbuild.2022.112312

Verbeke, S., Aerts, D., Rynders, G., & Ma, Y. (2019). *Summary of state of affairs in 2nd technical support study on the smart readiness indicator for buildings.* Study accomplished under the authority of the European Commission DG Energy 2019/SEB/R/1810610

Vigna, I., Pernetti, R., Pasut, W., & Lollini, R. (2018). New domain for promoting energy efficiency: Energy Flexible Building Cluster. *Sustainable Cities and Society*, *38*, 526–533. doi:10.1016/j.scs.2018.01.038

Vigna, I., Pernetti, R., Pernigotto, G., & Gasparella, A. (2020). Analysis of the building smart readiness indicator calculation: A comparative case-study with two panels of experts. *Energies*, *13*(11), 2796. doi:10.3390/en13112796

Wang, S. (2016). Making buildings smarter, grid-friendly, and responsive to smart grids. *Science and Technology for the Built Environment*, *22*(6), 629–632. doi:10.1080/23744731.2016.1200888

Xu, X., Chen, C., Zhu, X., & Hu, Q. (2018). Promoting acceptance of direct load control programs in the United States: Financial incentive versus control option. *Energy*, *147*, 1278–1287. doi:10.1016/j.energy.2018.01.028

Yaïci, W., Krishnamurthy, K., Entchev, E., & Longo, M. (2021). Recent advances in internet of things (IoT) infrastructures for building energy systems: A review. *Sensors (Basel)*, *21*(6), 1–40. doi:10.339021062152 PMID:33808558

KEY TERMS AND DEFINITIONS

BACS: Building Automation and Control System.
BMS: Building Management System.
CHP: Combined Heat and Power.
DHW: Domestic Hot Water.
DLC: Direct Load Control.
DR: Demand Response.
DSM: Demand Side Management.
EPBD: European Performance of Building Directive.
EPC: Energy Performance Certificate.

EV: Electric vehicles.

ICT: Information and Communications Technologies.

IoT: Internet of Things.

MC: Monitoring and Control.

PV: Photovoltaics.

SRI: Smart Readiness Indicator.

TBS: Technical Building System.

Chapter 7

Evolution of Smart Energy Grid System Using IoT:
Smart Grid, Online Power Monitoring in Buildings, Smart Sensors for Smart Grid Protection

P. Saranya
Rohini College of Engineering and Technology, India

R. Rajesh
Rohini College of Engineering and Technology, India

ABSTRACT

The IoT is a rapidly emerging research area. It refers to an infrastructure network that includes digital data, mechanical objects, computational devices, and sensors that have unique identities. IoT delivers many solutions in various domains by providing connection of devices through the internet. Recently electricity is very important in our day-to-day lives. The consumption of electricity is also rapidly increasing. It is necessary to improve the production of electricity and also reduce the wastage of electricity in transmission lines. The energy grid refers to the next generation power grids, with bi-directional or two-way flows of electricity through the communication interface or protocols. The energy management in grid ensures stability between the supply and demand, which is maintained for reducing the wastage of electricity. In order to achieve this reduction, it is necessary to monitor the parameters of the PV system by the IoT hardware. Specifically, the authors focus on IoT technologies for monitoring the parameters of PV systems such as voltage and current by sensors in IoT.

DOI: 10.4018/978-1-6684-7756-4.ch007

INTRODUCTION

The Internet of Things (IoT) is emerging rapidly and delivers numerous solutions in various domains. Current research on Internet of Things (IoT) mainly focuses on how to enable general objects and make them connected for sharing data or information. IoT allows sensing, identification, actuation, monitoring, decision making, communication, and management. Since IoT is the network of connected physical objects or devices. The definition of IoT by a researcher is an open and comprehensive network of intelligent objects that have the capacity to auto-organize, share information, data and resources, reacting and acting in face of situations and changes in the environment. With the help of the communication technologies such as wireless sensor networks (WSN) and Radio frequency identification (RFID), sharing of information takes place. Therefore, we can say IoT allows humans and things to be connected Anytime, Anyplace, with anything and anyone using any network and any service. According to our latest State of IoT—Spring 2022 report, released in May 2022.The number of global IoT connections grew by 8% in 2021 to 12.2 billion active endpoints, representing significantly lower growth than in previous years. Despite a booming demand for IoT solutions and positive sentiment in the IoT community as well as in most IoT end markets, IoT Analytics expects the chip shortage's impact on the number of connected IoT devices to last well beyond 2023. Other headwinds for IoT markets include the COVID-19 pandemic and general supply chain disruptions. In the end of 2022, the market for the Internet of Things is expected to grow 18% to 14.4 billion active connections. It is expected that by 2025, as supply constraints ease and growth further accelerates, there will be approximately 27 billion connected IoT devices. IoT cloud platforms are designed to be used in domains such as application development, device management, system management, heterogeneity management, data management, analytics, deployment, monitoring, visualization, and finally research purposes. IOT has many applications such as Creating better enterprise solutions, integrating smarter homes, innovating agriculture, building smarter cities, upgrading supply chain management, transforming healthcare, installing smart grids, Revolutionizing wearables, Integrating connected factories, Reshaping hospitality. As IoT technologies are used in our day-to-day activities from domestic to commercial sector, unavoidable challenges are also increasing.

One of the important applications of IoT is the Smart grid. SG is a data communications network which is integrated with the power grid to collect and analyse data that are acquired from transmission lines, distribution substations, and consumers. The IoT enabled smart grid allows transforming the conventional energy grids into modernized Smart Energy Grid systems. The IoT-enabled Smart Energy Grid system equipped with intelligent two-way flow of data communication can significantly improve the operation and control of the traditional energy grid system. These improvements address the reliability, flexibility, efficiency of the conventional grid system. In a smart grid environment, the system must provide services including the large-scale integration of distributed renewable energy resources, establishment of live, real-time data communication between consumers and service providers regarding tariff information and energy consumption, facility to collect and transfer statistics of system parameters for analysis and infrastructure to implement necessary actions based on those analyses. Smart Energy grid generates immense data and information that needs to be transferred, processed and stored for intelligent decision making and processing.

The smart grid is an unprecedented opportunity to shift the current energy industry into a new era of a modernized network where the power generation, transmission, and distribution are intelligently, responsively, and cooperatively managed through a bi-directional automation system. Although the domains of smart grid applications and technologies vary in functions and forms, they generally share common potentials such as intelligent energy curtailment, efficient integration of Demand Response, Distributed Renewable Generation, and Energy Storage. This paper presents a comprehensive review categorically on the recent advances and previous research developments of the smart grid paradigm.

The Energy management in smart grid ensures stability between the supply and demand which is maintained for reducing the wastage of electricity and also optimized use of electricity which ensures the reduction of power generation cost, reduction of power usage cost for consumers. In order to achieve this reduction, it is necessary to monitor the parameters of the PV battery system by the IOT hardware. Specifically, we focus on IoT technologies for monitoring the parameters of PV battery systems such as Voltage, Current by sensors in IoT. The IoT based monitoring systems can be used to achieve reliable, and low cost remote monitoring of power grids. The monitored data is transmitted using specific protocols in order to achieve efficient routing of data. Security vulnerability is one of the major concerns of the IoT enabled energy system. For improving the security of the system proper Key management is to be provided by the Polynomial Ring Unit Algorithm. In comparison with the existing work the proposed work is more reliable, scalable, robust in IoT based smart systems.

LITERATURE SURVEY

The concept of demand response management, reliability, and security issues related to smart grid based on typical application scenarios of 5G IoT was investigated but it did not cover DRM in different layers of smart grid and DRM algorithm. The challenges in the performance of the network were not covered. The Peak load shaving under demand side management was reviewed with a focus on energy management approaches in a smart IoT-based environment but failed to cover the telecommunication aspects. On the other hand, the reliance on smart homes on advanced communication infrastructure promotes more concerns regarding data integrity. Therefore, the paper dedicates a subsection to highlight the challenges and the state-of-the-art of cybersecurity. In IoT-enabled Smart Grid Systems Users, generators, and consumers may intelligently be integrated into the grid to provide efficient, secure, and economically feasible supplies of electricity according to consumer demand. The SG incorporates distributed intelligence, bi-directional-based infrastructure for communications, and power flow to improve system efficiency, reliability, and sustainability. Furthermore, the smart grid is a network that integrates digital computing capabilities and highly automated services into the already existing power system infrastructure. Empowering the transition toward the smart grid enhances the robustness and self-healing capabilities of the system.

A CSOA-based Residential Energy Management System in a Smart Grid considering distributed generators (DGs) for demand response. The study focused on optimizing energy consumption and reducing peak loads through the integration of DGs. Mohamed Deriche et al. (2019) proposed an IoT-based sensing system for remote monitoring of PV panels. The system aimed to enhance the performance and reliability of PV panels through real-time monitoring and fault detection. Shuang Xu et al. (2021) introduced a single-phase grid-connected PV system with golden sections-based maximum power point tracking (MPPT) algorithm. The algorithm optimized the power extraction from PV panels under varying environmental conditions. The monitoring and control system for a PV microgrid using IoT. The system enabled real-time monitoring, control, and optimization of PV generation and consumption in a microgrid setup. Wei Gao et al. (n.d.) proposed a fault identification method for photovoltaic arrays using a convolutional neural network (CNN) and a residual gated recurrent unit (GRU). The method aimed to detect and diagnose faults in PV arrays for improved system reliability.

Rajesh Vemulakonda et al. (2016) presented an algorithm for basic IoT architectures. Although not directly related to smart grids, this work provides insights into IoT architectures that can be applied to energy management systems. Nosratabadi et al. (2017) provided a comprehensive review of microgrid and virtual power plant concepts employed for distributed energy resource scheduling in power systems. The study discussed various scheduling strategies and their application in microgrid systems. Olivares et al. (2014) discussed trends in microgrid control. The paper highlighted different control techniques and strategies for the efficient operation and coordination of microgrids. Parhizi et al. (2015) conducted a state-of-the-art review on microgrids, covering various aspects such as operation, control, and management. The review provided insights into the current research trends and challenges in microgrid systems. Sharda Tripathi and Swades De (n.d.) discussed channel-adaptive transmission protocols for smart grid IoT communication. The study focused on developing communication protocols that adapt to changing channel conditions to ensure reliable and efficient communication in smart grid IoT systems. Arunkumari and Indra Gandhi (2017) provided an overview of high voltage conversion ratio DC-DC converter configurations used in DC microgrid architectures. The paper discussed different converter topologies and their application in DC microgrids. Arbab-Zavar et al. (2019) conducted a review of smart inverters for microgrid applications. The study highlighted the role of smart inverters in enhancing the stability and reliability of microgrid systems.

Sahar Ahmadzadeh et al. (2021) reviewed the communication aspects of demand response management for future 5G IoT-based smart grids. The review discussed communication protocols, architectures, and challenges in implementing demand response in smart grid systems. Jan T. Bialasiewicz (n.d.) presented a book chapter on renewable energy systems with photovoltaic power generators, focusing on their operation and modeling. The chapter provided insights into the modeling and analysis of PV systems in the context of renewable energy integration. Na Dong et al. (2019) proposed a novel convolutional neural network framework-based solar irradiance prediction method. The method aimed to improve solar irradiance forecasting accuracy using deep learning techniques. S. M. Abu Adnan Abir et al. (2021) discussed IoT-enabled smart energy grids, their applications, and their challenges. The paper highlighted the integration of IoT technologies in energy management systems to enable the efficient and sustainable operation of smart grids. This literature survey provides an overview of various studies related to smart grids, energy management systems, and their integration with IoT technologies. The references cover a range of topics, including demand response, PV panel monitoring, microgrid control, communication aspects, renewable energy systems, and cybersecurity.

Smart Grid

The Smart energy grid refers to the next generation power grids, with bi- directional or two way flows of electricity through the communication interface or protocols. The power flows to the consumers, big buildings, enterprises, etc. The Energy management in smart grid ensures stability between the supply and demand which is maintained for reducing the wastage of electricity and also optimized use of electricity which ensures the reduction of power generation cost, reduction of power usage cost for consumers. This work provides a real impact on the minimization of Line Power Losses. Power consumption is highly correlated with the occupants' behavior, therefore, the proposed method is capable of understanding its surrounding environment due to two-way communication between power utility and consumers and then take decisions to supply power according to the requirements. Supplying power according to the demand by using the concept of integrating IoT and Smart Grid will be more effective as compared to the existing methodology used in Pakistan. It will not only minimize losses and provide power-efficient systems but also maintain reliable cost and quality of power for consumers. The monitoring and optimized system which is described in this paper will minimize the factors of permanent losses which has fewer compatibility issues with the existing method of supplying electricity in India. This research supports energy management and downgrades transmission and distribution Line losses to improve power supply systems for better growth of electricity production in India.

The Internet has proved its existence in our lives, from interactions at a virtual level to social relationships. The IoT has added a new potential into the internet by enabling communications between objects and humans, making a smarter and intelligent planet. This has led to the vision of ''anytime, anywhere, anyway, anything'' communications practically in the true sense. To this end, it is observed that the IoT should be considered as the core part of the existing internet relying on its future direction, which is obviously to be exceptionally different from the current phase of the internet that we see and use in our lives. Hence, the architectural concept comes into the picture. Architecture is a framework of technology enabling things to interconnect and interact with similar or dissimilar objects by imposing humans to be a layer on it. In fact, it is clear that the current IoT paradigm, which is supportive toward M2M communications, is now getting limited by a number of factors. New formulations are inevitable for sustenance of IoT which is a strong notation for the researcher to come up with. From the above survey, it is found that publish/subscribe based IoT is flourishing nowadays and being successively used in many applications. In this perspective, it should be understood that people are solemnizing their thoughts in terms of vertical silos of architecture. If this trend continues for next few years, IoT may not achieve its goal related to flexibility, interoperability, concurrency, scalability, and addressability issues. Crowdsourcing may be incorporated into the architectural conciseness. Defense, military, intelligence services, robotics etc. fields are still undercover by IoT. Tourism, education, multimedia, governance, social aware, and context aware IoT architectures have not been functional at all. Vertical silos must be coincided with the horizontal perspective for effective measures of the IoT. Numerous technologies can be implemented to achieve successful control and automation in smart grids. Such technologies are imperative to facilitate the transition toward a well-functioned infrastructure from the perspective of grid designers and consumers. These technologies may include Automatic Voltage Regulation (AVR), Energy Management System (EMS), Automatic Generation Control (AGC), Advanced Metering Infrastructure (AMI), Meter Data Management (MDM), Distribution Management System (DMS), Geographical Information

System (GIS), Outage Management System (OMS), Wide Area Management System (WAMS), and Demand Side Management (DSM).

ONLINE POWER MONITORING IN BUILDINGS

Power monitoring system is the brain of the whole architecture of the IoT enabled System. Continues two-way flow of communication using IoT is responsible of online power monitoring which splits into five stages. In a grid system one or number of devices are switch-on at the same time that is why for monitoring Data Collection is the first stage which collects the data from the consumers and send information to SM through the internet connectivity. After analysis of switch on devices, it will convert it into a programmable language that is why digital conversion of the data is known as Digitization. SM must make intelligent decisions that power demand of which device or devices should be on priority according to the demand and occupants behavior. Therefore, a set of Decision Protocols will take decisions according to the prior demand of the consumer and send it to the Processing stage to process. SM will send power requests to the monitoring system and at the same time SM sends the signal to the main switchboard of the system to activate respective electrical paths automatically. The monitoring system and SM will communicate with each other through the internet. It helps the automatic switching system to turn on when it gets the signal from its own monitoring system. It will automatically close the paths of the electrical network to supply power which it receives from the Power Generation side. Main power supply switches of a system will start receiving power and they send it to the socket-boards to all the respective power-demanding appliances to provide Services. SM maintains complete information of the amount of receiving power in the system for billing and other records.

PV Power Generation Monitoring

The PV power generation monitoring system monitors the PV power generation devices, the grid-connected inverters, and the auxiliary AC/DC devices in the PV power generation system, and analyzes the conditions of the grid for connection, the power generation quality, and the power generation volume. This can realize the operation monitoring and power generation control of the PV power generation system. The PV power generation monitoring system monitors the operation conditions of the devices in real time, and triggers an audible and visual alarm on the monitoring interface for the abnormal signal generated by the device. This monitoring system can also monitor the power quality indexes in real time, including the voltage, frequency, power factor, three phase unbalance rate, the harmonic content and other critical ones, so as to make sure the power generation system supplies electric energy of reliable quality. Monitoring of PV power generation includes three parts of SCADA of PV power generation, power generation statistics, and generated energy management. (SCADA - supervisory Control and Data Acquisition)

The main functions of SCADA of PV power generation include data collection and processing, event and alarm, PV inverter operation monitoring, operation monitoring of the PV box type transformer, operation monitoring of the PV junction box, and power quality monitoring. Statistics and analysis of PV power generation include the current power generation, daily power generation, monthly power generation, accumulated power generation, accumulated CO_2 emission reduction, and generated power statistics and analysis.

Generated energy management includes locally and remotely controlled energy management. The locally controlled energy management includes the exchange power curve control, the smooth control active output, the reactive automatic voltage control, the emergency supporting dispatching of power, and the emergency shutdown dispatching; and the remotely controlled energy management includes the exchange power curve control, the emergency supporting dispatching of power, the emergency shutdown dispatching, and the reactive automatic dispatching of voltage.

The solar photovoltaic (PV) system has become the key attraction for the generation of clean, renewable electricity. Nevertheless, performance varies due to different parameters and environmental factors. Therefore, a remote and real- performance is required to evaluate its performance. The monitoring of the solar PV system can be achieved by sensors in IoT. The monitoring system uses real-time measured values to display power, current, voltage, temperature, and light intensity graphs, and it is also easy to track and view the database file to analyze the history of the collected data. The design work was divided into two main sections, hardware, and software. The hardware includes the creation of major units such as the power supply unit, the control unit and the sensor units while the software includes the database system and pulled the data out into private webpage and visualization on Grafana dashboard. The IoT based Solar Battery Monitoring System using two microcontrollers, Arduino UNO and NodeMCU. The data obtained will be stored in the local database and can be viewed through a web page that serves as a data log and through a visualization tool using Grafana. Throughout the system, users can easily track their solar PV system over the internet. A Grafana dashboard is a powerful open source analytical and visualization tool that consists of multiple individual panels arranged in a grid. The panels interact with configured data sources, including (but not limited to) AWS Cloud Watch, Microsoft SQL server, Prometheus, MySQL, InfluxDB, and many others.

Sensors in Smart Grid

Sensors for monitoring electrical parameters over an entire electricity network infrastructure play a fundamental role in protecting smart grids and improving the network's energy efficiency. When a short circuit takes place in a smart grid it has to be sensed as soon as possible to reduce its fault duration along the network and to reduce damage to the electricity infrastructure as well as personal injuries. Existing protection devices, which are used to sense the fault, range from classic analog electro-mechanics relays to modern intelligent electronic devices (IEDs). However, both types of devices have fixed adjustment settings (offline stage) and do not provide any coordination among them under real-time operation. The smart sensor is developed that offers the capability to update its adjustment settings during real-time operation, in coordination with the rest of the smart sensors spread over the network. The sensor and the coordinated protection scheme were tested in a standard smart grid (IEEE 34-bus test system) under different short circuit scenarios and renewable energy penetration.

Smart Sensors for Smart Grid Protection

In smart grids, several parameters must be measured, such as voltage, current, temperature, and phase, to be able to detect any parameter fluctuation in near real time and manage the corrective actions to assure grid reliability under fault conditions. Furthermore, the measured data must be readable by intelligent devices and contain a timestamp as well as the sensor location to facilitate decision support in smart grid operation. The relay-based smart sensor composed of several modules:

Data acquisition module: This module is in charge of monitoring and measuring the analogue signal in real time by means of the electricity transducers installed in the network.

Data conditioning: In this module, the analogue electrical signal is conditioned and converted into a digital signal. After the sampling stage, the root mean square (RMS) value of the sampled signal is calculated and used to obtain the fundamental component of the measured signal.

Microprocessor unit (MPU): This module is responsible for processing the digital signal in order to detect and activate the network breaker to isolate the faulted zone. This is the core of the sensor in which the smart-sensor settings are updated depending on the network conditions and fault situation. Inside the MPU, the optimization algorithm (the APS) is responsible for selecting the optimal setting parameters that minimize the operation time of the PR and BR of the faulted zone. When a fault occurs, only the PR of the faulted zone executes the APS in the MPU to determine the optimal setting parameters of the primary and backup smart sensors.

Moreover, the MPU algorithms are able to transform a physical measurement in an electric signal that could be processed, stored, and communicated to other devices through a bidirectional communication channel. Finally, digital measured data could be stored internally on the device for future local or remote treatment.

Synchronization module: An internal clock allows for the synchronization of the acquired digital data with an external time reference that could be shared with other devices, such as global positioning systems (GPS). Using measurement synchronization helps to improve the quality and accuracy of the measurement data. In smart grids, measurement synchronization is of great importance for operational and protection issues.

Communication module: The communication module is responsible for the peer-to-peer communication between the smart sensors. For communication issues, smart sensors use the IEC 61850 standard. When a fault takes place, the primary smart sensor communicates the optimal setting parameters to the backup smart sensor and activates the opening of the circuit breaker by GOOSE messages.

Additional module for metadata sensor storage: This module allows the device to perform supplementary tasks related to the following: smart-sensor description and identification capability (self-description and self-identification); quality control of the work achieved by the smart sensor; and operation error reporting (self-diagnostics, self-testing and self-validation).

Technical Losses and its Reduction

In an IoT enabled smart energy grid system, 22.5% of total losses of electricity in transmission and distribution Lines are technical losses which depend on the characteristics of electrical network and operation modes. Technical losses are subdivided into two types: Permanent losses and Variable losses. Almost 25% of technical losses are permanent losses which depends upon the following factors:-

- Open-circuit Losses
- Corona Losses
- Continuous load of measuring and controlling elements
- Leakage current losses
- Dielectric Losses

There will be no permanent losses for the time in which no data originates from the consumers. (1) defines the total losses in the transmission lines and these all losses should be minimized but only for that time duration when the Lines will not carry electric power. Open circuit Losses will be extremely minimized because the electrical network will only be close to supply electricity when the consumer's request. Corona losses become zero because it depends upon the voltage supplied.

Conventional Electricity Grids vs.Smart Grid

Currently, conventional electrical grids have minimal storage capabilities. They usually follow a demand-centric model, where companies reduce network voltage to allow usage by different consumers. When you factor in different variables, such as weather changes, wildlife damage, sabotage by humans, or natural disasters, it becomes easy to see that electrical grids are difficult to maintain. A smart grid, on the other hand, has self-healing capabilities. This simply means that the grid detects outage areas, and automatically re-routes electricity (if possible) while alerting repair teams. Since it allows two-way electricity flow, stakeholders can review the data that is fed into the grid and forecast changes in demand, plan for inclement weather and prepare contingency plans for prolonged outages. The aim is to create a grid that contains minimal outages and prevents them from turning into large-scale blackouts. New technologies will allow for faster response by emergency services, and by relying on distributed power generation, could result in the formation of a "smartgrid," where a community can power its essential services by itself in case of an emergency.

Smart Meters and Smart Grids Clean Energy Plan

The plan, which is expected to take effect from January 1, 2024, is focussed on building resilience into the company's electricity and gas networks and targets the meeting of California's goal of achieving carbon neutrality by 2045. Among the major investments detailed is the implementation of the next generation of smart meters in order to give customers more control, access and insights into their energy usage. Grid modernisation is planned with cutting-edge technologies to enable the integration of significantly more renewables generation, energy storage and electric vehicle (EV) charging, while grid automation and remote sensing tools and the replacement of ageing or failure-prone equipment are intended to cut the risk for power outages.

Cutting-Edge Energy Storage Technologies

With the increase in the use of hybrid and renewable energy sources within the scope of measures taken to reduce greenhouse gas emissions, the difficulties brought by daily and seasonal changes in transmission and distribution need to be tackled. Energy storage systems (ESS) are essential technologies because of the support they provide in times of need to overcome supplydemand balance challenges. For this reason, worldwide efforts are being made to develop more efficient energy storage systems. Energy storage facilities can be employed for various purposes in power systems such as reliability procurement, frequency regulation, or redressing fluctuations caused by uncertain and intermittent sources. These technologies deliver power in various scales and various response speeds. Even though pumped storage technology is the most common type of grid-scale energy storage, various ongoing studies are still looking for other efficient alternatives. Some emerging large-scale storage technologies have been proposed, or even tested as a prototype in small scale.

CHALLENGES IN DEPLOYING A SMART GRID

The idea of a smart grid is promising, but it's not without its challenges. The biggest challenge is from consumers, who often resist the installation of something as basic as a smart meter. As a result, governments or power companies are often forced to offer financial rewards or impose fines on customers who do not comply. There's also another bigger challenge to overcome: cybersecurity. There is always a risk that hackers can breach into a connected power grid, and divert resources, or worse, hijack parts of the grid.

Cyber Security of Smart Grids

There are many risks that Smart Grids can potentially obtain, and these could not only affect the organizations but will also affect regular customers. These risks possibly pose significant threats to individuals' privacy, such as sensitive information about customers, maybe at risk of getting information stolen or terminating the business for good. These risks are not just posed at using the internet but also affect customers at home while adversaries could possibly collect personal information. Due to the necessity to resolve the data security issues, we devoted this subsection to highlight the complexity of the widespread problems in cybersecurity. The advanced automation and communication capabilities in smart grids expose the entire system to cyber threats. Although the integration of smart grids empowers electric utilities and end-users and enhances the reliability and availability of the service with the ability to monitor and manage the behavior of the demands continually, it brings various security constraints and vulnerabilities. To ensure the security of the complete system, the key management for large amounts of devices in grid systems is very important. Recently, several studies were conducted related to the Key Management System (KMS). Existing surveys on smart grids discussed topics on Demand response management and cyber security. In contrast, this survey work deals with key management systems for smart grids, a very critical area where very less attention has been paid to. This survey showcases the importance of monitoring the parameters of PV Battery in smart grids and also focuses on the key management system that plays a defensive role against threats. The novelty in this paper is effectively monitoring the parameters of the PV battery system along with a proper Key management algorithm in the Smart energy grid system.

Security Initiative for Smart Grid

Hundreds of regulations, standards, and guidelines have already been created to define requirements for a recommended level of security and provide instruction on the best practices in smart grid security. These documents will continually be reviewed, scrutinized, revised, and improved. Additionally, new documents will be created to address new smart grid technologies when they are developed. The majority of these documents provide a tremendous wealth of knowledge in integrating security controls into smart grid components. Thus, smart grid security professionals must regularly monitor for new requirements and best practices.

Several states already have initiatives to promote, or even require, the deployment of smart grids. With the amount of federal money available, the remaining states will most likely create their own initiatives. California state law specifically states that smart grids should follow the best practices defined in several standards. By including similar verbiage in their own initiatives, state legislatures around the country will help create a more secure electrical infrastructure. Companies take different approaches in handling compliance. Larger companies may have separate compliance departments, whereas smaller companies may place that responsibility on the security departments. Whichever department is ultimately responsible, they will need to closely monitor their state legislature and utility regulatory body to ensure compliance. Being compliant with the state and local security regulations, as well as with other levels of regulation, may not guarantee the security of smart grids. The state and local security requirements will not be perfect, and companies should only view these requirements as setting a minimum level. Doing the bare minimum may be the most cost-effective approach upfront; however, a breach of security or privacy will likely cost significantly more than implementing appropriate controls.

Even after having put in place the most resilient and attack-resistant architecture possible, it is still essential to put in place an operational model that can respond effectively to attacks, intrusions and data exfiltration. Enterprise Geographic Information System (GIS) is the platform that creates and collects information about utility assets (cables, transformers, customers, etc.) and makes that information available to enterprise for monitoring and analysis (ESRI, 2011). SCADA systems that control and monitor devices used in power generation, management and distribution.

Customer information systems that monitor usage, perform billing, handle customer relationships and so on. Interfaces with external systems such as weather information, traffic information, satellite imagery, threat intelligence and so on.

Utilities use this combined information for a broad range of applications, including managing a comprehensive picture of the operating environment, detecting and analysing faults, planning and analysing the network, and managing security operations. For all these purposes, the utility must understand the relationship of its assets to each other. Since the smart grid is composed of two networks – the electric distribution network and the communications network – utilities must understand the physical, spatial and electronic relationships both within each of these networks and between these networks. For example, the communications network not only enables the collection and consolidation of information from the electricity distribution network, but also provides the means of distributing control information to substations, smart meters and other components in the electricity distribution network. Understanding these interconnections is essential not only in effective operational management but also in security management.

The GIS is particularly important in enabling the utility to understand the electric and communication networks and the relationship between them. It provides a means to monitor the operational and security health of the system, answering such questions as "what sensors have reported anomalous values for the past hour", where the anomaly may be in terms of the historical record for a particular sensor for a particular time period (day, week, month) or in terms of an abstracted pattern of values for sensors providing that particular function. This operational model of the system as a whole takes advantage of device information provided by the SCADA system. But it needs to go beyond that device-specific information to present both a comprehensive perspective on the grid and insight into specific operational and security issues that could affect the availability and safety of the grid. This visibility into the health of both the electric and the communication networks, as well as components within those networks, enables the smart grid to adapt quickly to prevent outages, whether those are the result of equipment failure, weather conditions, accidents, physical attacks or cyber security events.

The more comprehensive monitoring and control systems enabled by smart grid, particularly through the instrumentation of a larger number of more diverse sensors within the substation, can reduce the risk of such events. The instance of physical attacks on the grid, such as the attack on the PG&E (Pacific Gas and Electric) transmission station in Metcalf CA in April 2013, also demonstrates the importance of these more comprehensive operational systems that can detect and respond more quickly to damage to a particular facility in order to limit the impact to the grid as a whole.

FUTURE ENHANCEMENT

The prominent research in the Smart grid is an important dimension of the modern electricity system. Augmenting the smart IoT devices such as smart PMUs, smart meter, sensors with the node level intelligence will significantly contribute in efficient handling of big data footprints in future IoT communication. This work provides a real impact on the minimization of Line Power Losses. Power consumption is highly correlated with the occupants' behavior, therefore, the proposed method is capable of understanding its surrounding environment due to two-way-communication between power utility and consumers and then make decisions to supply power according to the requirements. Supplying power according to the demand by using the concept of integrating IoT and Smart Grid will be more effective as compared to the existing methodology used in Pakistan. It will not only minimize losses and provide power-efficient systems but also maintain reliable cost and quality of power for consumers. The monitoring and optimized system which is described in this paper will minimize the factors of permanent losses which has fewer compatibility issues with the existing method of supplying electricity in India.

This research supports energy management and downgrades transmission and distribution Line losses to improve power supply systems for better growth of electricity production in India. The main limitation in the research work is in the limited range of the RFID. Research is ongoing to enhance the range and test the solution using multiple PV panels.

CONCLUSION

The Internet has proved its existence in our lives, from interactions at a virtual level to social relationships. The IoT has added a new potential into the internet by enabling communications between objects and humans, making a smarter and intelligent planet. This has led to the vision of "anytime, anywhere, anyway, anything" communications practically in the true sense. To this end, it is observed that the IoT should be considered as the core part of the existing internet relying on its future direction, which is obviously to be exceptionally different from the current phase of the internet that we see and use in our lives. Hence, the architectural concept comes into the picture. Architecture is a framework of technology enabling things to interconnect and interact with similar or dissimilar objects by imposing humans to be a layer on it. In fact, it is clear that the current IoT paradigm, which is supportive toward M2M communications, is now getting limited by a number of factors. New formulations are inevitable for sustenance of IoT which is a strong notation for the researcher to come up with. From the above survey, it is found that publish/subscribe based IoT is flourishing nowadays and being successively used in many applications. An IOT based solution for monitoring PV panels using battery less RFID temperature sensors has been proposed. An SMTP email protocol has been used to send email alerts remotely. The proposed key management approach provides high protection of data with better stability. When the defined work is compared with the existing works, it is more robust with improved routing and key management in the IoT based grid system. The proposed research works provide better security with education training time and high efficiency.

REFERENCES

Abir, S. M. A. A., Anwar, A., Choi, J., & Kayes, A. S. (2021). IoT-Enabled Smart Energy Grid: Applications and Challenges. IEEE.

Ahmadzadeh, Parr, & Zhao. (2021). *A Review on Communication Aspects of Demand Response Management for Future 5G IoT-Based Smart Grids*. Academic Press.

Arbab-Zavar, B., Palacios-Garcia, E., Vasquez, J., & Guerrero, J. (2019). Smart inverters for microgrid applications: A review. *Energies*, *12*(5), 840. doi:10.3390/en12050840

Arunkumari, T., & Indragandhi, V. (2017). An overview of high voltage conversion ratio DC-DC converter configurations used in DC micro-grid architectures. *Renewable & Sustainable Energy Reviews*, *77*, 670–687. doi:10.1016/j.rser.2017.04.036

Betis, G., Cassandras, C. G., & Nucci, C. A. (2018). Smart cities. *Proceedings of the IEEE*, *106*(4), 513–517. doi:10.1109/JPROC.2018.2812998

Bi, S., & Zhang, Y. J. A. (2017). Graph-based cyber security analysis of state estimation in smart power grid. *IEEE Communications Magazine*, *55*(4), 176–183. doi:10.1109/MCOM.2017.1600210C

Bialasiewicz. (n.d.). *Renewable Energy Systems With Photovoltaic Power Generators: Operation and Modeling*. Academic Press.

Deriche, M. (2019). *An IOT based sensing system for remote monitoring of PV panels*. IEEE.

Dong, N., Chang, J-F., Wu, A-G., & Gao, Z-K. (2019). *A novel convolutional neural network framework based solar irradiance prediction method*. Elsevier.

Gao & Wai. (n.d.). *A novel fault identification method for photovoltaic array via convolutional neural network and residual gated recurrent unit*. Academic Press.

Hajimiragha, A. H., Gomis-Bellmunt, O., Saeedifard, M., & Palma-Behnke, R. (2014). Trends in Microgrid Control. *IEEE Transactions on Smart Grid, 5*(4), 1905–1919. doi:10.1109/TSG.2013.2295514

Kumar, M., Minai, A. F., Khan, A. A., & Kumar, S. (2000). *IoT based Energy Management System for Smart Grid*. IEEE.

Nosratabadi, S. M., Hooshmand, R.-A., & Gholipour, E. (2017). A comprehensive review on microgrid and virtual power plant concepts employed for distributed energy resources scheduling in power systems. *Renewable & Sustainable Energy Reviews, 67*, 341–363. doi:10.1016/j.rser.2016.09.025

Parhizi, S., Lotfi, H., Khodaei, A., & Bahramirad, S. (2015). State of the art in research on microgrids: A review. *IEEE Access : Practical Innovations, Open Solutions, 3*, 890–925. doi:10.1109/ACCESS.2015.2443119

Pramudhita, A. N., & Asmara, R. A. (2018). Internet of Things Integration in Smart Grid. IEEE.

Tiwari, V. (2021). *Monitoring and Control of PV Microgrid using IoT*. IEEE.

Tripathi & De. (n.d.). *Adaptive Transmission Protocols for Smart Grid IoT Communication*. IEEE.

Vemulakonda, R. (2016). *An algorithm for basic IoT Architectures*. ICETCSE.

Waseem, Kouser, Waqas, Imran, Hameed, & Bin Faheem. (2021). *CSOA-Based Residential Energy Management System in Smart Grid Considering DGs for Demand Response*. IEEE.

Xu, Shao, Cao, & Chang. (2021). *Single phase grid connected PV system with golden sections each based MPPT algorithm*. Academic Press.

Chapter 8
E-Voting:
Portable Fingerprint-Based Biometric Device for Elderly and Disabled People

Siddharth Chatterjee
Vellore Institute of Technology, India

Ishan Sagar Jogalekar
Vellore Institute of Technology, India

K. Lavanya
Vellore Institute of Technology, India

ABSTRACT

Biometric fingerprint devices used in electronic voting machines (EVMs) for voter verification and authentication eliminates two main threats towards present-day voting systems, which include illegal voting as well as repetition of votes. This application has extensive use in real world scenarios and helps to conduct fair and free elections. The person at the polling booth need not carry his ID, which contains his required details; only placing his finger on the device would allow the acquisition of an on-spot fingerprint from the voter – an authentic identification. The fingerprint reader would read details from the tag; the data is then passed onto the controlling unit for verification. The controller fetches the data from the reader and compares the data with pre-existing data stored during registration of voters using biometric. This prototype is based on IoT (internet of things), and the microprocessor platform uses Arduino Uno as the microchip and some TFT displays to successfully simulate the architecture for voting systems and consequently improve the traditional EVM-based voting.

DOI: 10.4018/978-1-6684-7756-4.ch008

1. INTRODUCTION

Many nations are still having difficulty enrolling and verifying voters. As a result, they're evaluating the negative impact on their democratic systems. Indeed, during the last ten years, biometric registration and voting technologies have grown in popularity. The goal is to achieve voter equality, founded on the idea of one person, one vote, which states that everyone's vote should be counted fairly.

In a biometric voting system, the voters are registered based on their unique physical characteristics like fingerprints and even facial or IRIS recognition. Using these biometric characteristics, a person is registered as a voter. Identity theft, voting fraud, and other forms of voter fraud and tampering are targeted by biometric technology. The biometric voting system aims to provide a unique list of voters with zero duplicate voters. In India, the voting system plays a major role during elections. Election Commission of India uses electronic voting machines for the election. According to the survey, in the 2014 general election, only 66.4% votes got registered. At the same time, voting systems have encountered with serious challenges in delivering voting confirmation messages and lack of awareness among people to precisely use their fundamental right "Right to Vote". For avoiding misconceptions on the election time, many advanced techniques are being proposed earlier, by efficiently using various methods. In this paper, we proposed a solution for solving various issues in the present voting system which effectively uses biometric identification as a major concept. The biometric identification will provide better trustworthy results in the election process.

Now, we are all aware of the existing electronic voting machine where the user has to press a button to cast the vote. But these machines have been criticized for being tempered with since the beginning (Study of Biometric Voting System, n.d.). So, the government is planning to introduce a fingerprint-based voting machine where users can cast the vote based on his/her fingerprint impression. This system will not only remove the possibility of duplicate votes but also provide any kind of implication.So, it is necessary and advised to authenticate the voter and its identification with another machine which will mark this fingerprint as voted and vote in the old machine so that anonymity of vote is also considered.

Biometric finger print devices used in Electronic Voting Machines (EVMs) for voter verification and authentication eliminates two main threats towards present-day voting system which includes illegal voting as well as repetition of votes. The application of the 'Fingerprint Based Biometric Voting Machine' has an extensive use in real world scenario and could help elections be made fair and free from rigging and further ensuring that the elections would no longer be a tedious and expensive job. The person at the polling booth need not carry his ID which would contain his required details; only placing his finger on the device would allow the acquisition of an on-spot fingerprint from the voter which serves as an authentic identification. The Finger Print reader would read details from the tag and the data is then passed on to the controlling unit for verification. The controller fetches the data from the reader and compares the data with pre-existing data stored during registration of voters using biometric. This prototype of ours based on IoT (Internet Of Things) and microprocessor platform is going to use Arduino Uno as the microchip and some TFT displays to successfully simulate the architecture for voting system and consequently improve the traditional EVM based voting.

The main aim is to develop the prototype that will secure and validate voters for any voting campaigns. As biometric verification and secure the data of voting locally.

The main prototype is divided into 2 parts. For convenience we are going with Arduino-Uno as micro controller and Biometric sensor - GT-511C3 and TFT display as voting display.

The rest of the paper is organized so that Section 2 surveys related works. The system design and implementation are presented in Section 3. Section 4 provides a thorough evaluation and Section 6 concludes the paper and sets the ground for future work.

2. LITERATURE SURVEY

The paper discusses the development and implementation of a new technology for voting machines. It devises a new modern approach which can replace the traditional mechanical voting system with a biometric one. The main objective is to design a biometric voting machine that uses an individual's fingerprint as the medium of identification. It aims to remove the traditional use of documents or voter ID at polling booth during elections. The project suggests a more modern system which is biometric in nature, and also less time consuming (Gujanatti et al., 2015).

The person at the polling booth needs only to place his finger on the device, thus allowing (Suralkar et al., 2019), the acquisition of an on spot fingerprint from the voter which serves as an identification. This finger print reader reads the details from the tag.

This project mainly focuses on developing an E-Voting system which is much more secure, verifiable and does not involve the requirement of too many trustworthy individuals at every level. They aim at using Blockchain to make voting much secure and also using ring signature and Fingerprint Authentication for additional security. HTML client, HTTP, TCP/IP, Application Server, Database Server, Blockchain (Namballa, 2020).

The main intention of this proposal is to offer security and to overcome the limitations that are in the conventional balloting system. Initially, within the consumer registration procedure, the voter details, along with their fingerprint, are saved within the serial monitor. Here, the serial monitor acts as a database. The voter desires to area their finger at the module on the polling booth, thus allowing the acquisition of a finger impression from the voter, which serves as identification (David et al., 2014).

The design incorporates a database which holds the personal data of every registered voter, the Graphic User Interface (GUI) which provides a user friendly interface. The proposed EVM also allows the voters to scan their fingerprint for authentication, which is then matched with an already saved image within a database. The software is implemented completely as a .NET managed code in C programming language with database Microsoft SQL Server support (Waili & Alkawaz, 2020).

A Fingerprint is an important identifier for the humans. This paper proposes finger print voting system with Arduino. The majority of the worldwide election were using a paper-based voting rather than using biometric system. The current voting process has safety problems such as authenticity of voters (Amrish et al., n.d.) In proposed system, a voter identity can be proved instantly. All voters' information was stored securely to register in the system.

Using RFID Tag voters information is stored and each user is delivered a voter's ID in the method of RFID Tag. The hardware proposal has a Finger print scanning sensor which is used to compare the finger print of the user with the pre-stored finger print of the user (Gandhi, 2014) During voting, both the finger prints are checked for matching and if it does not match, then an alert is given using buzzer. For the selection process Keypad is used. LCD is used for indication to the corresponding data for each key to the user.

The main aim of this project is to make voting secure using fingerprint verification and also to reduce malpractices. The details of the voter along with their fingerprint in stored in database. If the fingerprint matches with the stored fingerprint, the system checks the Aadhar number of the user and if authenticated, it checks if multiple votes have been cast. If the fingerprint matching is not correct "Matching failed" message will be displayed and if Aadhar number is not correct, then "Aadhar not match" message will be displayed (Khairnar & Kharat, 2016).

In this paper we provide security to online voting system with secure user authentication by providing biometric as well as password security to voter accounts. Basic idea behind this is to combine secret key with cover image on the basis of key image (Nigar & Islam, 2020). As a result such new image is produced by system called stego image which is quite same as cover image. The key image is a biometric measure, such as a fingerprint image. Extraction of stego image is take place at server side to perform the voter authentication.

This paper aims at creation of secure online voting system providing biometric security. Online voting system used for government elections. Online voting system is publicly available system so there are various types of attacks to hack this system. Propose a new secure online voting system by using biometric and steganographic authentication. The vote casting and recording also secure using homomorphic encryption, blind signature to solve the problem of voter votes hacking and destroying system (Kumar & Begum, 2011).

Electronic Voting Machine (EVM), Microcontroller, Fingerprint Authentication, Central Integrated Database Voting is an onerous task for the election commission to conduct free and fair polls in our country, the largest democracy in the world. A lot of money has been spent on this to make sure that the elections are rampage free (Chakraborty et al., 2021). But, now- a -days it has become very usual for some forces to indulge in rigging which may eventually lead to a result contrary to the actual verdict given by the people. In order to provide inexpensive solutions to the above, this project is implemented with the biometric system i.e. fingerprint scanning.

Biometric, Fingerprint, Minutiae, Electronic Voting, Database In this study, for the fingerprint authentication the minutiae based matching is considered for higher recognition accuracy. Also, the matching accuracy of fingerprint based authentication systems has been shown to be very high.

Fingerprint – based authentication systems continue to dominate the biometrics market by accounting for almost 52% of authentication systems based on biometric traits (Gentles & Sankaranarayanan, 2012).

A reliable Electronic Voting Machine (EVM) is proposed and implemented in this study, which is integrated with a biometric fingerprint scanner to ensure a secure election process (Patil, 2019). This paper provides a detailed description of the systematic development of the hardware and software used. The software part includes algorithm development and implementation. A thorough and in-depth understanding of the data and the communication protocols along with the pathways used for storage of data in the devices is provided.

3. PROPOSED MODEL

Components and Modules

In this section, multiple components have been used for Fingerprint based *Biometric voting system* development as the following:

1) *Microcontroller:* Arduino UNO is a micro controller board based on the ATmega328P. It has 14 digital input/output pins (of which 6 can be used as PWM outputs), 6 analog inputs, a 16 MHz ceramic resonator. It is used to control different sensors connected to it and it is very useful for validating sensors outputs with local system. It is programmed using Arduino-C language with different libraries.

2) *GT511C Biometric Sensor:* Using the SmackFinger 3.0 Algorithm, the GT-511C3 fingerprint sensor module detects fingerprints quickly and accurately. It runs on a voltage range of 3.3V to 6V and draws approximately 130mA. It commu- nicates at a baud rate of 9600 using the UART protocol. It is important component of system.

3) *TFT Display:* TFT display is LCD display with touch- screen facility. It is multicoloured LCD display with TFT layered sensor. It also provides memory with SD card facility and reset button.

Software Component

1) *Program Development:* The Arduino will connect to system once program is loaded, it will act as power source and serial monitor and securely storage device. Also considering the software, the program will encrypt the serial data which is captured from sensor. Basically in this system development software component is having very low index of contribution. As it is used to develop program and use to load into micro controller.

2) *Arduino - C:* Arduino Uno used ATmega processor. In order to control different sensors and carry out specific results we have to create program for processor. Arduino-C language is an enhanced version of embedded C language. Arduino platform provides different IDE for this purpose. Biometric sensor data also reads through controller temporary memory and then it sends to system memory,

Security

As in product we are including the biometric data the security issues may rises at such points. But to solve such issues encryption algorithms will act effectively.The final data is not going to display on TFT display, it will always appear on computer system. Within system the serial data will be encrypted securely. It will decrypt with only unique key. Security is important factor of this prototype and it is also research gap for this paper. Secure the voters data and their vote is important aspect for this. As system obtains most crucial data while voting like biometric information so, it is important to secure such data.

Encryption

For encryption and decryption "Fernet" cryptography algo- rithm is used. Fernet is built on top of a number of standard cryptography primitives. Specifically, it uses - AES in CBC mode with a 128-bit key for encryption; using PKCS7 padding. HMAC using SHA256 for authentication. Hence it is very difficult to attack such cryptography based encryption. So, data will be always securely stored. It is based with symmetric key encryption.

Fernet Algorithm

Fernet algorithm is symmetric encryption algorithm, where same key is used for encryption and decryption. Fernet al- gorithm is in build sub-package with python cryptography package. It uses SHA256 hashing technique for key generation and uses 128bit AES for generating cipher text. In the system resultant data and result of voting will be available through only serial monitor and then converted to CSV file once it is stored on system, python based program will encrypt the data to make it secure. The whole process is running through local system hence it is not exposed to the internet.

Procedural Working

1) Once device powered up, users can view the options for voting.
2) Voters should use biometric verification first in order to press voting option.
3) Once voters press specific option, user data will be stored and it will not any other options or duplicate votes.
4) For display results it will reflect on serial monitor only and it will securely. Store in system only.

Working on System

1) Once the code is uploaded the TFT display should display the candidate's name. When someone taps on a candidate name, the machine will ask to scan the fingerprint scanner.
2) The fingerprint is valid, then the user vote will be counted, but in case, the pattern does not match with the records of the database, access to cast a vote will be denied.
3) total number of votes for each candidate will be stored in EEPROM and a candidate having the highest number of votes will win.

RESULTS AND DISCUSSIONS

A Web Based Application was created as a part of this project. The application provides multiple facilities to the farmers including provision of relevant news related to agricultural activities of the farmer, provision of live data from the farm in graphical forms and Buy and Sell features by the means of which the farmer can use the data collected over the entire crop cycle to sell the crops directly to the consumers.

Using this data the consumers can make sure all the claims by the farmer are valid including claims of organic farming using minimal amounts of fertilizers and pesticides.

RESULTS

Biometric finger print devices used in Electronic Voting Machines (EVMs) for voter verification and authentication eliminates two main threats towards present-day voting system which includes illegal voting as well as repetition of votes. The application of the 'Fingerprint Based Biometric Voting Machine' has an extensive use in real world scenario and could help elections be made fair and free from rigging and further ensuring that the elections would no longer be a tedious and expensive job. The person at the polling booth need not carry his ID which would contain his required details; only placing his finger on the device would allow the acquisition of an on-spot fingerprint from the voter which serves as an authentic identification. The Finger Print reader would read details from the tag and the data is then passed on to the controlling unit for verification. The controller fetches the data from the reader and compares the data with pre-existing data stored during registration of voters using biometric. This prototype of ours based on IoT (Internet Of Things) and microprocessor platform is going to use Arduino Uno as the microchip and some TFT displays to successfully simulate the architecture for voting system and consequently improve the traditional EVM based voting.

7. CONCLUSION AND FUTURE SCOPE

The prototype for the project 'Fingerprint Based Voting Machine' was mainly intended to remove any present discrepancies related to duplicate and unregistered voting, which would subsequently help in conducting free and fair elections which should be the primary basis for a democratic country like India and set an example in the present world using advanced technology in an updated fashion.

REFERENCES

Amrish, Akash, Sukhi, & Jabamani. (n.d.). *Fingerprint and RFID Based Electronic Voting System.* EAM Engineer Department of Electrical and Electronics Engineering, R.M.K. Engineering College.

ChakrabortyS.BejD.RoyD.MahammadS. A. (2021). Designing of a Biometric Fingerprint Scanner-Based, Secure, and Low-Cost Electronic Voting Machine for India. Preprints. doi:10.20944/preprints202111.0177.v1

David, Ijomanta, Gil-Ozoudeh, & Chukwuebuka. (2014). A Biometric based Software Solution for E-Voting using networking. *Scholars Journal of Engineering and Technology, 2,* 874–881.

Gandhi, N. (2014). *Study on Security of Online Voting System Using Biometrics and Steganography.* Academic Press.

Gentles, D. S., & Sankaranarayanan, S. (2012). Application of Biometrics in Mobile Voting. *International Journal of Computer Network and Information Security., 4*(7), 57–68. Advance online publication. doi:10.5815/ijcnis.2012.07.07

Gujanatti, Tolanur, Nemagoud, Reddy, & Neelagund. (2015). A Finger Print based Voting System. *International Journal of Engineering Research Technology, 4*(5). doi:10.17577/IJERTV4IS050948

Khairnar, S. K., & Kharat, R. (2016). Survey on Secure Online Voting System. *International Journal of Computer Applications, 134*(13), 19–21. doi:10.5120/ijca2016908144

Kumar & Begum. (2011). A Novel design of Electronic Voting System Using Fingerprint. *International Journal of Innovative Technology Creative Engineering, 1.*

Namballa, M. (2020). Realtime Fingerprint based Voting System. *International Journal of Engineering Research & Technology (Ahmedabad), 9*(9). Advance online publication. doi:10.17577/IJERTV9IS090073

Nigar, N. N., & Islam, M. (2020). A Proposed Framework for Fingerprint-based Voting System in Bangladesh. JOIV. *International Journal on Informatics Visualization, 4*(1). Advance online publication. doi:10.30630/joiv.4.1.283

Patil, H. (2019). Mobile Based Voting Application. *International Journal for Research in Applied Science and Engineering Technology, 7*(5), 2181–2185. doi:10.22214/ijraset.2019.5366

Study of Biometric Voting System. (n.d.). https://researchtrend.net/ijet/pdf/ 28-S-812.pdf

Suralkar, Udasi, Gagnani, Tekwani, & Bhatia. (2019). *E-Voting Using Blockchain With Biometric Authentication.* Academic Press.

Waili, T. Z., & Alkawaz, A. (2020). Advanced Voting System Using Fingerprint. *International Journal on Perceptive and Cognitive Computing,* 6(2), 18–21. doi:10.31436/ijpcc.v6i2.172

APPENDIX: PROJECT CODEBASE

The entire codebase for the system and other relevant files have been uploaded in the given link.

https://github.com/ishanjogalekar/Biometric-Voting-System

Chapter 9

Regular Language Encryption for Secured Storage of Cloud Data in Smart Home–Based Cities

S. Muthurajkumar

(iD) https://orcid.org/0000-0003-3960-6926

Anna University, Chennai, India

R. Praveen

(iD) https://orcid.org/0000-0001-9048-6224

Anna University, Chennai, India

S. Yogeshwar

Anna University, Chennai, India

K. A. Muthukumaran

Anna University, Chennai, India

K. C. Abishek

Anna University, Chennai, India

ABSTRACT

The smart city is an evolution of a smart home. According to a report by ABI Research, almost 300 million smart homes have been installed around the world by 2022. The smart sensors of separate homes, various organizations are connected to make a city smart. The regular language encryption is privacy ensuring and at the same time proves to be secured against the keyword guessing attack (KGA). The authors propose a model in which they regulate the way the user wants to search and return results. They also provide privacy to the outsourced data by encrypting the content before being outsourced to the database server. The entire module is controlled by keyword generation center (KGC), which is responsible for approving the owners for uploading the files to the cloud server and the users for downloading the files from the same. In this work, the authors introduce a model to behave in a way where the approved user has the entire control over his data and also has the role of granting permission to the user who requests access for the particular data.

DOI: 10.4018/978-1-6684-7756-4.ch009

1. INTRODUCTION

Smart home and smart cities are evolved by implementing the IoT system in traditional homes and cities. There are variety of IoT devices are used to automate the home and change the way it is. Many leading manufacturers are helping the smart home with the smart devices like Kepler Gas and CO detector, Anova Precision cooker, SkyBell smart video doorbell, Misfit Bolt Bluetooth smart bulb, Parrot Wireless plant monitor, iGrill 2 Smart grill thermometer, Fitbit Surge Smart Watch, and many more in the era of IoT. These devices bring the intelligence and smartness into the smart home and smart cities environment. These devices are producing and process huge volume of data every day. The storage and security of the data must be given a high priority while building the smart cities. Cloud storage and cloud security helping us to handle this scenario in effective manner.

Cloud computing is an innovative technology that provides "pay as you use" kind of services with scalability, security, and usability to users. Without any restrictions regarding device, time, and place, it enables the users to gain access to the data stored in cloud system. When the data is accessed by a user group, the cloud system enables simultaneous synchronization of data improving the working process of the team members. It also saves the investment due to expensive storage facilities. Though cloud delivers ease and convenience, it often comes with the cost of security and privacy problems. Even though the provider assures safety and security to our data, an inner mind never always believes their assurance. The data we outsource are physically stored in different locations and the customer cannot have full control over respective data. The users are anxious regarding the security of their cloud data as they afraid of the possible intrusion by hackers and they can gain access to the information present in the document. Thus, the customers prefer adopting the idea of encrypting the data to ensure confidentiality.

Encrypting data is a technique of transforming the plain text data into non-understandable cipher text data. The outcome thus obtained is completely irrelevant from the actual data and it appears to be random and meaningless. Only the person with authorization is able to read the original message. This authorization is provided by a passphrase called key. Key in encryption is similar to the key in a lock, where the data which is encrypted (locked) has to be decoded (opened) with the help of the key. Decryption is the process of retrieving the original message from the encrypted message with the help of key.

In symmetry key or secret key cryptography, similar cryptographic key is used for both encrypting, and decrypting the cipher text. Blowfish, DES(Data Encryption Standard), and Triple-DES algorithms are examples of generally used symmetry key encryption algorithms.

In asymmetry key or public key cryptography, two different cryptographic keys are used. One key which is public key for the encryption process, and another key which is a private key for the process of decryption. The two keys are different from one another but they are mathematically related and hence makes the process of decryption feasible. Some of the commonly used Asymmetric Encryption algorithms are RSA algorithm, ECDSA algorithm, Diffie – Hellman Key agreement protocol, etc. The type of algorithm being used in our model is DES which is a secret key encryption process.

Hashing is a process of converting the key into unknown, unformatted and retraceable values. A hash function when implemented in a right way is a one-way function, which means a text which is hashed cannot be reversed or converted back into the same original text.

Hashing is mostly used for message digest, password verification and linking a file with its path without the actual path being visible. It is also found in the Compiler operations to differentiate different keywords being used.

In this model, hashing is used for the purpose of storing the search token, file access key and password in their hashed form. We have made use of Salt with hash which makes sure that no two hash values match at any point of time. Salting also makes it difficult to use lookup tables, rainbow tables and dictionary based attacks for cracking the hash value.

We have encountered the above mentioned problems in our model by incorporating SALT along with hash which decreases the chance of two input text with same hash values. An efficient storage mechanism can be used to handle the one way working of hash function.

2. LITERATURE SURVEY

V. Chang and M. Ramachandran (2016) have proposed a approach called as CCAF(Cloud Computing Adoption Framework) to achieve security for the data stored in remote cloud. Their approach has capability to be modified to suit any specific security need while the data is stored in the cloud. BPMN (Business Process Modeling Notation) method is used by this approach for simulating the security provided to the data.

Dawn X. S. et. al (2000) have proposed pragmatic solutions for searching in the data after encryption. They have described about cryptographic frameworks to facilitate both searching and security of the data in cipher-text form. The final cryptographic system of the proposed idea has proven security aspects.

Islam S. J. et. al. (2019) has proposed SSCSC which is an easy and secure cryptographic system for cloud computation. It is a preferable and secured authenticating system for cryptography oriented cloud system. There is an automatic encrypting and KEYs switching technique in the cloud side of the proposed system. Initially, newly produced KEYs are not sent to the end-users. Authentication for the users of the cloud system are done in three stages. Cloud Service Provider (CSP) triggers the encrypting function either manually or automatically at any moment after the users signed out from the cloud system. This approach ensured more security for both data and in avoiding intruders from accessing restricted data even though they had proper authorization.

Run Xie et. al. (2016) have proposed an encrypted data accessing framework against the attacks of insider in a cloud computing system. The paper proposed efficient cipher text accessing model with the designated tester by using keyword mapping to resist and prevent against inside keyword attack.

Bakhtiari M. et. al. (2013) have proposed secured search on encrypted data of cloud system. The paper proposed SSAE (Secure Searchable Based Asymmetric Encryption) function that provided indistinction when Adaptive-Chosen Cipher attack is made. This suggested encrypting model has the ability to search into the data in encrypted form without the need of decryption. It has been proven mathematically that the model is both safe and secure. Though the data can be searched without decryption, this technique used public key for encryption so that there may be a chance of key word guessing attack.

Q. Zheng, et. al. (2014) has proposed VABKS (Verifiable Attribute-based Keyword Search) for searching into the cloud data which is in encrypted form. The idea behind the suggested cryptographic approach is to allow end users for accessing the data when their credentials satisfies the access rules of owners of the data.

Chen R. et. al. (2016) has proposed keyword based encrypted data searching algorithm along with dual-server based asymmetric key encryption for cloud computing system. The suggested PEKS (Public Key Encryption with Keyword Search) approach has provided another level of security for cloud computing applications.

Su H. et. al. (2017) has proposed an approach to nullify Keyword Guessing Attack. The idea behind the approach is O2ABKS which is online/offline attribute-based encryption algorithm with keyword search capability. Novel design of ABKS enable it to work in both online and offline mode to increase efficiency. To challenge the KGA attack, index generating function of ABKS needs access to the secret key of owner of the data.

Xu P. et. al. (2013) have suggested fuzzy keyword based searching with public-key encryption. It has been improved from PEKS to provide an enhanced security model for nullifying KGA attack, by ensuring secrecy of the keyword used in searching of data after encryption.

Boneh D. et. al. (2004) have suggested a new approach for keyword searching with Public Key Encryption. It has defined and devised a model for enabling an user to give input a keyword to the cloud server. Based on the keyword the server tests whether the keyword is contained in the file without knowing any other details of the file.

Liu. Q. et. al. (2011) have proposed an approach that ensure security in unsecured cloud systems. The approach, which is called as Reliable Re-Encryption, uses timestamp based re-encryption model. It enables the cloud systems for automatic re-encrypting of the data, after the intimation from internal clock. But Cloud with large data requires additional time to search data in it. This model failed to consider this problem.

Cao. N. et. al. (2014) have suggested PMRS (Privacy-Preserving Multi-Keyword Ranked Search) into cloud data which is in the form of encryption. This approach is supposed to incur less cost for communication and computation activities of known background and cryptographic process that creates encrypted data. This approach has utilized inner-product method for quantitative evaluation of affinity of ranking files. The very poor standard deviation of MRSE that weakens the privacy of keyword is the major disadvantage of PMRS.

Xu. W. et. al. (2019) have proposed asymmetric key encryption with approved keyword searching. In this approach the cryptographic key used is revocable. This kind of revocable key is used here mainly to tackle the problems of KGA attack. For efficient revocation, Identity Based Encryption (IBE) technology was used.

Zhang Y. et. al. (2021) have proposed Blockchain based keyword searching with asymmetric key encryption to tackle KGA attacks in cloud system. The idea behind this approach is regularly replacing the existing key by renewing it with fresh one on every cloud server to prevent compromising of the encryption key. It uses storing of used keyword in a general Blockchain approach to tackle KGA attacks done via online mode.

Yang Y. et. al. (2020) have suggested an efficient and secure searching of regular language or plain text in the cloud system. It has an encrypting algorithms with the capability of searching of regular language. This capability has ensured security and the preservation of secrecy in accessing the data from the cloud system by successfully repelling KGA attacks. DFA (Deterministic Finite Automata) oriented data retrieving and encrypting of regular language are major merits of this approach when comparing the existing ones.

Liang K. et. al. (2016) have proposed an approach for preserving the privacy and searching of regular language in a cloud computing system with data encryption. It is achieved with the help of novel design of functional encrypting and a searching function based on encryption. Very speedy searching mechanism when comparing with existing searching schemes based on asymmetric key is the distinctive merit

Figure 1. Overall architecture model

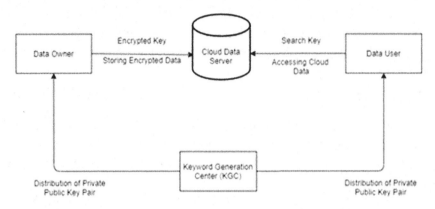

of this simple method. This merit is achieved mainly due to searching based on regular language. There are many works related to secured data storage in cloud (Indira Priya & Muthurajkumar, 2022; Muthurajkumar et al., 2022; Periasamy Nancy, 2020; Surya et al., 2022).

3. PROPOSED WORK

The figure. 1 shown in the overall architecture of the model. The number of users making use of cloud storage as a part of their working environment or personal use has been increasing and it is a field which has to be researched further upon. Though the rise in numbers doesn't mean the system is suitable for any user. There are people who feel that their data is not secure in a cloud environment as the storage server can be at any location which the user has no access to and he has no ideas how his data is handled and stored in the cloud server. Thus, it is crucial to provide foolproof security to the user data.

Hence, this project aims at providing a concept in small scale which can be scaled up and used for big data servers where the files are encrypted at the device using which the user uploads. The cloud will not be able to know what the contents of the file which is being outsourced. While downloading the file, the file has to be decrypted in the local system and saved in the desired location. Apart from this, making an approval based entry system with secure OTP verification makes the system much more secure from the point of being attacked by data intruders.

The system can be divided into four major modules namely,

- Data User

- Cloud Data Server
- Data Owner
- Keyword Generation Center (KGC)
  KGC:
  - Keyword Generation Center is responsible to generate and distribute the cryptographic keys of asymmetric encryption for every legitimate user.
  - It is also responsible for approving the Data Owners and Data Users who have registered to the service.

  Cloud Data Server:
  - The cloud data server is the place where the data or file given by owner of the data owner gets stored.
  - The file is stored in encrypted form thus the cloud server is not aware of what the contents of the file are and the contents are decrypted only after downloading from the server.
  - Thus the Cloud data server is isolated from the system but can be accessed using the Public, Private keys pairs.

  Data Owner:
  - It is the person who has the access to store sensitive data in the cloud data server.
  - He will upload a file to the cloud server which will be mapped with a search token.
  - When a data user requests for a file for access, the data user can authorize the person's request. Thus, the owner would send the search token for the requested file.
  - With the help of File ID, the owner will be able to delete the file stored in the database.

  Data User:
  - It is the person who gains the authorization from KGC and the Data owner to view files.
  - User will search for the file using the search token provided by owner of the data and requests for the file.
  - Once the data owner authorizes, he sends the private key for accessing the file which the user makes use of to download the encrypted file, decrypt it and store locally.
  - A data owner could also acts as data user and vise versa.

The workflow of data owner is depicted in figure. 2. The owner once upon registration has to be permitted by the KGC for the approval of his account. Once the account is approved, the owner is able to login to the system. An owner has the ability to upload file to the cloud server which will be encrypted before uploading the file. The owner can view his files present in the cloud. The owner can delete a file in the cloud server. The data owner too has the rights to provide access to users who request the file from the user. Thus, the owner upon his own will and risk, if he finds the user to be legit, he can also approve the user to access the file.

Data User

The workflow of data user is depicted in figure. 3. The user once upon registration has to be permitted by the KGC for the approval of his account. Once the account is approved, the user is able to login to the system. An end user could search for a file present on the cloud using the search token and the file id. Then the user can request the owner to ask his permission to access his files present in the cloud. Upon gaining the access, the user can be able to download the encrypted file into system which is then decrypted.

Figure 2. Workflow of data owner

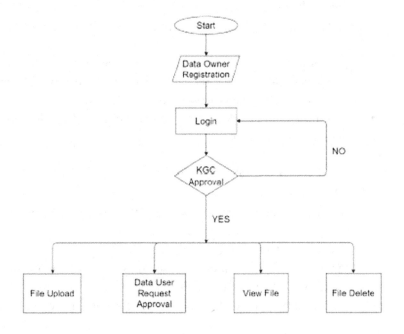

KGC

The KGC module is used to allocate the keys to the data user in terms of symmetric key way of working (explained in this model) and also for distribution of the Private Public cryptographic key pair in terms for public key encryption model. The entity is also used to approve the data owners and data users by checking them for any black marks or issues with the user or owner and approve their registration. It acts as the administrative entity in the model.

Figure 3. Workflow of data user

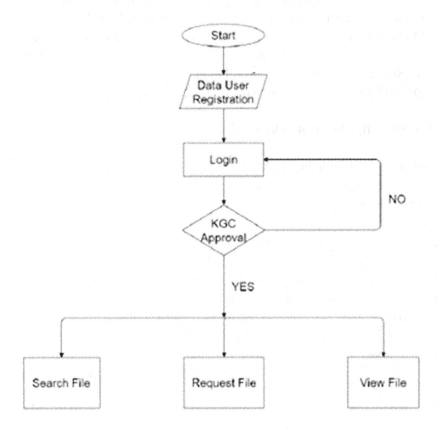

Cloud Data Server

The cloud data server in this model is used like a storage medium. The model is made in order for the cloud won't be able to aware of what are the contents of the file which is being outsourced. This makes the current implementation of cloud to be more reliable than any other implementation.

4. ENCRYPTION FOR SECURED STORAGE ALGORITHM

- Eclipse IDE for the system development.
  Ø The web pages are designed using JSP (Jakarta Servlet Pages).
  Ø The style sheet is designed using CSS (Cascading Style Sheets).
  Ø The communication with the database is established using Java Servlets.
- Xammp for hosting the project.
- MySQL is used as the database solution.
- Drive HQ is used as the cloud data server.

Cryptographic Hashing With Salt

Algorithm 1: Cryptographic Hashing with Salt
   Input: String denoting Password
   Output: Hash value of Password

```
 1:  import necessary packages
 2:  hexArray[] ¬ [0,1,2,3,4,5,6,7,8,9,A,B,C,D,E,F]
 3:  procedure Bytes_To_Hex(Byte_characters)
 4:    Hexa_characters [] ¬ length of Byte_characters * 2
 5:    for j and j < length of Byte_characters
 6:      V ¬ Byte_characters[j] & 0xFF
 7:      Hexa_characters[j*2] ¬ hexArray[v>>4]
 8:      Hexa_characters[j*2+1] ¬ hexArray[v & 0x0F]
 9:    end for
10:    Salt ¬ "123456"
11:    procedure hash(input)
12:      digest ¬ message digest of SHA-256
13:      digest ¬ add bytes of Salt
14:      digest ¬ add bytes of input
15:      output ¬ digest into bytes
16:      procedure Bytes_To_Hex(output)
```

The process of hashing with salt is used for the purpose of encrypting passwords and token text which is used for accessing the file. It is also used to generate key for the file uploaded by the owner and it serves to be the access key for the user to download the file. The input string is passed to the hash() function which chooses the message digest to be used for the implementation. The digest is updated with the byte values of Salt and byte values of the input string. The byte string is then passed to a function Bytes_To_Hex() which converts the bytes in binary form to hexadecimal. The final hash value will be of hexadecimal type and it is returned to the function call.

DES Ciphering

Algorithm 2: DES Ciphering for Encryption and Decryption
  Input: File which has to be encrypted or decrypted.
  Output: Ciphered file

```
1:  procedure Cipher (plainBlock[64], RoundKeys[16, 48],
cipherBlock[64])
2:     permute (64, 64, plainBlock, inBlock,
InitialPermutationTable)
3:     split (64, 32, inBlock, leftBlock, rightBlock)
4:     for (round = 1 to 16)
5:       mixer (leftBlock, rightBlock, RoundKeys[round])
6:         if (round!=16) swapper (leftBlock, rightBlock)
7:         end if
8:     end for
9:     combine (32, 64, leftBlock, rightBlock, outBlock)
10:    permute (64, 64, outBlock, cipherBlock,
FinalPermutationTable)
11:    procedure mixer (leftBlock[48], rightBlock[48],
RoundKey[48])
12:       copy (32, rightBlock, T1)
13:       function (T1, RoundKey, T2)
14:       exclusiveOr (32, leftBlock, T2, T3)
15:       copy (32, T3, rightBlock)
16:    procedure swapper (leftBlock[32], rigthBlock[32])
17:       copy (32, leftBlock, T)
18:       copy (32, rightBlock, leftBlock)
19:       copy (32, T, rightBlock)
20:    procedure function (inBlock[32], RoundKey[48],
```

153

```
outBlock[32])
21:     permute (32, 48, inBlock, T1,
ExpansionPermutationTable)
22:     exclusiveOr (48, T1, RoundKey, T2)
23:     substitute (T2, T3, SubstituteTables)
24:     permute (32, 32, T3, outBlock,
StraightPermutationTable)
25:   procedure substitute (inBlock[32], outBlock[48],
SubstitutionTables[8, 4, 16])
26:   for (i = 1 to 8)
27:       row ¬ 2 x inBlock[i x 6 + 1] + inBlock [i x 6 + 6]
28:       col ¬ 8 x inBlock[i x 6 + 2] + 4 x inBlock[i x 6 + 3]
+
29:       2 x inBlock[i x 6 + 4] + inBlock[i x 6 + 5]
30:       value = SubstitutionTables [i][row][col]
31:       outBlock[[i x 4 + 1] ¬ value / 8; value ¬ value mod 8
32:       outBlock[[i x 4 + 2] ¬ value / 4; value ¬ value mod 4
33:       outBlock[[i x 4 + 3] ¬ value / 2; value ¬ value mod 2
34:       outBlock[[i x 4 + 4] ¬ value
35:   end for
```

For the process of encrypting and decrypting the file, we made use of DES algorithm which is a symmetric algorithm. A symmetric algorithm makes use of only one key for both encrypting and decrypting processes. The 64 bit plain data input is given to an IP (Initial Permutation) module. Then IP process is done on the plain data. After that, the IP creates two permuted blocks which are equally half and called as RPT (Right Plain Text) and LPT (Left Plain Text). The next step is each RPT and LPT are subjected for 16 round encrypting procedure. Finally, RPT and LPT are combined, and FP (Final Permutation) is done one time on this block. The outcome of this entire procedure generates 64 bit encrypted data.

In our model, we have made use of SecretKeyFactory DES model. Here we would generate the secret key for the key which we have passed to the function. The key will be appended with a byte string called as initialization vector. A cipher object for the instance of DES algorithm with Cyclic Block Cipher and PKCS5 Padding is created. By mentioning the mode of operation either encryption and decryption, and passing the secret key and initialization vector the cipher is obtained. The cipher is then passed to the function call using a cipher stream.

Timer Based OTP Generation

The generator function is used to generate OTP for the system. The reminder function creates a timer object and schedules an event which calls the generator after a period of time as mentioned. Once the task is completed, the OTP will be replaced and the user cannot use the last generated OTP for further process.

Algorithm 3: Timer Based OTP Generation

Input: None

Output: Random Generated OTP

```
 1:  Server ¬ FTP server name
 2:  Port ¬ 21
 3:  User ¬ FTP Client User name
 4:  Password ¬ FTP Client Password
 5:  Filename ¬ name of the file to be uploaded
 6:  RemoteFile ¬ Server side location
 7:  FTPClient ftp()
 8:  ftp.connect(Server,Port)
 9:  ftp.login(User,Password)
10:  ftp.setFiletype(FTP.BINARY_FILE_TYPE)
11:  InputStream in ¬ FileInputStream(Filename.getabspath())
12:  ftp.storeFile(RemoteFile, in)
```

FTP Program for File Upload

The FTP client i.e. the local system is connected to the FTP server through port number 21. It requires the user name and password of the account to be used in the FTP server for login and access of files. The file to be uploaded is read using a file input stream object and the object is used to store the file in the remote location.

FTP Program for File Download

The FTP client i.e. the local system is connected to the FTP server through port number 21. It requires the user name and password of the account to be used in the FTP server for login and access of files. The file to be downloaded from the data server is read using a file output stream object and the object is used to store the file in the local storage location.

```
 1:    Server ¬ FTP server name
 2:    Port ¬ 21
 3:    User ¬ FTP Client User name
 4:    Password ¬ FTP Client Password
 5:    RemoteFile ¬ name of the file to be downloaded from data
server
 6:    Filename ¬ local machine location
 7:    FTPClient ftp()
 8:    ftp.connect(Server,Port)
 9:    ftp.login(User,Password)
10:    ftp.setFiletype(FTP.BINARY_FILE_TYPE)
11:    OutputStream out ¬ FileOutputStream(Filename.getabspath())
12:    ftp.storeFile(RemoteFile, out)
```

5. RESULTS AND DISCUSSIONS

The working of the system as explained in the implementation is proved to work properly in every possible case tested. The result messages and the emails received upon the successful registration, request of search token, and the access key are given below.

We have tried using various hashing algorithms to select the right one for our model. The most commonly used industry standard algorithm for hashing is SHA – 256 that provides either 64 digit hexadecimal value or 256 bit hash value. The graph in Figure. 4 shows the data relevant to the performance of the algorithms with different string length. The performance measure is done by testing the algorithm for 10 times for each string length and the average of them is taken and the graph is plotted (Table. 1).

Table 1. Hash algorithms comparison

	Time in Milliseconds for String of Varied Length					
Hash Algorithm	**5**	**8**	**16**	**32**	**64**	**128**
MD2	13	14	15	15	14	17
MD5	14	16	15	17	17	19
SHA – 1	16	19	20	16	18	20
SHA – 256	16	17	16	19	21	19
SHA – 512	15	16	18	17	18	18

Figure 4. Hash algorithms comparison

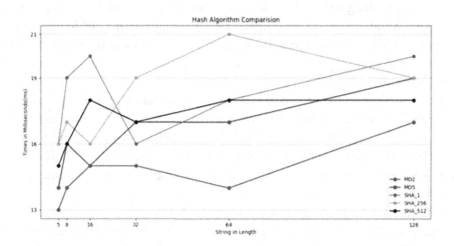

Table 2. Data encryption and decryption rate

File Size (in MB)	Time for Encryption (in ms)	Time for Decryption (in ms)
1	402.75	612.25
2	683.75	1144.75
5	1700.25	3363.5
10	3692.25	5208.25
20	6586	11364.5

Figure 5. Data encryption and decryption rate

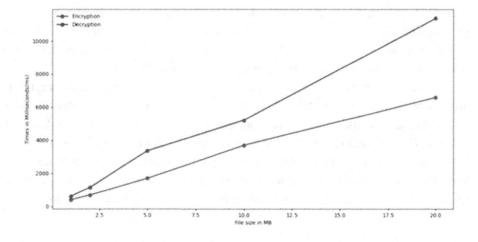

157

As from the graph in Figure. 4 and Table. 1. We can see that MD2 has an overall low time for hashing string of any length. This is because of the ease in use of the algorithm. Similar to MD5 takes less time for hashing strings of longer length. Though the MD hash algorithms are faster, but in real application they don't stand good for good security purposes. They are easily broken using brute force attempts of passwords.

The SHA algorithms prove to be secured than MD5 and MD2 algorithms though they consume some extra time. We have made use of SHA – 256 in our model. This is because we wanted to retain a 64 hexadecimal digit hash value for our process which has to be used as the key for DES algorithm for file encryption. The use of SHA – 512 could provide higher security but will increase the complexity of the overall model.

When the files have to be uploaded and downloaded from the server after encryption or decryption, the time for encrypt and decrypt process is overhead for the existing server time. So we tried to find how much overhead is being added when the size of the file increases. The graph from the Figure. 5 and Table. 2, shown that the time change is linear and time increases with increase in file size. Thus, larger files will have additional time for encryption and decryption in addition to the upload and download speed of the files.

The rate of upload and download will differ for every possible case as the network connection plays an important role in the file upload and download process. Thus, the data obtained by using the upload and download times will not be reliable to come to conclusion or take it into comparison.

6. CONCLUSION

We have come up with the application for smart homes/smart cities for storing encrypted data and decrypting after download which works only in a local host system. The file server can be accessed from different system, but the application is tied to the single host i.e. localhost. We have presented a robust approach of an advanced smart home based cities concept and implementation.

Our future works would include, trying to improve the encryption and decryption process by making use of much more powerful algorithms implemented in more efficient way. We could try to host the application and making it usable from different devices. This application could also be built into an Android application if such functionality is required for a mobile device. We could improve the application features like viewing the file from the application without downloading if the access is given, try to bring multi user working in a single file to bring a team based environment.

IslamS. J.ChaudhuryZ. H.IslamS. (2019). A Simple and Secured Cryptography System of Cloud Computing. 2019 IEEE Canadian Conference of Electrical and Computer Engineering (CCECE), 1-3. doi:10.1109/CCECE.2019.8861845

REFERENCES

Bakhtiari, M., Nateghizad, M., & Zainal, A. (2013). Secure Search Over Encrypted Data in Cloud Computing. *2013 International Conference on Advanced Computer Science Applications and Technologies*, 290-295. 10.1109/ACSAT.2013.64

Boneh, Crescenzo, & Ostrovsky. (2004). Public Key Encryption with Keyword Search. In *Advances in Cryptology – EUROCRYPT 2004*. Springer Berlin Heidelberg.

Cao, N., Wang, C., Li, M., Ren, K., & Lou, W. (2014, January). Privacy-Preserving Multi- Keyword Ranked Search over Encrypted Cloud Data. *IEEE Transactions on Parallel and Distributed Systems*, 25(1), 222–233. doi:10.1109/TPDS.2013.45

Chang & Ramachandran. (2016). Towards Achieving Data Security with the Cloud Computing Adoption Framework. *IEEE Transactions on Services Computing, 9*(1), 138-151. . doi:10.1109/TSC.2015.2491281

Chen, R., Mu, Y., Yang, G., Guo, F., & Wang, X. (2016, April). Dual-Server Public-Key Encryption With Keyword Search for Secure Cloud Storage. *IEEE Transactions on Information Forensics and Security, 11*(4), 789–798. doi:10.1109/TIFS.2015.2510822

Dawn Xiaoding Song, Wagner, & Perrig. (2000). Practical techniques for searches on encrypted data. *Proceeding 2000 IEEE Symposium on Security and Privacy*, 44-55. 10.1109/SECPRI.2000.848445

Indira Priya, P., & Muthurajkumar, S. (2022). Data Fault Detection in Wireless Sensor Networks Using Machine Learning Techniques. Wireless Personal Communications, 122(3), 2441–2462.

Liang, K., Huang, X., Guo, F., & Liu, J. K. (2016, October). Privacy-Preserving and Regular Language Search Over Encrypted Cloud Data. *IEEE Transactions on Information Forensics and Security, 11*(10), 2365–2376. doi:10.1109/TIFS.2016.2581316

Liu, Q., Tan, C. C., Wu, J., & Wang, G. (2011). Reliable Re-Encryption in Unreliable Clouds. *2011 IEEE Global Telecommunications Conference - GLOBECOM 2011*, 1-5. 10.1109/GLOCOM.2011.6133609

Muthurajkumar, S., Karthikeyan, C. A., Pradeep, K., & Hariharan, A. (2022). Privacy-Preserving Dynamic Task Scheduling for Autonomous Vehicles. In *Proceedings of 2nd International Conference on Artificial Intelligence: Advances and Applications. Algorithms for Intelligent Systems*. Springer. 10.1007/978-981-16-6332-1_55

Periasamy Nancy, S. (2020, March). Intrusion Detection Using Dynamic Feature Selection and Fuzzy Temporal Decision Tree Classification for Wireless Sensor Networks. *IET Communications*, *14*(5), 888–895. doi:10.1049/iet-com.2019.0172

Su, H., Zhu, Z., & Sun, L. (2017). Online/offline attribute-based encryption with keyword search against Keyword Guessing Attack. *2017 3rd IEEE International Conference on Computer and Communications (ICCC)*, 1487-1492. 10.1109/CompComm.2017.8322788

Surya, V. J., Muthurajkumar, S., Jitiendran, K., Ajithkumar, K., & Ibrahim, S. M. (2022). A Web Based Application for Optimization of Less than Truckload Problem. *2022 IEEE World Conference on Applied Intelligence and Computing (AIC)*, 813-817. 10.1109/AIC55036.2022.9848847

Xie, R., Xu, C., Li, F., & He, C. (2016). Ciphertext retrieval against insider attacks for cloud storage. *2016 2nd IEEE International Conference on Computer and Communications (ICCC)*, 202-206. 10.1109/CompComm.2016.7924693

Xu, Dong, Cao, & Shen. (2019). Revocable Public Key Encryption with Authorized Keyword Search. *2019 IEEE 3rd Information Technology, Networking, Electronic and Automation Control Conference (ITNEC)*, 857-860. . doi:10.1109/ITNEC.2019.8729491

Xu, P., Jin, H., Wu, Q., & Wang, W. (2013, November). Public-Key Encryption with Fuzzy Keyword Search: A Provably Secure Scheme under Keyword Guessing Attack. *IEEE Transactions on Computers*, *62*(11), 2266–2277. doi:10.1109/TC.2012.215

Yang, Zheng, Rong, & Guo. (2020). Efficient Regular Language Search for Secure Cloud Storage. *IEEE Transactions on Cloud Computing*, *8*(3), 805-818. . doi:10.1109/TCC.2018.2814594

Zhang, Y., Xu, C., Ni, J., Li, H., & Shen, X. S. (2021, October 1). Blockchain-assisted Public-key Encryption with Keyword Search against Keyword Guessing Attacks for Cloud Storage. *IEEE Transactions on Cloud Computing*, *9*(4), 1335–1348. Advance online publication. doi:10.1109/TCC.2019.2923222

Zheng, Q., Xu, S., & Ateniese, G. (2014). VABKS: Verifiable attribute-based keyword search over outsourced encrypted data. *IEEE INFOCOM 2014 - IEEE Conference on Computer Communications,* 522-530. 10.1109/INFOCOM.2014.6847976

Compilation of References

Abir, S. M. A. A., Anwar, A., Choi, J., & Kayes, A. S. (2021). IoT-Enabled Smart Energy Grid: Applications and Challenges. IEEE.

Abramowski, M. (2018, April). Application of data video recorder in reconstruction of road accidents. In *2018 XI International Science-Technical Conference Automotive Safety* (pp. 1-6). IEEE. 10.1109/AUTOSAFE.2018.8373327

Adamus, A., Šancer, J., Guřanová, P., & Zubíček, V. (2011). An investigation of the factors associated with interpretation of mine atmosphere for spontaneous combustion in coal mines. *Fuel Processing Technology, 92*(3), 663–670. doi:10.1016/j.fuproc.2010.11.025

Adford, A., Metz, L., & Chintala, S. (2015). Unsupervised representation learning with deep convolutional generative adversarial networks. arXiv preprint arXiv:1511.06434.

Ahmadzadeh, Parr, & Zhao. (2021). *A Review on Communication Aspects of Demand Response Management for Future 5G IoT-Based Smart Grids.* Academic Press.

Aishwarya, A. R., Rai, A., Charitha, Prasanth, M. A., & Savitha, S. C. (2015). An IoT Based Accident Prevention & Tracking System for Night Drivers. *International Journal of Innovative Research in Computer and Communication Engineering, 3*(4).

Al Dakheel, J., Del Pero, C., Aste, N., & Leonforte, F. (2020). Smart Buildings Features and Key Performance Indicators: A Review. *Sustainable Cities and Society, 61*, 102328. doi:10.1016/j.scs.2020.102328

Al-Zaidy, R., Fung, B. C., Youssef, A. M., & Fortin, F. (2012). Mining criminal networks from unstructured text documents. *Digital Investigation, 8*(3-4), 147–160. doi:10.1016/j.diin.2011.12.001

Amrish, Akash, Sukhi, & Jabamani. (n.d.). *Fingerprint and RFID Based Electronic Voting System.* EAM Engineer Department of Electrical and Electronics Engineering, R.M.K. Engineering College.

Apostolopoulos, V., Giorka, P., Martinopoulos, G., Angelakoglou, K., Kourtzanidis, K., & Nikolopoulos, N. (2022). Smart readiness indicator evaluation and cost estimation of smart retrofitting scenarios - A comparative case-study in European residential buildings. *Sustainable Cities and Society, 82*, 103921. doi:10.1016/j.scs.2022.103921

Araujo, J., Elson, R., & Anselmo, M. (2017). Assessment of the Impact of Microgrid Control Strategies in the Power Distribution Reliability Indices. *Journal of Control Automation and Electric System. .* doi:10.1007/s40313-017-0299-x

Arbab-Zavar, B., Palacios-Garcia, E., Vasquez, J., & Guerrero, J. (2019). Smart inverters for microgrid applications: A review. *Energies*, *12*(5), 840. doi:10.3390/en12050840

Arcos, A. (2021). An Energy Management System Design Using Fuzzy Logic Control: Smoothing the Grid Power Profile of a Residential Electro-Thermal Microgrid. *IEEE Access : Practical Innovations, Open Solutions*, *1*(17), 25172–25188. Advance online publication. doi:10.1109/ACCESS.2021.3056454

Arunkumari, T., & Indragandhi, V. (2017). An overview of high voltage conversion ratio DC-DC converter configurations used in DC micro-grid architectures. *Renewable & Sustainable Energy Reviews*, *77*, 670–687. doi:10.1016/j.rser.2017.04.036

Atanasiu, B., Despret, C., Economidou, M., Maio, J., Nolte, I., & Rapf, O. (2011). *Europe's Buildings under the Microscope, A Country-by-Country Review of the Energy Performance of Buildings, Buildings Performance Institute Europe*. BPIE.

Avila, C., Wu, T., & Lester, E. (2014). Petrographic characterization of coals as a tool to detect spontaneous combustion potential. *Fuel*, *125*, 173–182. doi:10.1016/j.fuel.2014.01.042

Bakhtiari, M., Nateghizad, M., & Zainal, A. (2013). Secure Search Over Encrypted Data in Cloud Computing. *2013 International Conference on Advanced Computer Science Applications and Technologies*, 290-295. 10.1109/ACSAT.2013.64

Bertheau, P., Hoffmann, M. M., Eras-Almeida, A., & Blechinger, P. (2020). *Assessment of Microgrid Potential in Southeast Asia Based on the Application of Geospatial and Microgrid Simulation and Planning Sustainable Energy Solutions for Remote Areas in the Tropics. In Green Energy and Technology*. Springer. doi:10.1007/978-3-030-41952-37

Betis, G., Cassandras, C. G., & Nucci, C. A. (2018). Smart cities. *Proceedings of the IEEE*, *106*(4), 513–517. doi:10.1109/JPROC.2018.2812998

Bhamidi, L., & Sivasubramani, S. (2019). Optimal Planning and Operational Strategy of a Residential Microgrid with Demand Side Management. *IEEE Systems Journal*, *1*(9). . doi:10.1109/JSYST.2019.2918410

Bharathi, G., & Padmanabhan, T. S. (2022). Planning and Optimization of Energy Scheduling in Cohesive Renewable Energy Microgrid to Meet Electric Load Demand of an Educational Institution. *Journal of Electrical Engineering & Technology*, *17*(6), 3207–3221. doi:10.100742835-022-01138-8

Bhatt., N., Sondhi, R., Arora, S. (2022). Droop Control Strategies for Microgrid: A Review. In *Advances in Renewable Energy and Electric Vehicles*. Springer. https://doi.org//978-981-16-1642-612 doi:10.1007

Bhattacharjee, S., Roy, P., Ghosh, S., Misra, S., & Obaidat, M. S. (2012). Wireless sensor network-based fire detection, alarming, monitoring and prevention system for Bord-and-Pillar coal mines. *Journal of Systems and Software, 85*(3), 571–581. doi:10.1016/j.jss.2011.09.015

Bialasiewicz. (n.d.). *Renewable Energy Systems With Photovoltaic Power Generators: Operation and Modeling.* Academic Press.

Bi, S., & Zhang, Y. J. A. (2017). Graph-based cyber security analysis of state estimation in smart power grid. *IEEE Communications Magazine, 55*(4), 176–183. doi:10.1109/MCOM.2017.1600210C

Boehm, V. A., Kim, J., & Hong, J. W. K. (2018). Holistic tracking of products on the blockchain using NFC and verified users. In *Information Security Applications: 18th International Conference, WISA 2017, Jeju Island, Korea, August 24-26, 2017, Revised Selected Papers 18* (pp. 184-195). Springer International Publishing. 10.1007/978-3-319-93563-8_16

Boneh, Crescenzo, & Ostrovsky. (2004). Public Key Encryption with Keyword Search. In *Advances in Cryptology – EUROCRYPT 2004.* Springer Berlin Heidelberg.

Botelle, R., Bhavsar, V., Kadra-Scalzo, G., Mascio, A., Williams, M. V., Roberts, A., Velupillai, S., & Stewart, R. (2022). Can natural language processing models extract and classify instances of interpersonal violence in mental healthcare electronic records: An applied evaluative study. *BMJ Open, 12*(2), e052911. doi:10.1136/bmjopen-2021-052911 PMID:35172999

Brock, A., Donahue, J., & Simonyan, K. (2021). BigGAN: Large Scale GAN Training for High Fidelity Natural Image Synthesis. *International Conference on Learning Representations.*

Byun, J. Y., Nasridinov, A., & Park, Y. H. (2014). Internet of things for smart crime detection. *Contemporary Engineering Sciences, 7*(15), 749–754. doi:10.12988/ces.2014.4685

Cachin, C. (2016, July). *Architecture of the hyperledger blockchain fabric* [Workshop session]. Distributed cryptocurrencies and consensus ledgers, IBM Research – Zurich, CH-8803 Ruschlikon, Switzerland. https://theblockchaintest.com/uploads/resources/IBM%20Resear ch%20-%20Architecture%20of%20the%20Hyperledger%20Blockchain% 20Fabric%20-%202016%20-%20July.pdf

Cano Basave, A. E., He, Y., Liu, K., & Zhao, J. (2013). *A weakly supervised bayesian model for violence detection in social media.* Academic Press.

Cao, N., Wang, C., Li, M., Ren, K., & Lou, W. (2014, January). Privacy-Preserving Multi-Keyword Ranked Search over Encrypted Cloud Data. *IEEE Transactions on Parallel and Distributed Systems, 25*(1), 222–233. doi:10.1109/TPDS.2013.45

Carli, R., Cavone, G., Ben Othman, S., & Dotoli, M. (2020). IoT Based Architecture for Model Predictive Control of HVAC Systems in Smart Buildings. *Sensors (Basel), 20*(3), 781. doi:10.339020030781 PMID:32023965

Caro, M. P., Ali, M. S., Vecchio, M., & Giaffreda, R. (2018, May). Blockchain-based traceability in Agri-Food supply chain management: A practical implementation. In *2018 IoT Vertical and Topical Summit on Agriculture-Tuscany (IOT Tuscany)* (pp. 1-4). IEEE. doi:10.1109/IOT-TUSCANY.2018.8373021

ChakrabortyS.BejD.RoyD.MahammadS. A. (2021). Designing of a Biometric Fingerprint Scanner-Based, Secure, and Low-Cost Electronic Voting Machine for India. Preprints. doi:10.20944/preprints202111.0177.v1

Chang & Ramachandran. (2016). Towards Achieving Data Security with the Cloud Computing Adoption Framework. *IEEE Transactions on Services Computing, 9*(1), 138-151. . doi:10.1109/TSC.2015.2491281

Changliang, L., Yanqun, W., Kang, B., & Weiliang, L. (2017). Energy management strategy research for residential microgrid considering virtual energy storage system at demand side. *IEEE International Conference on Electronic Measurement Instruments (ICEMI)*, 273-280, 10.1109/ICEMI.2017.8265790

Che, T., Li, Y., Zhang, R., Hjelm, R. D., Li, W., Song, Y., & Bengio, Y. (2017). Maximum-likelihood augmented discrete generative adversarial networks. arXiv preprint arXiv:1702.07983.

Chen, T.-H., Wu, P.-H., & Chiou, Y.-C. (2004). An early fire-detection method based on image processing. *Image Processing. ICIP'04. 2004 International Conference on*, 1707-1710.

Chen, R., Mu, Y., Yang, G., Guo, F., & Wang, X. (2016, April). Dual-Server Public-Key Encryption With Keyword Search for Secure Cloud Storage. *IEEE Transactions on Information Forensics and Security, 11*(4), 789–798. doi:10.1109/TIFS.2015.2510822

Church, C., Morsi, W. G., El-Hawary, M. E., Diduch, C. P., & Chang, L. C. (2011). Voltage collapse detection using Ant Colony Optimization for smart grid applications. *Electric Power Systems Research, 81*(8), 1723–1730. doi:10.1016/j.epsr.2011.03.010

COM. (2011). *112 Final. A Roadmap for Moving to a Competitive Low Carbon Economy in 2050.* European Commission.

COM. (2016). *763 Final. Accelerating Clean Energy Innovation.* European Commission.

COM. (2016). *860 Final, Annex 1. Accelerating Clean Energy in Buildings.* European Commission.

Cooper, M. C., Lambert, D. M., & Pagh, J. D. (1997). Supply chain management: More than a new name for logistics. *International Journal of Logistics Management, 8*(1), 1–14. doi:10.1108/09574099710805556

Cunbao, D., Jiren, W., Xuefeng, W., & Hanzhong, D. (2010). Spontaneous coal combustion producing carbon dioxide and water. *Mining Science and Technology (China), 20*(1), 82–87. doi:10.1016/S1674-5264(09)60165-4

David, Ijomanta, Gil-Ozoudeh, & Chukwuebuka. (2014). A Biometric based Software Solution for E-Voting using networking. *Scholars Journal of Engineering and Technology, 2*, 874–881.

Dawn Xiaoding Song, Wagner, & Perrig. (2000). Practical techniques for searches on encrypted data. *Proceeding 2000 IEEE Symposium on Security and Privacy*, 44-55. 10.1109/SECPRI.2000.848445

Deriche, M. (2019). *An IOT based sensing system for remote monitoring of PV panels*. IEEE.

Directive (EU) 2018/844 of the European Parliament and of the Council of 30 May 2018 Amending Directive 2010/31/EU on the Energy Performance of Buildings Directive 2012/27/EU on Energy Efficiency; L156/75; Official Journal of the European Union: Brussels, Belgium, 2018

Directive 2002/91/EU of the European Parliament and of the Council of 16 December 2002 on the Energy Performance of Buildings; L1/65; Official Journal of the European Union: Brussels, Belgium, 2003

Directive 2009/28/EC of the European Parliament and of the Council of 23 April 2009 on the Promotion of the Use of Energy from Renewable Sources; L140/16-62; Official Journal of the European Union: Brussels, Belgium, 2009.

Directive 2010/31/EU of the European Parliament and of the Council of 19 May 2010 on the energy performance of buildings; L153/13; Official Journal of the European Union: Brussels, Belgium, 2010

Directive 2012/27/EU of the European Parliament and of the Council of 25 October 2012 on Energy Efficiency; L315/1-56; Official Journal of the European Union: Brussels, Belgium, 2012.

Dong, N., Chang, J-F., Wu, A-G., & Gao, Z-K. (2019). *A novel convolutional neural network framework based solar irradiance prediction method.* Elsevier.

Effective Control Strategy in Microgrid. (n.d.). In *International Conference on Intelligent Computing and Smart Communication Algorithms for Intelligent Systems.* Springer. https://doi.org/10.1007/ 978-981-15-0633-8 94

ENER/C3/2016-554. VITO. Support for Setting up a Smart Readiness Indicator for Buildings and Related Impact Assessment. (2020). Available online: https://smartreadinessindicator.eu/

Energybiz. (n.d.). http://www.energybiz.com/article/11/11/prevention-and-control-module-spontaneous-combustion-coal-coal-yards

Final Report, S. R. I. (2020). *European Commission, Final report on the technical support to the development of a smart readiness indicator for buildings.* Publications Office of the European Union.

FinExtra. (2017, July 19). *Borsa Italiana partners IBM on securities data blockchain system for SMEs.* The finextra blog. https://www.finextra.com/newsarticle/30848/borsa-italiana-partners-ibm-on-securities-data-blockchain-system-for-smes

Fokaides, P. A., Panteli, C., & Panayidou, A. (2020). How are the smart readiness indicators expected to affect the energy performance of buildings: First evidence and perspectives. *Sustainability (Basel)*, *12*(22), 9496. doi:10.3390u12229496

Gandhi, N. (2014). *Study on Security of Online Voting System Using Biometrics and Steganography.* Academic Press.

Gao & Wai. (n.d.). *A novel fault identification method for photovoltaic array via convolutional neural network and residual gated recurrent unit.* Academic Press.

Gentles, D. S., & Sankaranarayanan, S. (2012). Application of Biometrics in Mobile Voting. *International Journal of Computer Network and Information Security.*, *4*(7), 57–68. Advance online publication. doi:10.5815/ijcnis.2012.07.07

Gretton, A., Borgwardt, K. M., Rasch, M. J., Schölkopf, B., & Smola, A. (2012). A kernel two-sample test. *Journal of Machine Learning Research*, *13*(1), 723–773.

Gujanatti, Tolanur, Nemagoud, Reddy, & Neelagund. (2015). A Finger Print based Voting System. *International Journal of Engineering Research Technology, 4*(5). doi:10.17577/IJERTV4IS050948

Guo, J., Lu, S., Cai, H., Zhang, W., Yu, Y., & Wang, J. (2018, April). Long text generation via adversarial training with leaked information. *Proceedings of the AAAI Conference on Artificial Intelligence*, *32*(1). doi:10.1609/aaai.v32i1.11957

Hafeez, G., Wadud, Z., Khan, I., Khan, I., Shafiq, Z., Usman, M., & Khan, M. (2020). Efficient energy management of IoT-enabled smart homes under price-based demand response program in smart grid. *Sensors (Basel)*, *20*(11), 3155. doi:10.339020113155 PMID:32498402

Hajimiragha, A. H., Gomis-Bellmunt, O., Saeedifard, M., & Palma-Behnke, R. (2014). Trends in Microgrid Control. *IEEE Transactions on Smart Grid*, *5*(4), 1905–1919. doi:10.1109/TSG.2013.2295514

Heinen, S., Elzinga, D., Kim, S. K., & Ikeda, Y. (2011). Impact of Smart grid technology on peak load to 2050. International Energy Agency.

Hofer, J., Svetozarevic, B., & Schlueter, A. (2017). Hybrid AC/DC building microgrid for solar PV and battery storage integration. *IEEE Second International Conference on DC Microgrids (ICDCM)*, 188-191. 10.1109/ICDCM.2017.8001042

IBM. (2017). *Maersk and IBM unveil first industry-wide cross border supply chain solution on blockchain* [Press release]. www-03.ibm.com/press/us/en/ pressrelease/51712.wss

IEA EBC Annex 67. (n.d.). Available online: http://www.annex67.org/

Indira Priya, P., & Muthurajkumar, S. (2022). Data Fault Detection in Wireless Sensor Networks Using Machine Learning Techniques. Wireless Personal Communications, 122(3), 2441–2462.

Janhunen, E., Pulkka, L., Säynäjoki, A., & Junnila, S. (2019). Applicability of the Smart Readiness Indicator for Cold Climate Countries. *Buildings*, *9*(4), 102. doi:10.3390/buildings9040102

Jones, S. G. (2022). *The evolution of domestic terrorism. Statement before the House Judiciary Subcommittee on Crime.* Terrorism, and Homeland Security CSIS-Center for Strategic and International Studies Washington.

Jun, D., Jingyu, Z., Yanni, Z., & Ruilin, G. (2014). Study on Coal Spontaneous Combustion Characteristic Temperature of Growth Rate Analysis. *Procedia Engineering*, *84*, 796–805. doi:10.1016/j.proeng.2014.10.498

Kamilaris, A., Fonts, A., & Prenafeta-Boldú, F. X. (2019). The rise of blockchain technology in agriculture and food supply chains. *Trends in Food Science & Technology*, *91*, 640–652. doi:10.1016/j.tifs.2019.07.034

Karazeev, A. (2017). *Generative adversarial networks (GANs): Engine and applications*. https://blog. statsbot. co/generativeadversarial-networks-ga ns-engine-and-applications-f96291965b47

Karim, M. (2019). State of the art in bigdata applications in microgrid: A review. *Advanced Engineering Informatics*, *100945*. Advance online publication. doi:10.1016/j.aei.2019.100945

Karras, T., Laine, S., Aittala, M., Hellsten, J., Lehtinen, J., & Aila, T. (2021). StyleGAN2: Analyzing and Improving the Image Quality of StyleGAN. In *Proceedings of the IEEE/CVF Conference on Computer Vision and Pattern Recognition (CVPR)* (pp. 10665-10675). Academic Press.

Khairnar, S. K., & Kharat, R. (2016). Survey on Secure Online Voting System. *International Journal of Computer Applications*, *134*(13), 19–21. doi:10.5120/ijca2016908144

Khalifeh, H., Moran, P., Borschmann, R., Dean, K., Hart, C., Hogg, J., Osborn, D., Johnson, S., & Howard, L. M. (2015). Domestic and sexual violence against patients with severe mental illness. *Psychological Medicine*, *45*(4), 875–886. doi:10.1017/S0033291714001962 PMID:25180908

Kim, M., Hilton, B., Burks, Z., & Reyes, J. (2018, November). Integrating blockchain, smart contract-tokens, and IoT to design a food traceability solution. In *2018 IEEE 9th annual information technology, electronics and mobile communication conference (IEMCON)* (pp. 335-340). IEEE. https://doi: 10.1109/IEMCON.2018.8615007

Kim, C. J., & Sohn, C. H. (2016). Effects of wind barrier design and closed coal storage on spontaneous ignition of coal stockpiles. *Journal of Loss Prevention in the Process Industries*, *40*, 529–536. doi:10.1016/j.jlp.2016.02.009

Kim, S. Y., Lim, J., Na, T., & Kim, M. (2019). Video Super-Resolution Based on 3D-CNNS with Consideration of Scene Change. *2019 IEEE International Conference on Image Processing (ICIP)*, 2831-2835. 10.1109/ICIP.2019.8803297

Kinoshita, H., Yagi, M., Takahashi, S., & Hagiwara, T. (2022, July). A Method for Classifying Road Narrowing Conditions Based on Features of Surrounding Vehicles and Piled Snow in In-vehicle Camera Videos. In *2022 IEEE International Conference on Consumer Electronics-Taiwan* (pp. 299-300). IEEE. 10.1109/ICCE-Taiwan55306.2022.9868980

Krug, E. G., Mercy, J. A., Dahlberg, L. L., & Zwi, A. B. (2002). The world report on violence and health. *Lancet*, *360*(9339), 1083–1088. doi:10.1016/S0140-6736(02)11133-0 PMID:12384003

Kuang, D., Brantingham, P. J., & Bertozzi, A. L. (2017). Crime topic modeling. *Crime Science*, *6*(1), 1–20. doi:10.118640163-017-0074-0

Kumar & Begum. (2011). A Novel design of Electronic Voting System Using Fingerprint. *International Journal of Innovative Technology Creative Engineering, 1.*

Kumar, M., Minai, A. F., Khan, A. A., & Kumar, S. (2000). *IoT based Energy Management System for Smart Grid.* IEEE.

Kyoto Protocol, United Nations Climate Change. (n.d.). *Kyoto Protocol—Targets for the First Commitment Period.* Available online: https://unfccc.int/process/the-kyoto-protocol

Lamb, A. M., Alias Parth Goyal, A. G., Zhang, Y., Zhang, S., Courville, A. C., & Bengio, Y. (2016). Professor forcing: A new algorithm for training recurrent networks. Advances in Neural Information Processing Systems, 29.

Lin, K., Li, D., He, X., Zhang, Z., & Sun, M. T. (2017). Adversarial ranking for language generation. *Advances in Neural Information Processing Systems*, 30.

Lin, Q., Wang, H., Pei, X., & Wang, J. (2019). Food safety traceability system based on blockchain and EPCIS. *IEEE Access : Practical Innovations, Open Solutions*, 7, 20698–20707. doi:10.1109/ACCESS.2019.2897792

Liu, Y., Guo, L., Wang, C., & Hou, R. (2021). Application of Optimization Techniques in the Design and Operation of Microgrid. In Design, Control, and Operation of Microgrids in Smart Grids Power Systems. Springer. 10.1007/978-3-030-64631-83

Liu, J., Wang, W., Zhang, Y., & Xu, X. (2019). Energy Management for Households Considering Uncertainty in Solar Irradiance with Various Probability Distribution. *Journal of Electrical Engineering & Technology*, *14*(5), 1943–1956. doi:10.100742835-019-00243-5

Makhzani, A., Shlens, J., Jaitly, N., Goodfellow, I., & Frey, B. (2016). Adversarial Autoencoders. In *Proceedings of the 33rd International Conference on Machine Learning (ICML)* (pp. 1558-1566). Academic Press.

Mallidi, S. K. R., & Vineela, V. V. (2018). IoT based smart vehicle monitoring system. *Int. J. Adv. Res. Comput. Sci*, *9*(2), 738–741. doi:10.26483/ijarcs.v9i2.5870

Mao, Z., Zhu, H., Zhao, X., Sun, J., & Wang, Q. (2013). Experimental study on characteristic parameters of coal spontaneous combustion. *Procedia Engineering*, *62*, 1081–1086. doi:10.1016/j.proeng.2013.08.164

Märzinger, T., & Österreicher, D. (2019). Supporting the Smart Readiness Indicator—A Methodology to Integrate a Quantitative Assessment of the Load Shifting Potential of Smart Buildings. *Energies*, *12*(10), 1955. doi:10.3390/en12101955

Ma, Y., Zhou, Y., Zhang, J., & Piao, C. (2018). Economic Dispatch of Islanded Microgrid Considering a Cooperative Strategy Between Diesel Generator and Battery Energy Storage System. *Journal of Shanghai Jiaotong University (Science)*, *23*(5), 593–599. doi:10.100712204-018-1988-8

Mensa, E., Colla, D., Dalmasso, M., Giustini, M., Mamo, C., Pitidis, A., & Radicioni, D. P. (2020). Violence detection explanation via semantic roles embeddings. *BMC Medical Informatics and Decision Making*, *20*(1), 1–13. doi:10.118612911-020-01237-4 PMID:33059690

Mishra, S., Kwasnik, T., Anderson, K., & Wood, R. (2021). *Microgrid's Role in Enhancing the Security and Flexibility of City Energy Systems. In Flexible Resources for Smart Cities*. Springer. doi:10.1007/978-3-030-82796-0 4

Mohler, G., & Brantingham, P. J. (2018, April). Privacy preserving, crowd sourced crime Hawkes processes. In *2018 International Workshop on Social Sensing (SocialSens)* (pp. 14-19). IEEE. 10.1109/SocialSens.2018.00016

Moseley, P. (2017). EU Support for Innovation and Market Uptake in Smart Buildings under the Horizon 2020 Framework Programme. *Buildings*, *7*(4), 105. doi:10.3390/buildings7040105

Nakamoto, S. (2008). *Bitcoin: A Peer-to-Peer Electronic Cash System*. www.bitcoin.org

Namballa, M. (2020). Realtime Fingerprint based Voting System. *International Journal of Engineering Research & Technology (Ahmedabad)*, *9*(9). Advance online publication. doi:10.17577/IJERTV9IS090073

Ndwali, P.K., Njiri, J., & Wanjiru, E.M. (2021). Economic Model Predictive Control of Microgrid Connected Photovoltaic-Diesel Generator backup Energy System Considering Demand Side Management. *J. Electric Eng Technology*. https://doi.org/s42835-021-00801-w doi:10.1007/s

Ndwali, P. K., Njiri, J. G., & Wanjiru, E. M. (2020). Optimal Operation Control of Microgrid Connected Photovoltaic-Diesel Generator Backup System Under Time of Use Tariff. *J Control Autom Electric Syst*, *31*(4), 1001–1014. doi:10.100740313-020-00585-w

Nigar, N. N., & Islam, M. (2020). A Proposed Framework for Fingerprint-based Voting System in Bangladesh. JOIV. *International Journal on Informatics Visualization*, *4*(1). Advance online publication. doi:10.30630/joiv.4.1.283

Nimaje, D., & Tripathy, D. (2016). Characterization of some Indian coals to assess their liability to spontaneous combustion. *Fuel*, *163*, 139–147. doi:10.1016/j.fuel.2015.09.041

Ni, Y., Barzman, D., Bachtel, A., Griffey, M., Osborn, A., & Sorter, M. (2020). Finding warning markers: Leveraging natural language processing and machine learning technologies to detect risk of school violence. *International Journal of Medical Informatics*, *139*, 104137. doi:10.1016/j.ijmedinf.2020.104137 PMID:32361146

Nosratabadi, S. M., Hooshmand, R.-A., & Gholipour, E. (2017). A comprehensive review on microgrid and virtual power plant concepts employed for distributed energy resources scheduling in power systems. *Renewable & Sustainable Energy Reviews*, *67*, 341–363. doi:10.1016/j.rser.2016.09.025

Osorio, J., & Beltran, A. (2020, July). Enhancing the Detection of Criminal Organizations in Mexico using ML and NLP. In *2020 International Joint Conference on Neural Networks (IJCNN)* (pp. 1-7). IEEE. 10.1109/IJCNN48605.2020.9207039

Palensky, P., & Dietrich, D. (2011). Demand side management: Demand response, intelligent energy systems, and smart loads. *IEEE Transactions on Industrial Informatics*, 7(3), 381–388. doi:10.1109/TII.2011.2158841

Pandey, R., & Mohler, G. O. (2018, November). Evaluation of crime topic models: topic coherence vs spatial crime concentration. In *2018 IEEE International Conference on Intelligence and Security Informatics (ISI)* (pp. 76-78). IEEE. 10.1109/ISI.2018.8587384

Pandiyaraju, V., Logambigai, R., Ganapathy, S., & Kannan, A. (2020). An energy efficient routing algorithm for WSNs using intelligent fuzzy rules in precision agriculture. *Wireless Personal Communications*, 112(1), 243–259. doi:10.100711277-020-07024-8

Pandiyaraju, V., Perumal, P. S., Kannan, A., & Ramesh, L. S. (2017). Smart terrace gardening with intelligent roof control algorithm for water conservation. *Pakistan Journal of Agricultural Sciences*, 54(2), 451–455. doi:10.21162/PAKJAS/17.4903

Parhizi, S., Lotfi, H., Khodaei, A., & Bahramirad, S. (2015). State of the art in research on microgrids: A review. *IEEE Access : Practical Innovations, Open Solutions*, 3, 890–925. doi:10.1109/ACCESS.2015.2443119

Parsania, P. S., & Virparia, D. P. V. (2014). A review: Image interpolation techniques for image scaling. *International Journal of Innovative Research in Computer and CNommunication Engineering*, 2(12), 7409–7414.

Patil, H. (2019). Mobile Based Voting Application. *International Journal for Research in Applied Science and Engineering Technology*, 7(5), 2181–2185. doi:10.22214/ijraset.2019.5366

Pazmin˜o, I., Ochoa, D., Minaya, E. P., & Mera, H. P. (2022). Use of Battery Energy Storage Systems to Enhance the Frequency Stability of an Islanded Microgrid Based on Hybrid Photovoltaic-Diesel Generation. Sustainability, Energy and City. CSE City. Lecture Notes in Networks and Systems, 379. 10.1007/978-3-030-94262-55

Pearson, S., May, D., Leontidis, G., Swainson, M., Brewer, S., Bidaut, L., Frey, J. G., Parr, G., Maull, R., & Zisman, A. (2019). Are distributed ledger technologies the panacea for food traceability? *Global Food Security*, 20, 145–149. doi:10.1016/j.gfs.2019.02.002

Perumal, S., & Velmurugan, T. (2018). Preprocessing by contrast enhancement techniques for medical images. *International Journal of Pure and Applied Mathematics*, 118(18), 3681–3688.

PHOENIX. Horizon 2020 project. (n.d.). Available online: https://eu-phoenix.eu/

Pramudhita, A. N., & Asmara, R. A. (2018). Internet of Things Integration in Smart Grid. IEEE.

Qian, M., Hongquan, W., Yongsheng, W., & Yan, Z. (2008). SVM Based Prediction of Spontaneous Combustion in Coal Seam. *Computational Intelligence and Design. ISCID'08. International Symposium on*, 254-257. 10.1109/ISCID.2008.193

QuillHash Team. (2019). Will Hyperledger be the Platform that Successfully Brings Blockchain into the Enterprises? *The Medium Blog.* https://medium.com/quillhash/will-hyperledger-be-the-platform-that-successfully-brings-blockchain-into-the-enterprises-c 7759e38cc61

Rajendran, T. (2022, January). Road Obstacles Detection using Convolution Neural Network and Report using IoT. In *2022 4th International Conference on Smart Systems and Inventive Technology (ICSSIT)* (pp. 22-26). IEEE. 10.1109/ICSSIT53264.2022.9716337

Ramallo-González, A. P., Tomat, V., Fernández-Ruiz, P. J., Zamora-Izquierdo, M. A., & Skarmeta-Gómez, A. F. (2020). Conceptualisation of an IoT Framework for Multi-Person Interaction with Conditioning Systems. *Energies*, *13*(12), 3094. doi:10.3390/en13123094

Ramezani, B., Silva, M. G. D., & Simões, N. (2021). Application of smart readiness indicator for Mediterranean buildings in retrofitting actions. *Energy and Building*, *249*, 111173. doi:10.1016/j.enbuild.2021.111173

Romano, Y., Elad, M., & Milanfar, P. (2021). ConSinGAN: Learning a Conditional SinGAN from a Single Natural Image. *International Conference on Machine Learning (ICML).*

Sabry, K., & Emad, M. (2021, December). Road Traffic Accidents Detection Based On Crash Estimation. In *2021 17th International Computer Engineering Conference (ICENCO)* (pp. 63-68). IEEE. 10.1109/ICENCO49852.2021.9698968

Salah, K., Nizamuddin, N., Jayaraman, R., & Omar, M. (2019). Blockchain-based soybean traceability in agricultural supply chain. *IEEE Access : Practical Innovations, Open Solutions*, *7*, 73295–73305. doi:10.1109/ACCESS.2019.2918000

Sandeep, K., Ravikumar, P., & Ranjith, S. (2017, July). Novel drunken driving detection and prevention models using Internet of things. In *2017 International Conference on Recent Trends in Electrical, Electronics and Computing Technologies (ICRTEECT)* (pp. 145-149). IEEE. 10.1109/ICRTEECT.2017.38

Sane, N. H., Patil, D. S., Thakare, S. D., & Rokade, A. V. (2016). Real time vehicle accident detection and tracking using GPS and GSM. *International Journal on Recent and Innovation Trends in Computing and Communication*, *4*(4), 479–482.

Sanjeev, P., Padhy, N. P., & Agarwal, P. (2017). Effective control and energy management of isolated DC microgrid. *IEEE Power Energy Society General Meeting*, 1-5. 10.1109/PESGM.2017.8273786

Santos, D., & Ferreira, J. C. (2019). IoT Power Monitoring System for Smart Environments. *Sustainability (Basel)*, *11*(19), 5355. doi:10.3390u11195355

Saranya, P., & Maheswari, R. (2023). Proof of Transaction (PoTx) Based Traceability System for an Agriculture Supply Chain. *IEEE Access : Practical Innovations, Open Solutions*, *11*, 10623–10638. doi:10.1109/ACCESS.2023.3240772

Schultz, R. R., & Stevenson, R. L. (1996, June). Extraction of high-resolution frames from video sequences. *IEEE Transactions on Image Processing*, *5*(6), 996–1011. doi:10.1109/83.503915 PMID:18285187

Seo, S., Chan, H., Brantingham, P. J., Leap, J., Vayanos, P., Tambe, M., & Liu, Y. (2018, December). Partially generative neural networks for gang crime classification with partial information. In *Proceedings of the 2018 AAAI/ACM Conference on AI, Ethics, and Society* (pp. 257-263). 10.1145/3278721.3278758

Sheikholeslami, M., Shahidehpour, M., Paaso, A., & Bahramirad, S. (2020). Challenges of Modeling and Simulation of Clustered Bronzeville Community Microgrid (BCM) and IIT Campus Microgrid (ICM) Using RTDS. *IEEE Power Energy Society General Meeting (PESGM)*, 1-5. 10.1109/PESGM41954.2020.9281885

Shetgaonkar, P. R., & NaikPawar, VGauns, R. (2015). Proposed Model for the Smart Accident Detection System for Smart Vehicles using Arduino board, Smart Sensors, GPS and GSM. *Int. J. Emerg. Trends Technol. Comput. Sci*, *4*, 172–176.

Siano, P. (2014). Demand response and smart-grids – A survey. *Renewable & Sustainable Energy Reviews*, *30*, 461–478. doi:10.1016/j.rser.2013.10.022

Simeon, A., & Chowdhury, S. (2020). Protection Challenges in a Standalone Microgrid: Case Study of Tsumkwe Microgrid. *IEEE PES/IAS Power Africa*, 1-5. doi:.2020.9219972 doi:10.1109/PowerAfrica49420

Singh, R. V. K. (2013). Spontaneous heating and fire in coal mines. *Procedia Engineering*, *62*, 78–90. doi:10.1016/j.proeng.2013.08.046

Sornsoontorn, C. (n.d.). *How do GANs intuitively work?* Available: https://hackernoon.com/how-do-gans-intuitively-work-2dda07f2 47a1

Study of Biometric Voting System. (n.d.). https://researchtrend.net/ijet/pdf/ 28-S-812.pdf

Sumner, S. A., Mercy, J. A., Dahlberg, L. L., Hillis, S. D., Klevens, J., & Houry, D. (2015). Violence in the United States: Status, challenges, and opportunities. *Journal of the American Medical Association*, *314*(5), 478–488. doi:10.1001/jama.2015.8371 PMID:26241599

Suralkar, Udasi, Gagnani, Tekwani, & Bhatia. (2019). *E-Voting Using Blockchain With Biometric Authentication*. Academic Press.

Syed, D., Zainab, A., Ghrayeb, A., Refaat, S. S., Abu-Rub, H., & Bouhali, O. (2021). Smart Grid Big Data Analytics: Survey of Technologies, Techniques, and Applications. *IEEE Access : Practical Innovations, Open Solutions*, *9*, 59564–59585. doi:10.1109/ACCESS.2020.3041178

Terroso-Saenz, F., González-Vidal, A., Ramallo-González, A. P., & Skarmeta, A. F. (2019). An open IoT platform for the management and analysis of energy data. *Future Generation Computer Systems*, *92*, 1066–1079. doi:10.1016/j.future.2017.08.046

Tian, F. (2016, June). An agri-food supply chain traceability system for China based on RFID & blockchain technology. In *2016 13th international conference on service systems and service management (ICSSSM)* (pp. 1-6). IEEE. 10.1109/ICSSSM.2016.7538424

Tiwari, V. (2021). *Monitoring and Control of PV Microgrid using IoT*. IEEE.

Tomat, V., Ramallo-González, A. P., & Skarmeta Gómez, A. F. (2020). A comprehensive survey about thermal comfort under the IoT paradigm: Is crowdsensing the new horizon? *Sensors (Basel)*, *20*(16), 4647. doi:10.339020164647 PMID:32824790

Tomat, V., Vellei, M., Ramallo-González, A. P., González-Vidal, A., Le Dréau, J., & Skarmeta-Gómez, A. (2022). Understanding patterns of thermostat overrides after demand response events. *Energy and Building*, *271*, 112312. doi:10.1016/j.enbuild.2022.112312

Toyoda, K., Mathiopoulos, P. T., Sasase, I., & Ohtsuki, T. (2017). A novel blockchain-based product ownership management system (POMS) for anti-counterfeits in the post supply chain. *IEEE Access : Practical Innovations, Open Solutions*, *5*, 17465–17477. doi:10.1109/ACCESS.2017.2720760

Tripathi & De. (n.d.). *Adaptive Transmission Protocols for Smart Grid IoT Communication*. IEEE.

Umuhoza, J., Zhang, Y., Zhao, S., & Mantooth, H. A. (2017). An adaptive control strategy for power balance and the intermittency mitigation in battery-PV energy system at residential DC microgrid level. *IEEE Applied Power Electronics Conference and Exposition*, *1341345*, 1341–1345. Advance online publication. doi:10.1109/APEC.2017.7930870

Vanamoorthy, M., & Chinnaiah, V. (2020). Congestion-free transient plane (CFTP) using bandwidth sharing during link failures in SDN. *The Computer Journal*, *63*(6), 832–843. doi:10.1093/comjnl/bxz137

Vanamoorthy, M., Chinnaiah, V., & Sekar, H. (2020). A hybrid approach for providing improved link connectivity in SDN. *The International Arab Journal of Information Technology*, *17*(2), 250–256. doi:10.34028/iajit/17/2/13

Vasluianu, O., Faida, C. N., Flangea, R., Giorgian, N., & Marinescu, M. (2019). Microgrid System for a Residential Ensemble. *22nd International Conference on Control Systems and Computer Science (CSCS)*, 375-379, 10.1109/CSCS.2019.00067

Vemulakonda, R. (2016). *An algorithm for basic IoT Architectures*. ICETCSE.

Verbeke, S., Aerts, D., Rynders, G., & Ma, Y. (2019). *Summary of state of affairs in 2nd technical support study on the smart readiness indicator for buildings*. Study accomplished under the authority of the European Commission DG Energy 2019/SEB/R/1810610

Vigna, I., Pernetti, R., Pasut, W., & Lollini, R. (2018). New domain for promoting energy efficiency: Energy Flexible Building Cluster. *Sustainable Cities and Society*, *38*, 526–533. doi:10.1016/j.scs.2018.01.038

Vigna, I., Pernetti, R., Pernigotto, G., & Gasparella, A. (2020). Analysis of the building smart readiness indicator calculation: A comparative case-study with two panels of experts. *Energies*, *13*(11), 2796. doi:10.3390/en13112796

Waili, T. Z., & Alkawaz, A. (2020). Advanced Voting System Using Fingerprint. *International Journal on Perceptive and Cognitive Computing*, *6*(2), 18–21. doi:10.31436/ijpcc.v6i2.172

Wang, Y., Sun, Y.-M., Yan, Y., & Ma, Y. (2010). Design of Wireless Sensor Networks in prevention of combustion on coal gangue based on pseudo-parallel genetic algorithms. *Advanced Computational Intelligence (IWACI), Third International Workshop on, 2010*, 294-298. 10.1109/IWACI.2010.5585211

Wang, H., Wang, J., Wang, J., Zhao, M., & Yang, J. (2018). GraphGAN: Graph Representation Learning with Generative Adversarial Nets. In *Proceedings of the 27th International Joint Conference on Artificial Intelligence (IJCAI)* (pp. 4176-4182). 10.1609/aaai.v32i1.11872

Wang, S. (2016). Making buildings smarter, grid-friendly, and responsive to smart grids. *Science and Technology for the Built Environment*, *22*(6), 629–632. doi:10.1080/23744731.2016.1200888

Wang, X., Gerber, M. S., & Brown, D. E. (2012, April). Automatic crime prediction using events extracted from twitter posts. In *International conference on social computing, behavioral-cultural modeling, and prediction* (pp. 231-238). Springer. 10.1007/978-3-642-29047-3_28

Wang, Y., Tian, F., Huang, Y., Wang, J., & Wei, C. (2015). Monitoring coal fires in Datong coalfield using multi-source remote sensing data. *Transactions of Nonferrous Metals Society of China*, *25*(10), 3421–3428. doi:10.1016/S1003-6326(15)63977-2

Waseem, Kouser, Waqas, Imran, Hameed, & Bin Faheem. (2021). *CSOA-Based Residential Energy Management System in Smart Grid Considering DGs for Demand Response*. IEEE.

Wong, W.-T., & Hsu, S.-H. (2006). Application of SVM and ANN for image retrieval. *European Journal of Operational Research*, *173*(3), 938–950. doi:10.1016/j.ejor.2005.08.002

Wood, G. (2014). *Ethereum: a secure decentralised generalised transaction ledger* (Vol. 151). Ethereum Project Yellow Paper. https://files.gitter.im/ethereum/yellowpaper/VIyt/Paper.pdf

Wu, J., Xue, C., Zhao, Z., & Liu, B. (2012, July). Effect of camera angle on precision of parameters for traffic accident in video detection. In *2012 Third International Conference on Digital Manufacturing & Automation* (pp. 347-350). IEEE. 10.1109/ICDMA.2012.84

Xie, C., Sun, Y., & Luo, H. (2017, August). Secured data storage scheme based on block chain for agricultural products tracking. In *2017 3rd International Conference on Big Data Computing and Communications (BIGCOM)* (pp. 45-50). IEEE. 10.1109/BIGCOM.2017.43

Xie, J., Xue, S., Cheng, W., & Wang, G. (2011). Early detection of spontaneous combustion of coal in underground coal mines with development of an ethylene enriching system. *International Journal of Coal Geology*, *85*(1), 123–127. doi:10.1016/j.coal.2010.10.007

Xu, Shao, Cao, & Chang. (2021). *Single phase grid connected PV system with golden sections each based MPPT algorithm.* Academic Press.

Xu, X., Chen, C., Zhu, X., & Hu, Q. (2018). Promoting acceptance of direct load control programs in the United States: Financial incentive versus control option. *Energy, 147,* 1278–1287. doi:10.1016/j.energy.2018.01.028

Yaïci, W., Krishnamurthy, K., Entchev, E., & Longo, M. (2021). Recent advances in internet of things (IoT) infrastructures for building energy systems: A review. *Sensors (Basel), 21*(6), 1–40. doi:10.339021062152 PMID:33808558

Yang, X., Li, M., Yu, H., Wang, M., Xu, D., & Sun, C. (2021). A trusted blockchain-based traceability system for fruit and vegetable agricultural products. *IEEE Access : Practical Innovations, Open Solutions, 9,* 36282–36293. doi:10.1109/ACCESS.2021.3062845

Yang, Y., Li, Z., Hou, S., Gu, F., Gao, S., & Tang, Y. (2014). The shortest period of coal spontaneous combustion on the basis of oxidative heat release intensity. *International Journal of Mining Science and Technology, 24*(1), 99–103. doi:10.1016/j.ijmst.2013.12.017

Yuan, L., & Smith, A. C. (2011). CO and CO 2 emissions from spontaneous heating of coal under different ventilation rates. *International Journal of Coal Geology, 88*(1), 24–30. doi:10.1016/j.coal.2011.07.004

Yuan, Y., & Wang, F. Y. (2016). Blockchain: The state of the art and future trends. *Acta Automatica Sinica, 42*(4), 481–494. doi:10.16383/j.aas.2016.c160158

Yu, B., Guo, J., Zhou, C., Gan, Z., & Yu, Y. (2017). A Review on Microgrid Technology with Distributed Energy. *International Conference on Smart Grid and Electrical Automation (ICSGEA),* 143-146. a.10.1109/ICSGEA.2017.152

Yu, L., Zhang, W., Wang, J., & Yu, Y. (2017, February). Seqgan: Sequence generative adversarial nets with policy gradient. *Proceedings of the AAAI Conference on Artificial Intelligence, 31*(1). doi:10.1609/aaai.v31i1.10804

Zhang, Y., Gan, Z., & Carin, L. (2016). Generating text via adversarial training. In NIPS workshop on Adversarial Training (Vol. 21, pp. 21-32). Academic Press.

Zhang, J., Choi, W., Ito, T., Takahashi, K., & Fujita, M. (2016). Modelling and parametric investigations on spontaneous heating in coal pile. *Fuel, 176,* 181–189. doi:10.1016/j.fuel.2016.02.059

Zhang, Y., Gan, Z., Fan, K., Chen, Z., Henao, R., Shen, D., & Carin, L. (2017, July). Adversarial feature matching for text generation. In *International Conference on Machine Learning* (pp. 4006-4015). PMLR.

Zhao, G. (2011). Predictions for coal spontaneous combustion stage based on an artificial neural network. *Computational Intelligence and Security (CIS), Seventh International Conference on,* 386-389. 10.1109/CIS.2011.92

Zhao, J., Li, C., & Wang, L. (2020). Hadoop-Based Power Grid Data Quality Verification and Monitoring Method. *Journal of Electrical Engineering & Technology*. Advance online publication. doi:10.100742835-022-01171-7

Zhu, S., & Xie, Y. (2019, May). Crime event embedding with unsupervised feature selection. In *ICASSP 2019-2019 IEEE International Conference on Acoustics, Speech and Signal Processing (ICASSP)* (pp. 3922-3926). IEEE. 10.1109/ICASSP.2019.8682285

Zhuang, L., & Ji-Ren, W. (2011). The Technology of Forecasting and Predicting the Hidden Danger of Underground Coal Spontaneous Combustion. *Procedia Engineering*, *26*, 2301–2305. doi:10.1016/j.proeng.2011.11.2438

Zhu, J., He, N., & Li, D. (2012). The relationship between oxygen consumption rate and temperature during coal spontaneous combustion. *Safety Science*, *50*(4), 842–845. doi:10.1016/j.ssci.2011.08.023

About the Contributors

Vanamoorthy Muthumanikandan, B.E., M.E., Ph.D., is working as a Senior Assistant Professor(Grade II) in the School of Computing Science and Engineering, at Vellore Institute of Technology, Chennai, India. He received his B.E and M.E degree in Computer Science and Engineering discipline. He received his Ph.D degree in Computer Science and Engineering from MIT Campus, Anna University. His areas of interests include Networking, Software Defined Networking and Network Function Virtualization. He published many papers in reputed journals and conferences.

T. Sudarson Rama Perumal is working as an Associate Professor in the Department of Electronics and Communication Engineering in Rohini College of Engineering, Kanniyakumari. He completed his PhD in Anna University, Chennai. His active research interests include wirless adhoc networks, image processing, bio medical imaging and networking.

* * *

Muthukumaran A. received B.E. degree in Computer Science and Engineering from Department of Computer Technology, MIT Campus, Anna University, Chennai.

Abishek C. received B.E .degree in Computer Science and Engineering from Department of Computer Technology, MIT Campus, Anna University, Chennai.

Lavanya K. is working as Associate Professor in VIT, Vellore. Research Interests include Big Data Analytics, Deep Learning and NoSQL Databases.

Saranya P., ME, is an Assistant Professor Department of Computer Science and Engineering, Rohini College of Engineering and Technology.

Shunmuga Perumal P. has completed his B.E. in Information Technology from Manonmaniam Sundaranar University, Tirunelveli, Tamil Nadu. He has pursued

M.E. in VLSI Design and Ph.D from Anna University, Chennai. Currently, he is working as a senior Assistant Professor at the School of Information Technology and Engineering, Vellore Institute of Technology, Vellore, India. His research interests include deep learning based perception systems for autonomous vehicles/advanced driver assistance systems, real-time driving dataset collection and labelling, internet of things.

Renugadevi Pandiyan received her B.E. (EEE) from Ganadhipathy Tulsis Engineering College, Vellore, India, MTech in Embedded Systems and Technologies from Veltech University Chennai. She is currently doing her PHD in VIT University Chennai. Her research interests in Bigdata Technology, Smart Microgrid Systems and Renewable Energy Resources.

Maheswari R. is Professor and Head of the Department, Cyber-Physical System, Centre for Smart Grid Technologies, School of Computer Science and Engineering, Vellore Institute of Technology, Chennai. She has professional experience of more than 22 years of working in Industry and in various prestigious institutions. She has published seven patents in her research domain and has received many awards like Outstanding FOSSEE Contributor Award and Best eSim Contribution Award from IIT Bombay & MHRD, Govt. of India, Best Faculty Award, Best achiever award, Best researcher award, Best Alumni Chapter Award, Best paper and Excellent paper awards, Best Club Coordinator award. She has published more than 70 research works in various Books, Book Chapters, Magazine articles and International Journals. She is a certified Knime Analyst. She actively co-ordinated Institution accreditation activities like NBA, ISO certification, NAAC, ABET. She has created her own footprint by contributing her work in FOSSEE (Free and Open Source Software for Education) such as esim, Scilab, R tool. She has received funds more than INR 80 Lakhs from various funding agencies and consultancy project works like like DST, Fundboon Technology, Exhibition hall proposal at Gujarat Institute of Disaster Management in collaboration with NID (National Institute of Design) Gujarat, Microsoft internship projects, Byjus, etc. She visited various countries like Hong Kong, Singapore, Malaysia etc. for presenting her research contributions as well as to give the keynote address. Acted as a resource person, panel member, chief guest, guest of honor, and given a plenary talk in various industries, and national and international institutions as a part of training, seminars, workshops and conferences. She has been an active reviewer in various International Journals and Conferences. Her teaching and research expertise covers a wide range of subject areas including IoT, Embedded Systems, Processor level architecture, High-Performance Computing, Reconfigurable Computing, Artificial Intelligence, Machine Learning, etc.

Srimathi R. received her B.E. (EEE) from the Bharathiar University, India, M.Tech in Power Electronics and Drives from SASTRA University, Thanjavur, India and her Ph.D in Electrical Engg from VIT Chennai. She is currently a Assistant Professor Senior with the School of Electrical and Electronic Engineering, VIT Chennai. Her research interests include smart LED lighting systems, Energy savings in buildings, Power converters for DC microgrids, Power train systems for EV and Control techniques for converters.

R. Rajesh, ME, Ph.D., is Principal of Rohini College of Engineering & Technology.

Deeksha S. is doing her undergraduate degree in Computer Science and Engineering.

Ganapathy S. has completed his M.E. and PhD from Anna University, Chennai. Currently he is working as an Associate Professor in VIT University-Chennai Campus. His areas of interest are Artificial Intelligence, Wireless Sensor Network, Data Mining, and Recommendation systems.

Muthurajkumar S. has completed his M.E. and PhD from Anna University, Chennai. Currently he is working as Assistant Professor in Anna University, Chennai. His areas of interest are Cloud Networks, Artificial Intelligence, Wireless Sensor Network and Data Mining.

Yogeshwar S. received B.E. degree in Computer Science and Engineering from Department of Computer Technology, MIT Campus, Anna University, Chennai.

Muthumanikandan V. is working as Assistant Professor Senior Grade-2 in the School of Computer Science and Engineering, Vellore Institute of Technology, Chennai. His area of interests are including Computer Network and Security.

Pattabiram Venkatasubbu received his B.E. (CSE) from Madras University, India, ME in Computer Applications from Bharathidasan University and Ph.D. in Data Mining from Bharathiyar University. He is currently working as a Professor with the School of Computer Science and Engineering, VIT University Chennai. His research interests in Data Mining, Data Science and Analytics, Machine Learning and Deep Learning.

Index

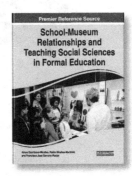

Are You Ready to
Publish Your Research ?

IGI Global
PUBLISHER of TIMELY KNOWLEDGE

IGI Global offers book authorship and editorship opportunities across 11 subject areas, including business, computer science, education, science and engineering, social sciences, and more!

Benefits of Publishing with IGI Global:

- Free one-on-one editorial and promotional support.

- Expedited publishing timelines that can take your book from start to finish in less than one (1) year.

- Choose from a variety of formats, including Edited and Authored References, Handbooks of Research, Encyclopedias, and Research Insights.

- Utilize IGI Global's eEditorial Discovery® submission system in support of conducting the submission and double-blind peer review process.

- IGI Global maintains a strict adherence to ethical practices due in part to our full membership with the Committee on Publication Ethics (COPE).

- Indexing potential in prestigious indices such as Scopus®, Web of Science™, PsycINFO®, and ERIC – Education Resources Information Center.

- Ability to connect your ORCID iD to your IGI Global publications.

- Earn honorariums and royalties on your full book publications as well as complimentary content and exclusive discounts.

Join Your Colleagues from Prestigious Institutions, Including:

Australian National University

MIT Massachusetts Institute of Technology

JOHNS HOPKINS UNIVERSITY

HARVARD UNIVERSITY

COLUMBIA UNIVERSITY IN THE CITY OF NEW YORK

Printed in the United States
by Baker & Taylor Publisher Services